Ancient China Simplified
By Edward Harper Parker

PREFACE

Boswell once remarked to Dr. Johnson that "the history of England is so strange that, if it were not well vouched as it is, it would be hardly credible." To which Johnson replied in his usual style: "Sir, if it were told as shortly, and with as little preparation for introducing the different events, as the history of the Jewish kings, it would be equally liable to objections of improbability." Dr. Johnson went on to illustrate what he meant, by specific allusion to the concessions to Parliament made by Charles I. "If," he said, "these had been related nakedly, without any detail of the circumstances which generally led to them, they would not have been believed."

This is exactly the position of ancient Chinese history, which may be roughly said to coincide in time with the history of the Jewish kings. The Chinese Annals are mere diaries of events, isolated facts being tumbled together in order of date, without any regard for proportion. Epoch-making invasions, defeats, and cessions of territory are laconically noted down on a level with the prince's indiscretion in weeping for a concubine as he would weep for a wife; or the Emperor's bounty in sending a dish of sacrificial meat to a vassal power by express messenger. In one way there is a distinct advantage in this method, for, the historian being seldom tempted to obtrude his own opinion or comments, we are left a clear course for the formation of our own judgments upon the facts given. On the other hand, it is unfortunate that what may be called the philosophy of history has never been seized by the Chinese mind: the annalists do not trouble themselves with the rights and aspirations of the masses; the results to general policy that naturally follow upon increase of population, perfecting of arms and munitions of war, admixture of foreign blood with the body politic, and such like matters. The heads of events being noted, it seems to be left to the reader to fill in the details from his imagination, and from his knowledge of contemporary affairs. For instance, suppose the reign of Queen Victoria were to begin after this fashion:—"1837, 5th moon, Kalends, Victoria succeeded: 9th moon, Ides, Napoleon paid a visit: 28th day, London flooded; 10th moon, 29th day, eclipse of the sun"; and so on. At the time, and for many years—possibly centuries—afterwards, there would be accurate general traditional, or even written, information as to who Victoria was; why Napoleon paid a visit; in what particular way the flood affected England generally; from what parts the eclipse was best visible, etc. These details would fade in distinctness with each successive generation; commentators would come to the rescue; then commentators upon commentators; and discussions as to which man was the most trustworthy of them all.

Under these circumstances it is difficult enough for the Chinese themselves to construct a series of historical lessons, adequate to guide them in the conduct of modern affairs, out of so heterogeneous a mass of material. This difficulty is, in the case of Westerners, more than doubled by the strange, and to us inharmonious, sounds of Chinese proper names: moreover, as they are monosyllabical, and many of them exactly similar when expressed in our letters, it is almost impossible to remember them, and to distinguish one from the other. Thus most persons who make an honest endeavour by means of translations to master the leading events in ancient Chinese history soon throw down the book in despair; while even specialists, who may wish to shorten their labours by availing themselves of others' work, can only get a firm grip of translations by comparing them with the originals: it is thus really impossible to acquire anything at all approaching an accurate understanding of Chinese antiquity without possessing in some degree the controlling power of a knowledge of the pictographs.

It is in view of all these difficulties that an attempt has been made in this book to extract principles from isolated facts; to avoid, so far as is possible, the use of Chinese proper names; to introduce these as sparingly and gradually as is practicable when they must be used at all; to describe the general trend of events and life of the people rather than the personal acts of rulers and great officers; and, generally, to put it into the power of any one who can only read English, to gain an intelligible notion of what Chinese antiquity really was; and what principles and motives, declared or tacit, underlay it. It is with this object before me that I have ventured to call my humble work "Ancient China Simplified," and I can only express a hope that it will really be found intelligible.

EDWARD HARPER PARKER.

18, GAMBIER TERRACE, LIVERPOOL, May 18, 1908.

AIDS TO MEMORY

There is much repetition in the book, the same facts being presented, for instance, under the heads of Army, Religion, Confucius, and Marriages. This is intentional, and the object is to keep in the mind impressions which in a strange, ancient, and obscure subject are apt to disappear after perusal of only one or two casual statements.

The Index has been carefully prepared so that any allusion or statement vaguely retained in the mind may at once be confirmed. The chapter headings, or contents list, which itself contains nearly five per cent of the whole letterpress, is so arranged that it omits no feature treated of in the main text.

In the earlier chapters uncouth proper names are reduced to a minimum, but the Index refers by name to specific places and persons only generally mentioned in the earlier pages. For instance, the states of Lu and CHÊNG on pages 22 and 29: it is hard enough to differentiate Ts'i, Tsin, Ts'in, and Ts'u at the outstart, without crowding the memory with fresh names until the necessity for it absolutely arises.

The nine maps are inserted where they are most likely to be useful: it is a good plan to refer to a map each time a place is mentioned, unless the memory suffices to suggest exactly where that place is. After two or three patient references, situations of places will take better root in the mind.

The chapters are split up into short discussions and descriptions, because longer divisions are apt to be tedious where ancient history is concerned. And the narrative of political movement is frequently interrupted by the introduction of new matter, in order to provide novelty and stimulate the imagination. Moreover, all chapters and all subjects converge on one general focus. On page 15 of "China, her Diplomacy, etc." (John Murray, 1901), I have confessed how tedious I myself had found ancient Chinese history, and how its human interest only begins with foreign relations. I have, however, gone systematically through the mill once more, and my present object is to present general results only obtainable at the cost of laboriously picking out and resetting isolated and often apparently unconnected records of fact.

NAMES OF CHIEF LOCALITIES

CHOU: at first a principality in South Shen Si and part of Kan Suh, subject to Shang dynasty; afterwards the imperial dynasty itself.

TS'IN: principality west of the above. When the Chou dynasty moved its capital east into Ho Nan, Ts'in took possession of the old Chou principality.

TSIN: principality (same family as Chou) in South Shan Si (and in part of Shen Si at times).

TS'I: principality, separated by the Yellow River from Tsin and

Yen; it lay in North Shan Tung, and in the coast part of Chih Li.

TS'U: semi-barbarous principality alone preponderant on the Yang- tsz River.

WU: still more barbarous principality (ruling caste of the same family as Chou, but senior to Chou) on the Yang-tsz embouchure and Shanghai coasts.

YÜEH: equally barbarous principality commanding another embouchure in the Hangchow-Ningpo region. Wu and Yüeh were at first subordinate to Ts'u.

YEN: principality (same family as Chou) in the Peking plain, north of the Yellow River mouth,

SHUH and PA: in no way Chinese or federal; equivalent to Central and Eastern Sz Ch'wan province.

CHÊNG: principality in Ho Nan (same family as Chou).

SUNG: principality taking in the four corners of Ho Nan, Shan Tung, An Hwei, and Kiang Su (Shang dynasty family).

CH'ÊN: principality in Ho Nan, south of Sung (family of the Ploughman Emperor, 2250 B.C., preceding even the Hia dynasty).

WEI: principality taking in corners of Ho Nan, Chih Li, and Shan Tung (family of the Chou emperors).

TS'AO: principality in South-west Shan Tung; neighbour of Lu, Wei, and Sung (same family as Chou).

TS'AI: principality in Ho Nan, south of CH'ÊN (same family as Chou).

LU: principality in South-west Shan Tung, between Ts'ao and Ts'i (its founder was the brother of the Chou founder).

HÜ: very small principality in Ho Nan, south of Cheng (same obscure eastern ancestry as Ts'i),

K'I: Shan Tung promontory and German sphere (of Hia dynasty descent); it is often confused with, or is quite the same as, another principality called Ki (without the aspirate).

The above are practically all the states whose participation in Chinese development has been historically of importance,

NAMES OF CHIEF PERSONAGES

CONFUCIUS: after 500 B.C. premier of Lu; traced his descent back through the Chou dynasty vassal ruling family of Sung to the Shang dynasty family.

TSZ-CH'AN: elder contemporary of Confucius; premier of Cheng; traced his descent through the vassal ruling family of Cheng to the Chou dynasty family: date of death variously stated.

KWAN-TSE: died between 648 and 643 B.C., variously stated; premier of Ts'i; traced his descent to the same clan as the ruling dynasty of Chou.

YEN-TSZ: died 500 B.C.; premier of Ts'i; traced his descent to a local clan, apparently eastern barbarian by origin.

WEI YANG: died 338 B.C.; premier of Ts'in; was a concubine-born prince of the vassal state of Wei, and was thus of the imperial Chou dynasty clan.

SHUH HIANG: lawyer and minister of Tsin; belonged to one of the "great families" of Tsin; was contemporary with Tsz-ch'an. HIANG SÜH: diplomat of the state of Sung; pedigree not ascertained,

KI-CHAH: son, brother, and uncle of successive barbarian kings of Wu, whose ancestors, however, were the same ancestors as the orthodox imperial rulers of the Chou dynasty; contemporary of Tsz- ch'an.

NAMES OF THE SO-CALLED "FIVE PROTECTORS"

(ONLY THE TWO FIRST OF THE FIVE WERE SO OFFICIALLY; THE TWO LAST WERE SO, EVEN OFFICIALLY, THOUGH NEVER COUNTED AMONGST THE FIVE.)

1. MARQUESS OF Ts'i (not of imperial Chou clan, perhaps of "Eastern Barbarian" origin).

2. MARQUESS OF TSIN (imperial Chou clan).

3. DUKE OF SUNG (imperial Shang dynasty descent),

4. "KING" OF T'SU (semi-barbarian, but with remote imperial Chinese legendary descent).

5. EARL OF TS'IN (semi-Tartar, with legendary descent from remote imperial Chinese).

6. "KING" OF Wu (semi-barbarian, but of imperial Chou family descent).

7. "KING" OF YÜEH (barbarian, but with legendary descent from ultra-remote imperial Chinese).

CHAPTER I.OPENING SCENES

The year 842 B.C. may be considered the first accurate date in Chinese history, and in this year the Emperor had to flee from his capital on account of popular dissatisfaction with his tyrannical ways: he betook himself northward to an outlying settlement on the Tartar frontier, and the charge of imperial affairs was taken over by a regency or duumvirate.

At this time the confederation of cultured princes called China— or, to use their own term, the Central Kingdom—was a very different region from the huge mass of territory familiar to us under those names at the present day. It is hardly an exaggeration to say that civilized China, even at that comparatively advanced period, consisted of little more than the modern province of Ho Nan. All outside this flat and comparatively riverless region inhabited by the "orthodox" was more or less barbaric, and such civilization as it possessed was entirely the work of Chinese colonists, adventurers, or grantees of fiefs in partibus infidelium (so to speak). Into matters of still earlier ancient history we may enter more deeply in another chapter, but for the present we simply take China as it was when definite chronology begins.

The third of the great dynasties which had ruled over this limited China had, in 842 B.C., already been on the imperial throne for practically three hundred years, and, following the custom of its predecessors, it had parcelled out all the land under its sway to vassal princes who were, subject to the general imperial law and custom, or ritual, together with the homage and tribute duty prescribed thereunder, all practically absolute in their own domains. Roughly speaking, those smaller fiefs may be said to have corresponded in size with the walled-city and surrounding district of our own times, so well known under the name of hien. About a dozen of the larger fiefs had been originally granted to the blood relations of the dynastic founder in or after 1122 B.C.; but not exclusively so, for it seems to have been a point of honour, or of religious scruple, not to "cut off the sacrifices" from ruined or disgraced reigning families, unless the attendant circumstances were very gross; and so it came to pass that successive dynasties would strain a point in order to keep up the spiritual memory of decayed or rival houses.

Thus, at the time of which we speak (842 B.C.), about ten of the dozen or so of larger vassal princes were either of the same clan as the Emperor himself, or were descended from remoter branches of that clan before it secured the imperial throne; or, again, were descended from ministers and statesmen who had assisted the founder to obtain empire; whilst the two or three remaining great vassals were lineal representatives of previous dynasties, or of their great ministers, keeping up the honour and the sacrifices of bygone historical personages. As for the minor fiefs, numbering somewhere between a thousand and fifteen hundred, these play no part in political history, except as this or that one of them may have been thrust prominently forward for a moment as a pawn in the game of ambition played by the greater vassals. Nominally the Emperor was direct suzerain lord of all vassals, great or small; but in practice the greater vassal princes seem to have been what in the Norman feudal system were called "mesne lords"; that is, each one was surrounded by his own group of minor ruling lords, who, in turn, naturally clung for protection to that powerful magnate who was most immediately accessible in case of need; thus vassal rulers might be indefinitely multiplied, and there is some vagueness as to their numbers.

Just as the oldest civilizations of the West concentrated themselves along the banks of the Euphrates and the Nile, so the most ancient Chinese civilization is found concentrated along the south bank of the Yellow River. The configuration of the land as shown on a modern map assists us to understand how the industrious cultivators and weavers, finding the flat and so-called loess territory too confined for their ever-increasing numbers, threw out colonies wherever attraction offered, and wherever the riverine systems gave them easy access; whether by boat and raft; or whether—as seems more probable, owing to the scanty mention of boat-travel—by simply following the low levels sought by the streams, and tilling on their way such pasturages as they found by the river-sides. When it is said that the earliest Chinese we know of clung to the Yellow River bed, it must be remembered that "the River" (as they call it simply) turned sharp to the north at a point in Ho Nan province very far to the west of its present northerly course, near a city marked in the modern maps as Jung-t&h, in lat. 35 degrees N., long, 114 degrees E., or thereabouts; moreover, its course further north lay considerably to the westward of the present Grand Canal, taking possession now of the bed of the Wei River, now of that of the Chang River, according to whether we regard it before or after the year 602 B.C.; but always entering the Gulf near modern Tientsin. Hence we need not be surprised to find that the Conqueror or Assertor of the dynasty had conferred upon a staunch adviser, of alien origin, and upon two of his most trusty relatives, the three distant fiefs which commanded both sides of the Yellow River mouth, at that time near the modern Tientsin. There was no Canal in those days, and the river which runs past Confucius' birth-place, and now goes towards feeding the Grand Canal, had then a free course south-east towards the lakes in Kiang Su province to the north of Nanking. It will be noticed that quite a network of tributary rivers take their rise in Ho Nan province, and trend in an easterly direction towards the intricate Hwai River system. The River Hwai, which has a great history in the course of Chinese development, was in quite recent times taken possession of by the Yellow River for some years, and since then the Grand Canal and the lakes between them have so impeded its natural course that it may be said to have no natural delta at all; to be dissipated in a dedalus of salt flats, irrigation channels, and marshes: hence it is not so obvious to us now why the whole coast-line was at the period we are now describing, when there was no Grand Canal, quite beyond the reach of Chinese colonization from the Yellow River valley: this was only possible in two directions—firstly to the south, by way of the numerous ramifications of the Han River, which now, as then, joins the Yang-tsz Kiang at Hankow; and secondly to the south- east, by way of the equally numerous ramifications of the Hwai River, which entered the sea in lat. 34ø N. No easy emigration to the westward or south-westward was possible in those comparatively roadless days, for not a single river pointed out the obvious way to would-be colonists.

Accustomed as we now are to regard China as one vast homogeneous whole, approachable to us easily from the sea, it is not easy for us to understand the historical lines of expansion without these preliminary explanations. Corea and Japan were totally unknown even by name, and even Liao Tung, or "East of the River Liao," which was then inhabited by Corean tribes, was, if known by tradition at all, certainly only in communication with the remote Chinese colony, or vassal state, in possession of the Peking plain: on the other hand, this vassal state itself (if it had records of its own at all), for the three centuries previous to 842 B.C., had no political relations with the federated Chinese princes, and nothing is known of its internal doings, or of its immediate relations (if any) with Manchus and Coreans. The whole coast-line of Shan Tung was in the hands of various tribes of "Eastern Barbarians." True, a number of Chinese vassal rulers held petty fiefs to the south and the east of the two highly civilized principalities already described as being in possession of the Lower Yellow River; but the originally orthodox rulers of these petty colonies are distinctly stated to have partly followed barbarian usage, even despite their own imperial clan origin, and to have paid court to these two greater vassals as mesne lords, instead of direct to the Emperor. South of these, again, came the Hwai group of Eastern barbarians in possession of the Lower Hwai valley, and the various quite unknown tribes of Eastern barbarians occupying the marshy salt flats and shore accretions on the Kiang Su coast right down to the River Yang-tsz mouth.

As we shall see, a century or two later than 842 B.C. powerful semi-Chinese states began to assert themselves against the federated orthodox Chinese princes lying to their north; but, when dated history first opens, Central China knew nothing whatever of any part of the vast region lying to the south of the Yang-tsz; nothing whatever of what we now call Yiin Nan and Sz Ch'wan, not to say of the Indian and Tibetan dominions lying beyond them; fortiori nothing of Formosa, Hainan, Cochin-China, Tonquin, Burma, Siam, or the various Hindoo trading colonies advancing from the South Sea Islands northwards along the Indo-Chinese coasts; nothing whatever of Tsaidam, the Tarim Valley, the Desert, the Persian civilization, Turkestan, Kashgaria, Tartary, or Siberia.

It is, and will here be made, quite clear that the whole of the left bank of the Yellow River was in possession of various Turkish and Tartar-Tibetan tribes. The only exception is that the south-west corner of Shan Si province, notably the territory enclosed between the Yellow River and the River F&n (which, running from the north, bisects Shan Si province and enters the Yellow River about lat. 35" 30' N., long. 110 degrees 30' E.) was colonized by a branch of the imperial family quite capable of holding its own against the Tartars; in fact, the valley of this river as far north as P'ing-yang Fu had been in semi-mythical times (2300 B.C.) the imperial residence. It will be noticed that the River Wei joins the Yellow River on its right bank, just opposite the point where this latter, flowing from the north, bends eastwards, the Wei itself flowing from the west. This Wei Valley (including the sub- valleys of its north-bank tributaries) was also in 842 B.C. colonized by an ancient Chinese family—not of imperial extraction so far as the reigning house was concerned—which, by adopting Tartar, or perhaps Tartar—Tibetan, manners, had for many generations succeeded in acquiring a predominant influence in that region. Assuming that—which is not at all improbable—the nomad horsemen in unchallenged possession of the whole desert and Tartar expanse had at any time, as a consequence of their raids in directions away from China westward, brought to China any new ideas, new commercial objects, or new religious notions, these novelties must almost necessarily have filtered through this semi-Chinese half-barbarous state in possession of the Wei Valley, or through other of their Tartar kinsmen periodically engaged in raiding the settled Chinese cultivators farther east, along the line of what is now the Great Wall, and the northern parts of Shan Si and Chih Li provinces.

We shall allude in a more convenient place and chapter to specific traditions touching the supposed journeys about 990 B.C. of a Chinese Emperor to Turkestan; the alleged missions from Tonquin to a still earlier Chinese Emperor or Regent; and the pretended colonization of Corea by an aggrieved Chinese noble-all three events some centuries earlier than the opening period of dated history of which we now specially speak. For the present we ignore them, as, even if true, these events have had, and have now, no specific or definite influence whatever on the question of Chinese political development as expounded here. It seems certain that for many centuries previous to 842 B.C. the ruling and the literary Chinese had known of the existence of at least the Lower Yang-tsz and its three mouths (the Shanghai mouth and the Hangchow mouth have ceased long ago to exist at all): they also seem to have heard in a vague way of "moving sands" beyond the great northerly bend of the Yellow River in Tartarland. It is not even impossible that the persistent traditions of two of their very ancient Emperors having been buried south of the Yang-tsz—one near the modern coast treaty-port of Ningpo, the other near the modern riverine treaty-port of Ch'ang-sha—may be true; for nothing is more likely than that they both met their death whilst exploring the tributaries of the mysterious Yang-tsz Kiang lying to their south; because the father of the adventurous Emperor who is supposed to have explored Tartary in ggo B.C. certainly lost his life in attempting to explore the region of Hankow, as will be explained in due course.

All this, however, is matter of side issue. The main point we wish to insist upon, by way of introduction, in endeavouring to give our readers an intelligible notion of early Chinese development, is that Chinese beginnings were like any other great nation's beginnings—like, for instance, the Greek beginnings; these were centred at first round an extremely petty area, which, gradually expanding, threw out its tentacles and branches, and led to the final inclusion of the mysterious Danube, the gloomy Russian plain, the Tin Islands, Ultima Thule, and the Atlantic coasts into one fairly harmonious Graeco-Roman civilization. Or it may be compared to the development of the petty Anglo-Saxon settlements and kingdoms and sub-kingdoms, and their gradual political absorption of the surrounding Celts. In any case it may be said that there is nothing startlingly new about it; it followed a normal course.

CHAPTER II.SHIFTING SCENES

Having now seen how the Chinese people, taking advantage of the material and moral growth naturally following upon a settled industrial existence, and above all upon the exclusive possession of a written character, gradually imposed themselves as rulers upon the ignorant tribes around them, let us see to what families these Chinese emigrant adventurers or colonial satraps belonged. To begin with the semi-Tartar power in the River Wei Valley— destined six hundred years later to conquer the whole of China as we know it to-day—the ruling caste claimed descent from the most ancient (and of course partly mythological) Emperors of China; but for over a thousand years previous to 842 B.C. this remote branch of the Chinese race had become scattered and almost lost amongst the Tartars. However, a generation or two before our opening period, one of these princes had served the then ruling imperial dynasty as a sort of guardian to the western frontier, as a rearer of horses for the metropolitan stud, and perhaps even as a guide on the occasion of imperial expeditions into Tartarland. The successor of the Emperor who was driven from his capital in 842 B.C. about twenty years later employed this western satrap to chastise the Tartar nomads whose revolt had in part led to the imperial flight. After suffering some disasters, the conductors of this series of expeditions were at last successful, and in 815 B.C. the title of "Warden of the Western Marches" was officially conferred on the ruler for the time being of this western state, who in 777 B.C. had the further honour of seeing one of his daughters married to the Emperor himself. This political move on the part of the Emperor was unwise, for it led indirectly to the Tartars, who were frequently engaged in war with the Warden, interfering in the quarrels about the imperial succession, in which question the Tartars naturally thought they had a right to interfere in the interests of their own people. The upshot of it was that in 771 B.C. the Emperor was killed by the Tartars in battle, and it was only by securing the military assistance of the semi-Tartar Warden of the Marches that the imperial dynasty was saved. As it was, the Emperor's capital was permanently moved east from the immediate neighbourhood of what we call Si-ngan Fu in Shen Si province to the immediate neighbourhood of Ho-nan Fu in the modern Ho Nan province; and as a reward for his services the Warden was granted nearly the whole of the original imperial patrimony west of the Yellow River bend and on both sides of the Wei Valley. This was also in the year 771 B.C., and this is really one of the great pivot-points in Chinese history, of equal weight with the almost contemporaneous founding of Rome, and the gradual substitution of a Roman centre for a Greek centre in the development and civilization of the Far West. The new capital was not, however, a new city. Shortly after the imperial dynasty gained the possession of China in 1122 B.C., it had been surveyed, and some of the regalia had been taken thither; this, with a view of making it one of the capitals at least, if not the sole capital.

As Chinese names sound uncouth to our Western ears, and will, therefore, in these introductory chapters only be used sparingly and gradually, it becomes correspondingly difficult to explain historical phenomena adequately whilst endeavouring to avoid as far as possible the use of such unintelligible names: it will be well, then, to sum up the situation, and even repeat a little, so that the reader may assimilate the main points without fatigue or repulsion. The reigning dynasty of Chou had secured the adhesion of the thousand or more of Chinese vassal princes in 1122 B.C., and had in other words "conquered" China by invitation, much in the same way, and for very much the same general reasons, that William III. had' accepted the conquest of the British Isles; that is to say, because the people were dissatisfied with their legitimate ruler and his house. But, before this conquest, the vassal princes of Chou had occupied practically the same territory, and had stood in the same relation to the imperial dynasty subsequently ousted by them in 1122, that the Wardens of the Marches occupied and stood in when the imperial house of Chou in turn fled east in 771 B.C. The Shang dynasty thus ousted by the Chou princes in 1122, had for like misgovernment driven out the Hia dynasty in 1766 B.C. Thus, at the time when the Wardens of the Marches (whose real territorial title was Princes of Ts'in) practically put the imperial power into commission in 771 B.C., the two old-fashioned dynasties of Shang and Chou had already ruled patriarchally for almost exactly one thousand years, and nothing of either a very startling, or a very definite, character had taken place at all within the comparatively narrow area described in our first chapter.

From this date of 771 B.C., and for five hundred years more down to 250 B.C., when the Chou dynasty was extinguished, the rule of the feudal Emperors of China was almost purely nominal, and except in so far as this or that powerful vassal made use of the moral, and even occasionally of the military power of the metropolitan district when it suited his purpose, the imperial ruler was chiefly exercised in matters of form and ritual; for under all three patriarchal dynasties it was on form and ritual that the idea of government had always been based. Of course the other powerful satraps—especially the more distant ones, those not bearing the imperial clan-name, and those more or less tinged with barbarian usages—learning by degrees what a helpless and powerless personage the Emperor had now become, lost no time in turning the novel situation to their own advantage: it is consequently now that begins the "tyrant period," or the period of the "Five Dictators," as the Chinese historians loosely term it: that is to say, the period during which each satrap who had the power to do so took the lead of the satrap body in general, and gave out that he was restoring the imperial prestige, representing the Emperor's majesty, carrying out the behests of reason, compelling the other vassals to do their duty, keeping up the legitimist sacrifices, and so on. In other words, the population of China had grown so enormously, both by peaceful in-breeding and by imperceptible absorption of kindred races, that more elbow-room was needed; more freedom from the shackles of ritual, rank, and feudal caste; more independence, and more liberty to take advantage of local or changed traditions. Besides all this, the art of writing, though still clumsy, expensive, and confined in its higher and literary aspects to the governing classes, had recently become simplified and improved; the salt trade, iron trade, fish industry, silk industry, grain trade, and art of usury had spread from one state to the other, and had developed: though the land roads were bad or non-existent, there were great numbers of itinerant dealers in cattle and army provisions. In a word, material civilization had made great strides during the thousand years of patriarchal rule immediately preceding the critical period comprised between the year 842 B.C. and the year 771 B.C. The voices of the advocates and the preachers of ancient patriarchal virtues were as of men crying in a wilderness of substantial prosperity and manly ambition. Thus political and natural forces combined with each other to prepare the way for a radical change, and this period of incipient revolution is precisely the period (722-480) treated of in Confucius' history, the first history of China—meagre though it be—which deals with definite human facts, instead of "beating the air" (as the Chinese say) with sermons and ritualistic exhortations.

CHAPTER III.THE NORTHERN POWERS

We have already alluded to a princely family, of the same clan- name as the Chou Emperor, which had settled in the southern part of modern Shan Si province, and had thus acted as a sort of buffer state to the imperial domain by keeping off from it the Tartar- Turk tribes in the north. This family was enfeoffed by the new Chou dynasty in 1106 B.C. to replace the extremely ancient princely house which had reigned there ever since the earliest Emperors ruled from that region (2300 B.C.), but which had resisted the Chou conquest, and had been exterminated. Nothing definite is known of what transpired in this principality subsequently to the infeoffment of 1106 B.C., and prior to the events of 771 B.C., at which latter date the ruling prince, hearing of the disaster to his kinsman the Emperor, went to meet that monarch's fugitive successor, and escorted him eastwards to his new capital. This metropolis had, as we have explained already, been marked out some 340 years before this, and had continued to be one of the chief spiritual and political centres in the imperial domain; but for some reason it had never before 771 B.C. been officially declared a capital, or at all events the capital. Confucius, in his history, does not mention at all the petty semi-Tartar state of which we are now speaking before 671 B.C., and all that we know of its doings during this century of time is that rival factions, family intrigues, and petty annexations at the cost of various Tartar tribes, and of small, but ancient, Chinese principalities, occupied most of its time. It must be repeated here, however, that, notwithstanding Tartar neighbours, the valley of the River Fen had been the seat of several of China's oldest semi-mythical emperors-possibly even of dynasties,-and at no time do the Tartars seem to have ever succeeded in ousting the Chinese from South Shan Si. The official name of the region after the Chou infeoffment of 1106 B.C. was the State of Tsin, and it was roughly divided off to the west from its less civilized colleague Ts'in by the Yellow River, on the right bank of which Tsin still possessed a number of towns. It is particularly difficult for Europeans to realize the sharp distinction in sound between these two names, the more especially because we have in the West no conception whatever of the effect of tone upon a syllable It may be explained, however, that the sonant initial and even-voiced tone in the one case, contrasted with the surd initial and the scaled tone in the other, involves to the Chinese mind a distinction quite as clear in all dialects as the European distinction in all languages between the two states of Prussia and Russia, or between the two peoples Swedes and Swiss: it is entirely the imperfection of our Western alphabet, not at all that of the spoken sounds or the ideographs, that is at fault.

The Yellow River, running from north to south, not only roughly separated from each other these two Tartar-Chinese buffer states in the north-west, but the same Yellow River, flowing east, and its tributary, the River Wei, also formed a rough boundary between the two states of Tsin and Ts'in (together) to the north, and the innumerable petty but ancient Chinese principalities surrounding the imperial domain to the south. These principalities or settlements were scattered about among the head-waters of the Han River and the Hwai River systems, and their manifest destiny, if they needed expansion, clearly drove them further southwards, following the courses of all these head-waters, towards the Yang- tsz Kiang. But, more than that, the Yellow River, after thus flowing east for several hundred miles, turned sharp north in long. 114ø E., as already explained, and thence to the north-east formed a second rough boundary between Tsin and nearly all the remaining orthodox Chinese states. Tsin's chief task was thus to absorb into its administrative system all the Tartar raiders that ventured south to the Yellow River.

But there was a third northern state engaged in the task of keeping back the Tartar tribes, and in developing a civilization of its own-based largely, of course, upon Chinese principles, but modified so as to meet local exigencies. This was the state of Ts'i, enclosed between the Yellow River to the west and the sea to the east, but extending much farther north than the boundaries of modern Shan Tung province, if, indeed, the embouchure of the Yellow River, near modern Tientsin, did not form its northern boundary; but the promontory or peninsula, as well as all the coast, was still in the hands of "barbarian" tribes (now long since civilized and assimilated), of which for many centuries past no separate trace has remained. We have no means of judging now whether these "barbarians" were uncultured, close kinsmen of the orthodox Chinese; or remote kinsmen; or quite foreign. When the Chou principality received an invitation by acclamation to conquer and administer China in 1122, an obscure political worthy from these eastern parts placed his services as adviser and organizer at the command of the new Chou Emperor, in return for which important help he received the fief of Ts'i. Although obscure, this man traced his descent back to the times when (2300 B.C.) his ancestors received fiefs from the most ancient Emperors. From that time down to the year 1122 B.C., and onwards to the events of 771 B.C., nothing much beyond the fact of the Chou infeoffment is recorded; but after the Emperor had been killed by the Tartar- Tibetans, this state of Ts'i also began to grow restive; and the seventh century before Christ opens with the significant statement that "Ts'in, Tsin, and Ts'i, now begin to be powerful states." Of the three, Tsin alone bore the imperial Chou clan-name of Ki.

North of the Yellow River, where it then entered the sea near the modern treaty-port of Tientsin, there was yet another great vassal state, called Yen, which had been given by the founders of the Chou dynasty to a very distinguished blood relative and faithful supporter: this noble prince has been immortalized in beautiful language on account of the rigid justice of his decisions given under the shade of an apple-tree: it was the practice in those days to render into popular song the chief events of the times, and it is not improbable, indeed, that this Saga literature was the only popular record of the past, until, as already hinted, after 827 B.C., writing became simplified and thus more diffused, instead of being confined to solemn manifestoes and commandments cast or carved on bronze or stone.

"Oh! woodman, spare that tree,
Touch not a single bough,
His wisdom lingers now."

The words, singularly like those of our own well-known song, are known to every Chinese school-boy, and with hundreds, even thousands, of other similar songs, which used to be daily quoted as precedents by the statesmen of that primitive period in their political intercourse with each other, were later pruned, purified, and collated by Confucius, until at last they received classical rank in the "Book of Odes" or the "Classic of Poetry," containing a mere tenth part of the old "Odes" as they used to be passed from mouth to ear.

Even less is known of the early days of Yen than is known of Ts'in, Tsin, and Ts'i; there is not even a vague tradition to suggest who ruled it, or what sort of a place it was, before the Chou prince was sent there; all that is anywhere recorded is that it was a very small, poor, and feeble region, dovetailed in between Tsin and Ts'i, and exposed north to the harassing attacks of savages and Coreans (i.e. tribes afterwards enumerated as forming part of Corea when the name of Corea became known). The mysterious region is only mentioned here at all on account of its distinguished origin, in order to show that the Chinese cultivators had from the very earliest times apparently succeeded in keeping the bulk of the Tartars to the left bank of the Yellow River all the way from the Desert to the sea; because later on (350 B.C.) Yen actually did become a powerful state; and finally, because if any very early notions concerning Corea and Japanese islands had ever crept vaguely into China at all, it must have been through this state of Yen, which was coterminous with Liao Tung and Manchuria. The great point to remember is, the extensive territory between the Great Wall and the Yellow River then lay almost entirely beyond the pale of ancient China, and it was only when Ts'in, Tsin, Ts'i, and Yen had to look elsewhere than to the Emperor for protection from Tartar inroads that the centre of political gravity was changed once and for ever from the centre of China to the north.

We know nothing of the precise causes which conduced to unusual Tartar activity at the dawn of Chinese true history: in the absence of any Tartar knowledge of writing, it seems impossible now that we ever can know it. Still less are we in a position to speculate profitably how far the movements on the Chinese frontier, in 800-600 B.C., may be connected with similar restlessness on the Persian and Greek frontiers, of which, again, we know nothing very illuminating or specific. It is certain that the Chinese had no conception of a Tartar empire, or of a coherent monarchy, under the vigorous dominion of a great military genius, until at least five centuries after the Tartars, killed a Chinese Emperor in battle as related (771 B.C.). It is even uncertain what were the main race distinctions of the nomad aggregations, loosely styled by us "Tartars," for the simple reason that the ambiguous Chinese terminology does not enable us to select a more specific word. Nevertheless, the Chinese do make certain distinctions; and, as what remains of aboriginal populations in the north, south, east, and west of China points strongly to the probability of populations in the main occupying the same sites that they did 3000 years ago (unless where specific facts point to a contrary conclusion), we may fairly assume that the distribution was then very much as now-beginning from the east, (1) Japanese, (2) Corean, (3) Tungusic, (4) Mongol-Turkish, (5) Turkish, (6) Turkish-Tibetan, and Mongol-Tibetan (or Mongol-Turkoid Tibetan), (7) Tibetan. The Chinese use four terms to express these relative quantities, which may be called X, Y, Z, and A. The term "X," pure and simple, never under any circumstances refers to any but Tibetans (of whom at this time the Chinese had no recorded knowledge whatever except by name); but "X + Y" also refers to tribes in Tibetan regions. The term "West Y" seems to mean Tibetan-Tartars, and the term "North Y" seems to mean Mongoloid- Tunguses. There is a third Y term, "Dog Y," evidently meaning Tartars of some kind, and not Tibetans of any sort. The term "Z" never refers to Tibetans, pure or mixed, but "Y + Z" loosely refers to Turks, Mongols, and Tunguses. The terms "Red Z", "White Z," and "North Z" seem to indicate Turks; and what is more, these colour distinctions—probably of clothing or head-gear-continue to quite modern times, and always in connection with Turks or Mongol-Turks. The fourth term "A" never occurs before the third century before Christ, and refers to all Tartars, Coreans, etc.; but not to Tibetans: it need not, therefore, be discussed at present. The modern province of Sz Ch'wan was absolutely unknown even by name; but several centuries later, as we shall shortly see, it turned out to be a state of considerable magnitude, with quite a little imperial history of its own: probably it was with this unknown state that the bulk of the

Tibetans tried conclusions, if they tried them with China at all.

Be that as it may, the present wish is to make clear that at the first great turning-point in genuine Chinese history the whole of north and west China was in the hands of totally unknown powers, who completely shut in the Middle Kingdom; who only manifested themselves at all in the shape of occasional bodies of raiders; and who, if they had any knowledge, direct or indirect, of India, Tibet, Turkestan, Siberia, Persia, etc., kept it strictly to themselves, and in any case were incapable of communicating it in writing to the frontier Chinese populations of the four buffer states above enumerated.

CHAPTER IV. THE SOUTHERN POWER

But the collapse of the imperial power in 771 B.C. led to restlessness in the south as well as in the north, north-western, and north-eastern regions: except for a few Chinese adventurers and colonists, these were exclusively inhabited by nomad Tartars, and perhaps some Tibetans, destitute of fixed residences, cities, and towns; ignorant of cultivation, agriculture, and letters; and roving about from pasture to pasture with their flocks and herds, finding excitement and diversion chiefly in periodical raids upon their more settled southern and western neighbours. The only country south of the federated Chinese princes in Ho Nan province (as we now call it) was the "Jungle" or "Thicket," a term which vaguely designated the lower waters of the Han River system, much as, with ourselves, the "Lowlands" or the "Netherlands" did, and still does, designate the outlying marches of the English and German communities. "Jungle" is still the elegant literary name for Hu Peh, just as Ts'in, Tsin, and Ts'i are for Shen Si, Shan Si, and Shan Tung. The King of the Jungle, like the Warden of the Western Marches, traced his descent far back to the same ancient monarchs whose blood ran also in the veins of the imperial house of Chou; and moreover this Jungle King's ancestors had served the founders of the Chou dynasty in 1150 B.C., whilst they were still hesitating whether to accept the call to empire: hence in later times (530 B.C.) the King made it a grievance that his family had not received from the founder of the Chou dynasty presents symbolical of equality of birth, as had the Tsin and Lu (South Shan Tung) houses. If any tribes, south, south-east, or south-west of this vague Jungle, whose administrative centre at first lay within a hundred miles' radius of the modern treaty-port of Ich'ang, were in any way known to Central China, it was and must have been entirely through this kingdom of the Jungle, and in a second-hand or indirect way. The Jungle was as much a buffer to the south as Ts'in was to the north-west, Tsin to the north, and Ts'i to the north-east. The bulk of the population was in one sense non- Chinese; that is, it was probably a mixture of the many uncivilized mountain tribes (all speaking monosyllabic and tonic dialects like the Chinese) who still survive in every one of the provinces south of the Yang-tsz Kiang; but the ruling caste, whose administrative centre lay to the north of these tribes, though affected by the grossness of their barbarous surroundings, were manifestly more or less orthodox Chinese in origin and sympathy, and, even at this early period (771 B.C.), possessed a considerable culture, a knowledge of Chinese script, and a general capacity to live a settled economical existence. As far back as 880 B.C. the King of the Jungle is recorded to have governed or conciliated the populations between the Han and the Yang-tsz Rivers; but, though he arrogated to himself for a time the title of "Emperor" or "King" in his own dominions, he confessed himself to be a barbarian, and disclaimed any share in the honorific system of titles, living or posthumous, having vogue in China, reserving it for his successors to assert higher rights when they should feel strong enough. Like an eastern Charlemagne, he divided his empire between his three sons; and this empire, which gradually extended all along the Yang-tsz down to its mouths, may have included in one of its three subdivisions a part at least of the Annamese race, as will be suggested more in detail anon.

The first really historical king, who once more arrogated the supreme title in 704 B.C., took advantage of imperial weakness to extend his conquests not only to the south but to the north of the River Han, attacking petty Chinese principalities, and boldly claiming recognition by the Emperor of equality in title. "I am a barbarian," said he, "and I will avail myself of the dissensions among the federal princes to inspect Chinese ways for myself." The Emperor displayed some irritation at this claim of equal rank, but the King retorted by referring to the services rendered by his (the King's) ancestor, some five hundred years earlier, to the Emperor's ancestor, virtual founder of the Chou dynasty. In 689 B.C. the next king moved his capital from its old site above the Ich'ang gorges to the commanding central situation now known as King-thou Fu, just above the treaty-port of Sha-shi': this place historically continues the use of the old word Jungle (King), and has been all through the present Manchu dynasty (1644-1908) the military residence of a Tartar-General with a Banner garrison; that is, a garrison of privileged Tartar soldiers living in cantonments, and exempt from the ordinary laws, or, at least, the application of them. It is only in 684 B.C. that the Jungle state is first honoured with mention in Confucius' history: it was, indeed, impossible then to ignore its existence, because, for the first time in the annals of China, Chinese federal princes between the Han River and the westernmost head-waters of the Hwai River had been deliberately annexed by these Jungle "barbarians." History for the next 450 years from this date consists mainly of the intricate narration how Ts'in, Tsin, Ts'i, and the Jungle struggled, first for hegemony, and finally for the possession of all China, The Jungle was now called Ts'u.

CHAPTER V.EVIDENCE OF ECLIPSES

Having now shown, as shortly and as intelligibly as we can, how the germs of Chinese development were sown at the dawn of true history, let us proceed to examine how far that history, as it has come down to us, contains within it testimony to its own truth. We shall revert to the description of wars and ambitions in due course; but, as so obscure a subject as early Chinese civilization is only palatable to most Western readers in small, varied, and sugared doses, we shall for the moment vary the nourishment offered, and say a few words upon eclipses. Confucius, whose bald "Spring and Autumn" annals, as expanded by three separate commentators (one a junior contemporary of himself), is really the chief authority for the period 722-468 B.C., was born on the 20th day after the eclipse of the sun which took place in the 10th month of 552 B.C., or the 27th of the 8th moon as worked out to-day (for 1908 this means the 22nd September). Confucius himself records thirty-seven eclipses of the sun between 720 and 481, those of 709, 601, and 549 being total. Of course, as Confucius primarily recorded the eclipses as seen from his own petty vassal state of Lu in Shan Tung province (lat. 35" 40' N., long, 117" E.), any one endeavouring to identify these eclipses, and to compare them with Julian or Gregorian dates, must, in making the necessary calculations, bear this important fact in mind. It so happens that nearly one-third of Confucius' thirty-seven eclipses are recorded as having taken place between the two total eclipses of 601 and 549. This being so, I referred the list to an obliging officer attached to the Royal Observatory, who has kindly furnished me with the following comparative list:-

CONFUCIUS' DATE. OPPOLZER'S JULIAN DATE.

B.C. 601, 7th moon.—-600, September 20.

" 599, 4th " —-598, March 5.

" 592, 6th " —-591, April 17.
" 575, 6th " —-574, May 9.
" 574, 12th " —-573, October 22.
" 559, 2nd " —-558, January 14.
" 558, 8th " —-557, June 29.
" 553, 10th " —-552, August 31.
" 552, 9th "
" 552, 10th " —-551, August 20.
" 550, 2nd " —-549, January 5.
" 549, 7th " —-548, April 19.

It will be observed that there is no Oppolzer's date to compare with the first of the two eclipses of 552; this is because I omitted to notice that there had been recorded in the "Springs and Autumns" two so close together, and therefore I did not include it in the list sent to the Observatory; but with the exception of the total eclipse of 601, all the other eclipses, so far as days of the moon and month go, are as consistent with each other as are modern Chinese dates with European (Julian) dates. As regards the year, Oppolzer's dates are the "astronomical" dates, that is, the astronomical year—x is the same as the year (x + 1) B.C.; or, in other words, the year of Christ's birth is, for certain astronomical exactitude purposes, interpolated between the years 1 B.C. and A.D. 1, as we vulgarly compute them: that is to say, the eclipses of the sun recorded 2,400 years ago by Confucius, from notes and annals preserved in his native state's archives as far back as 700 B.C., are found to be almost without exception fairly correct, with a uniform "error" of about one month, despite the fact that attempts were made by the First August Emperor to destroy all historical literature in 213 B.C. This being so in the matter of a dozen eclipses, there still remain two dozen for specialists to experiment upon, not to mention comets and other celestial phenomena. From this collateral evidence, imperfect though it be, we are reasonably entitled to assume that the three expanded versions of Confucius' history are trustworthy, or at the very least written in the best of faith.

Just as our mathematicians find no difficulty either in foretelling or retrospecting eclipses to a minute, so does the ancient "sixty" cycle, which the Chinese have from time immemorial used for computing or noting days and years, enable them, or for the matter of that ourselves, to calculate back unerringly any desired day. Thus, suppose the 1st January, 1908, is the 37th day of the perpetual cycle of sixty days; then, if the Chinese historians say that an eclipse took place on the first day of the new moon, which began the 9th Chinese month of the year corresponding in the main to our 800 B.C., and that the 1st day of the moon was also the 37th day of the sixty-day perpetual cycle, all we have to do is take roughly six cycles for each year, six thousand cycles for each thousand years, allowing at the same time two extra cycles every third year for intercalary moons, and then dealing with the fractions or balance of days. If our calculation does not bring the two 37th cyclic days together accurately, we must of course go into the question of how and when the Chinese calendars were altered, a subject that will be treated of in a subsequent chapter. It must be remembered that there can never be any question of so much as a whole year being involved in the balance of error; for, with the Chinese as with us, one year, whenever modified, always means that space of time, however irregularly computed at each end of it, within which two solstices and two equinoxes have taken place, Voltaire, in the article on "China" of his Universal Dictionary, remarks that "of 32 ancient Chinese eclipses, 28 have been identified by Western mathematicians"; and M. Edouard Chavannes, who has given a great deal of time and labour to working out the mysteries of the Chinese calendar, does not hesitate to claim accuracy to the very day (29th August) for the eclipse of the sun recorded in the Book of Odes (as re-edited by Confucius) as having taken place on the 28th cyclic day of the beginning of the both moon in 776 B.C. (i.e. of—775). This eclipse is of course not recorded in the "Springs and Autumns," which begins with the year 722 B.C.

The Chou dynasty, which came into power in 1122, for the second time put back the year a month because the calendar was getting confused. That is, they made what we should call January begin the legal year instead of February; or the still more ancient March; but some of the vassals either used computations of their own, or kept up those handed down by the two dynasties previous to that of Chou: hence in the Confucian histories, as expanded, there are frequent discrepancies in consequence of events apparently copied from the records of one vassal state having been reported to the historian of a second vassal state without steps having been taken to adjust the different new years.

CHAPTER VI.THE ARMY

As the struggle for pre-eminency which we are about to describe involved bloodthirsty combats extending almost uninterruptedly over five centuries, it may be of interest to inquire of what consisted the paraphernalia of warfare in those days. It appears that among the Chinese federal princes, who, as we have seen, only occupied in the main the flat country on the right bank of the Yellow River, war-chariots were invariably used, which is the more remarkable in that after the Conquest in 220 B.C. of China by the First August Emperor of Ts'in, and down to this day, war-chariots have scarcely ever once been even named, at least as having been marshalled in serious battle array. The Emperor alone was supposed in true feudal times to possess a force of 10,000 chariots, and even now a "10,000-chariot" state is the diplomatic expression for "a great power," "a power of the first rank," or "an empire." No vassal was entitled to more than 1000 war-chariots. In the year 632 B.C., when Tsin inflicted a great defeat upon its chief rival Ts'u, the former power had 700 chariots in the field. In 589 B.C. the same country, with 800 chariots included in its forces, marched across the Yellow River and defeated the state of Ts'i, its rival to the east. Again in 632 Tsin offered to the Emperor 100 chariots just captured from Ts'u, and in 613 sent 800 chariots to the assistance of a dethroned Emperor. The best were made of leather, and we may assume from this that the wooden ones found it very difficult to get safely over rough ground, for in a celebrated treaty of peace of 589 B.C. between the two rival states Tsin and Ts'i, the victor, lying to the west, imposed a condition that "your ploughed furrows shall in future run east and west instead of north and south," meaning that "no systematic obstacles shall in future be placed in the way of our invading chariots."

One of the features in many of the vassal states was the growth of great families, whose private power was very apt to constrain the wishes of the reigning duke, count, or baron. Thus in the year 537, when the King of Ts'u was meditating a treacherous attack upon Tsin, he was warned that "there were many magnates at the behest of the ruler of Tsin, each of whom was equal to placing 100 war-chariots in the field." So much a matter of course was it to use chariots in war, that in the year 572, when the rival great powers of Ts'u and Tsin were contesting for suzerainty over one of the purely Chinese principalities in the modern Ho Nan province, it was considered quite a remarkable fact that this principality in taking the side of Ts'u brought no chariots with the forces led against Tsin. In 541 a refugee prince of Ts'u, seeking asylum in Tsin, only brought five chariots with him, on which the ruler, ashamed as host of such a poor display, at once assigned him revenue sufficient for the maintenance of 100 individuals. It so happened that at the same time there arrived in Tsin a refugee prince from Ts'in, bringing with him 1000 carts, all heavily laden. On another occasion the prince (not a ruler) of a neighbouring state, on visiting the ruler of another, brings with him as presents an eight-horsed chariot for the reigning prince, a six-horsed conveyance for the premier, a four-horsed carriage for a very distinguished minister in the suite, and a two-horsed cart for a minor member of the mission.

Besides the heavy war-chariots, there were also rather more comfortable and lighter conveyances: in one case two generals are spoken of ironically because they went to the front playing the banjo in a light cart, whilst their colleague from another state— the very state they were assisting—was roughing it in a war- chariot. These latter seem to have connoted, for military organization purposes, a strength of 75 men each, and four horses; to wit, three heavily armed men or cuirassiers in the chariot itself, and 72 foot-soldiers. At least in the case of Tsin, a force of 37,500 men, which in the year 613 boldly marched off three hundred or more English miles upon an eastern expedition, is so described. On the other hand, thirty years later, a small Ts'u force is said to have had 125 men attached to each chariot, while the Emperor's chariots are stated to have had 100 men assigned to each. In the year 627 a celebrated battle was fought between the rival powers of Ts'in and Tsin, in which the former was utterly routed; "not a man nor a wheel of the whole army ever got back." War-chariots are mentioned as having been in use at least as far back as 1797 B.C. by the Tartar-affected ancestors of the Chou dynasty, nearly 700 years before they themselves came to the imperial power. The territory north of the River Wei, inhabited by them, is all yellow loess, deeply furrowed by the stream in question, and by its tributaries: there is no apparent reason to suppose that the gigantic cart-houses used by the Tartars, even to this day, had any historical connection with the swift war- chariots of the Chinese.

Little, if anything, is said of conveying troops by boat in any of the above-mentioned countries north of the Yang-tsz River. None of the rivers in Shen Si are navigable, even now, for any considerable stretches, and the Yellow River itself has its strict limitations. Later on, when the King of Ts'u's possessions along the sea coast, embracing the delta of the Yang-tsz, revolted from his suzerainty and began (as we shall relate in due course) to take an active part in orthodox Chinese affairs, boats and gigantic canal works were introduced by the hitherto totally unknown or totally forgotten coast powers; and it is probably owing to this innovation that war-chariots suddenly disappeared from use, and that even in the north of China boat expeditions became the rule, as indeed was certainly the case after the third century B.C.

Some idea of the limited population of very ancient China may be gained from a consideration of the oldest army computations. The Emperor was supposed to have six brigades, the larger vassals three, the lesser two, and the small ones one; but owing to the loose way in which a Shi, or regiment of 2,500 men, and a Kun, or brigade of 12,500 men, are alternately spoken of, the Chinese commentators themselves are rather at a loss to estimate how matters really stood after the collapse of the Emperor in 771: but though at much later dates enormous armies, counting up to half a million men on each side, stubbornly contended for mastery, at the period of which we speak there is no reason to believe that any state, least of all the imperial reserve, ever put more than 1000 chariots, or say, 75,000 men, into the field on any one expedition.

Flags seem to have been in use very much as in the West. The founder of the Chou dynasty marched to the conquest of China carrying, or having carried for him, a yellow axe in the left, and a white flag in the right hand. In 660 one of the minor federal princes was crushed because he did not lower his standard in time; nearly a century later, this precedent was quoted to another federal prince when hard-pressed, in consequence of which a sub- officer "rolled up his master's standard and put it in its sheath." In 645 "the cavaliers under the ruler's flag "—defined to mean his body-guard—were surrounded by the enemy.

During the fifth century B.C., when the coast provinces, having separated from the Ts'u suzerainty, were asserting their equality with the orthodox Chinese princes, and two rival "barbarian" armies were contending for the Shanghai region, one royal scion was indignant when he saw the enemy advance "with the flag captured in the last battle from his own father the general." Flags were used, not only to signal movements of troops during the course of battle, but also in the great hunts or battues which were arranged in peace times, not merely for sport, but also in order to prepare soldiers for a military life.

For victories over the Tartars in 623, the Emperor presented the ruler of Ts'in with a metal drum; and it seems that sacrificing to the regimental drum before a fight was a very ancient custom, which has been carried down to the present day. In 1900, during the "Boxer" troubles, General (now Viceroy) Yiian Shi-k'ai is reported to have sacrificed several condemned criminals to his drum before setting out upon his march.

CHAPTER VII.THE COAST STATES

Before we enter into a categorical description of the hegemony or Protector system, under which the most powerful state for the time being held durbars "in camp," and in theory maintained the shadowy rights of the Emperor, we must first introduce the two coast states of the Yang-tsz delta, just mentioned as having asserted their independence of Ts'u, each state being in possession of one of the Great River branches, In ancient times the Yang-tsz was simply called the Kiang ("river"), just as the Yellow River was simply styled the Ho (also "river"). In those days the Great River had three mouths-the northernmost very much as at present, except that the flat accretions did not then extend so far out to sea, and in any case were for all practical purposes unknown to orthodox China, and entirely in the hands of "Eastern barbarians"; the southerly course, which branched off near the modern treaty-port of Wuhu in An Hwei province, emerging into the sea at, or very near, Hangchow; and the middle course, which was practically the combined beds of the Soochow Creek and the Wusung River of Shanghai. Before the Chou dynasty came to power in 1122 B.C., the grandfather of the future founder, as a youth, displayed such extraordinary talents, that, by family arrangement, his two eldest brothers voluntarily resigned their rights, and exiled themselves in the Jungle territory, subsequently working their way east to the coast, and adopting entirely, or in part, the rude ways of the barbarous tribes they hoped to govern. We can understand this better if we picture how the Phoenician and Greek merchants in turn acted when successively colonizing Marseilles, Cadiz, and even parts of Britain. Excepting doubtful genealogies and lists of rulers, nothing whatever is heard of this colony until 585 B.C.—say, 800 years subsequent to the original settlement. A malcontent of Ts'u had, as was the practice among the rival states of those, times, offered his services to the hated Tsin, then engaged in desperate warfare with Ts'u: he proposed to his new master that he should be sent on a mission to the King of Wu (for that was, and still is, for literary purposes, the name of the kingdom comprising Shanghai, Soochow, and Nanking) in order to induce him to join in attacking Ts'u. "He taught them the use of arrows and chariots," from which we may assume that spears and boats were, up to that date, the usual warlike apparatus of the coast power. Its capital was at a spot about half-way between Soochow and Nanking, on the new (British) railway line; and it is described by Chinese visitors during the sixth century B.C. as being "a mean place, with low-built houses, narrow streets, a vulgar palace, and crowds of boats and wheelbarrows." The native word for the country was something like Keugu, which the Chinese (as they still do with foreign words, as, for instance, Ying for "England") promptly turned into a convenient monosyllable Ngu, or Wu. The semi-barbarous King was delighted at the opening thus given him to associate with orthodox Chinese princes on an equal footing, and to throw off his former tyrannical suzerain. He annexed a number of neighbouring barbarian states hitherto, like himself, belonging to Ts'u; paid visits to the Emperor's court, to the Ts'u court, and to the petty but highly cultivated court of Lu (in South Shan Tung), in order to "study the rites"; and threw himself with zest into the whirl of interstate political intrigue. Confucius in his history hardly alludes to him as a civilized being until the year 561, when the King died; and as his services to China (i.e. to orthodox Tsin against unorthodox Ts'u) could not be ignored, the philosopher- historian condescends to say "the Viscount of Wu died this year." It must be explained that the Lu capital had been celebrated for its learning ever since the founder of the Chou dynasty sent the Duke of Chou, his own brother, there as a satrap (1122 B.C.). Confucius, of course, wrote retrospectively, for he himself was only born in 551 and did not compose his "Springs and Autumns" history for at least half a century after that date. The old Lu capital of K'uh-fu on she River Sz (both still so called) is the official headquarters of the Dukes Confucius, the seventy-sixth in descent from the Sage having at this moment direct semi-official relations with Great Britain's representative at Wei-hai-wei. It must also be explained that the vassal princes were all dukes, marquises, earls, viscounts, or barons, according to the size of their states, the distinction of their clan or gens, and the length of their pedigrees; but the Emperor somewhat contemptuously accorded only the courtesy title of "viscount" to barbarian "kings," such as those of Ts'u and Wu, very much as we vaguely speak of "His Highness the Khedive," or (until last year) "His Highness the Amir," so as to mark inequality with genuine crowned or sovereign heads.

The history of the wars between Wu and Ts'u is extremely interesting, the more so in that there are some grounds for believing that at least some part of the Japanese civilization was subsequently introduced from the east coast of China, when the ruling caste of Wu, in its declining days, had to "take flight eastwards in boats to the islands to the east of the coast." But we shall come to that episode later on. In the year 506 the capital of Ts'u was occupied by a victorious Wu army, under circumstances full of dramatic detail. But now, in the flush of success, it was Wu's turn to suffer from the ambition of a vassal. South of Wu, with a capital at the modern Shao-hing, near Ningpo, reigned the barbarian King of Yiieh (this is a corrupted monosyllable supposed to represent a dissyllabic native word something like Uviet); and this king had once been a 'vassal of Ts'u, but had, since Wu's conquests, transferred, either willingly or under local compulsion, his allegiance to Wu. Advances were made to him by Ts'u, and he was ultimately induced to declare war as an ally of Ts'u. There is nothing more interesting in our European history than the detailed account, full of personal incident, of the fierce contests between Wu and Yiieh. The extinction of Wu took place in 483, after that state had played a very commanding part in federal affairs, as we shall have occasion to specify in the proper places. Yiieh, in turn, peopled by a race supposed to have ethnological connection with the Annamese of Vietnam or "Southern Yiieh," became a great power in China, and in 468 even transferred its capital to a spot on or near the coast, very near the German colony of Kiao Chou in Shan Tung. But its predominance was only successfully asserted on the coasts; to use the historians' words: "Yiieh could never effectively administer the territory comprised in the Yang-tsz Kiang and Hwai River regions."

It was precisely during this barbarian struggle, when federated China, having escaped the Tartars, seemed to be running the risk of falling into the clutches of southern pirates, that Confucius flourished, and it is in reference to the historical events sketched above-(1) the providential escape of China from Tartardom, (2) the collapse of the imperial Chou house, (3) the hegemony or Protector system, (4) the triumph of might over rite (right and rite being one with Confucius), and (5) the desirability of a prompt return to the good old feudal ways—that he abandoned his own corrupt and ungrateful principality, began his peripatetic teaching in the other orthodox states, composed a warning history full of lessons for future guidance, and established what we somewhat inaccurately call a "religion" for the political guidance of mankind.

CHAPTER VIII.FIRST PROTECTOR OF CHINA

The first of the so-called five hegemons or lords-protector of the federated Chinese Empire (after the collapse of the imperial power, and its consequent incapacity to protect the vassal states from the raids of the Tartars and other barbarians) was the Lord of Ts'i, whose capital was at the powerful and wealthy city of Lin-tsz (lat. 37ø, long. 118ø 30'; still so called on the modern maps), in Shan Tung province. Neither the Yellow River nor the Grand Canal touched Shan Tung in those days, and Lin-tsz was evidently situated with reference to the local rivers which flow north into the Gulf of "Pechelee," so as to take full political advantage of the salt, mining, and fishing industries. A word is here necessary as to this Protector's pedigree: we have seen that his ancestor, thirteen generations back, had inspired with his counsels and courage the founder of the imperial Chou dynasty in 1122 B.C.; he had further given to the new Emperor a daughter of his own in marriage, had served him as premier, and had finally been enfeoffed in reward for his services as Marquess of Ts'i, the economic condition of which far-eastern principality he had in a very few years by his energy as ruler mightily improved, notably with reference to the salt and fish industries, and to general commerce. The Yellow River, then flowing along the bed of what is now called the Chang River, and the sea, respectively, were the western and eastern limits of this state, which embraced to the north the salt flats now under the administration of a special Tientsin Commissioner, and extended south to the present Manchu Tartar-General's military garrison at Ts'ing-thou Fu. Of course, later on, during the five-hundred-year period of unrest, extensions and cessions of territory frequently took place, both within and beyond these vague limits, usually at the expense of Lu and other small orthodox states. Across the Yellow River, whose course northwards, as already stated, lay considerably to the west of the present channel, was the extensive state of Tsin; and south was the highly ritual and literary Weimar of China, the unwarlike principality of Lu, destined in future times to be glorified by Confucius.

Scarcely anything is recorded of a nature to throw specific light upon the international development of these far-eastern parts. But in the year 894 B.C. the reigning prince of Ts'i was boiled alive at the Emperor's order for some political offence, and his successor thereupon moved his capital, only to be transferred back to the old place by his son thirty-five years later. The imperial flight of 842 naturally caused some consternation even in distant Ts'i, and in 827 the next Emperor on his accession commanded the reigning Marquess of Ts'i to assist in chastising the Western Tartars. When this last Emperor's grandson was driven from his old hereditary domain in 771, and the semi-Tartar ruler of Ts'in took possession of the same, as already narrated, Ts'i was still so inconsiderable a military power that even two generations after that event, in the year 706, it was fain to apply for assistance against Northern Tartar raids to one of the small Chinese principalities in the Ho Nan province. (Roughly speaking, "Northern Tartars" were Manchu-Mongols, and "Western Tartars" were Mongol-Turks.) In 690 the prince, whose sister had married the neighbouring ruler of Lu, made an armed attack by way of vengeance upon the descendant of the adviser who had counselled the Emperor to boil his ancestor alive in 894: his power was now so considerable that the Emperor commissioned him to act with authority in the matter of a disputed succession to a minor Chinese principality. This was in the year 688 B.C., and it was the first instance of a vassal acting as dictator or protector on behalf of the Emperor; only, however, in a special or isolated case. Two years later this prince of Ts'i was himself assassinated, and the disputes between his sons regarding the succession terminated with the advent to the throne of one of the great characters in Chinese history, who was magnanimous and politic enough to take as his adviser and premier a still greater character, and one that almost rivals Confucius himself in fame as an author, a statesman, a benefactor of China; and a moralist.

This personage, who, like most Chinese of the period, carried many names, is most generally known as the philosopher Kwan-tsz, and his chief writings have survived, in part at least, until our own day. He was, in fact, a distant scion of the reigning imperial family of Chou, and bore its clan name of Ki. Here it may be useful to state parenthetically that most prominent men in all the federated states seem to have belonged to a narrow aristocratic circle, among whose members the craft of government, the knowledge of letters, and the hereditary right to expect office, was inherent; at the same time, there was never at any date anything in the shape of a priestly or military caste, and power appears to have been always within the reach of the humblest, so long as the aspirant was competent to assert himself.

The new ruler of Ts'i officially proclaimed himself Protector in the year 679 B.C., which is one of the fixed dates in Chinese history about which there is no cavil or doubt, He soon found himself embroiled in war with the Tartars, who were raiding both the state to his north in the Peking plain, and also the minor state, south of the Yellow River, that his predecessor has protected specially in 688. This was the state of Wei (imperial clan), through or near the capital town of which, near the modern Wei-hwei Fu, the Yellow River then ran northwards.

The way these successive Protectors of China afterwards exercised their preponderant influence in a general sense was this: When it appeared to them, or when any orthodox vassal state complained to them, that injustice was being done; whether in matters of duty to the Emperor, right of succession, legitimacy of birth, great crime, or inordinate ambition; the recognized Protector summoned a durbar, usually somewhere within the territory of the central area, or China proper as previously defined, and consulted with the princes, his colleagues, as to what course should be pursued. A distinction was drawn between "full-dress durbars" and "military durbars"; the etiquette in either case was very minute, and external behaviour at least was exquisitely courteous, though treachery was far from rare, and treaties never lasted long unbroken. But to return to the First Protector. Towards the end of his glorious reign of forty-three years the Marquess of Ts'i grew arrogant, vainglorious, and licentious, so much so that his western neighbour, the powerful state of Tsin, declined to attend the durbars. Of the other great powers Ts'in (to the west of Tsin) was much too far off to take active part in these parliaments; Ts'u was too busy in spreading civilization among the barbarous states or tribes south of the Yang-tsz. The Emperor was practically a roi fainéant by this time, and, curiously enough, less is known of what went on within his dominions or appanage after the western half of it fell to Ts'in in 771, than of what transpired in the territories of his three menacing vassals to the north, north-west, and north-east, and of his half- civilized satrap to the south. The fact is, all four rising powers were now carefully engaged in watching each other, and in playing a profound political game around their prey. This prey was the eastern half of the Emperor's original domain (the western half now, since 771 B.C., belonging to Ts'in) and the dozen or so of purely Chinese, highly cultured, vassal states making up the rest of modern Ho Nan province, together with small parts or wedges of modern Chih Li, Shan Tung, An Hwei, and Kiang Su. From first to last none of these ritual and literary states showed any real fight; there is hardly a single record of a really crushing victory gained by any one of them. The fighting instincts all lay with the new Chinese, that is, with the Chinese adventurers who had got their hand well in with generations of fighting against barbarians—Tartars, Tunguses, Annamese, Shans, and what not—and had invigorated themselves with good fresh barbarian blood. The fact is, the population of China had enormously increased; the struggle for life and food was keener; the old patriarchal appetite for ritual was disappearing; the people were beginning to assert themselves against the land-owners; the land-owners were encroaching upon the power of the ruling princes; and China was in a parlous state.

CHAPTER IX.POSITION OF ENVOYS

It was a fixed rule in ancient China that envoys should be treated with courtesy, and that their persons should be held sacred, whether at residential courts, in durbar, or on the road through a third state. During the wars of the sixth century B.C. between Tsin in the north and Ts'u in the south, when these two powers were rival aspirants to the Protectorate of the original and orthodox group of principalities lying between them, and were alternately imposing their will on the important and diplomatic minor Chinese state of CHÊNG (still the name of a territory in Ho Nan), there were furnished many illustrations of this recognized rule. The chief reason for thus making a fighting-ground of the old Chinese principalities was that it was almost impossible for Ts'u to get conveniently at any of the three great northern powers, and equally difficult for Ts'in, Tsin, and Ts'i to reach Ts'u, without passing through one or more Chinese states, mostly bearing the imperial clan name, and permission had to be asked for an army to pass through, unless the said Chinese state was under the predominancy of (for instance) Tsin or Ts'u. It was like Germany and Italy with Switzerland between them, or Germany and Spain with France between them. Another important old Chinese state was Sung, lying to the east of CHÊNG. Both these states were of the highest caste, the Earl of CHÊNG being a close relative of the Chou Emperor, and the Duke of Sung being the representative or religious heir of the remains of the Shang dynasty ousted by the Chou family in I 122 B.C., magnanimously reinfeoffed "in order that the family sacrifices might not be entirely cut off" together with the loss of imperial sway. In the year 595 B.C. Sung went so far as to put a Ts'u envoy to death, naturally much to the wrath of the rising southern power. Ts'u in turn arrested the Tsin envoy on his way to Sung, and tried in vain to force him to betray his trust. In 582 Tsin, in a fit of anger, detained the CHÊNG envoy, and finally put him to death for his impudence in coming officially to visit Tsin after coquetting with Tsin's rival Ts'u. All these irregular cases are severely blamed by the historians. In 562 Ts'u turned the tables upon Tsin by putting the CHÊNG envoy to death after the latter had concluded a treaty with Tsin. Confucius joins, retrospectively of course, in the chorus of universal reprobation. In 560 Ts'u tried to play upon the Ts'i envoy a trick which in its futility reminds us strongly of the analogous petty humiliations until recently imposed by China, whenever convenient occasion offered, upon foreign officials accredited to her. The Ts'i envoy, who was somewhat deformed in person, was no less an individual than the celebrated philosopher Yen-tsz, a respected acquaintance of Confucius (though, of course, much his senior), and second only to Kwan-tsz amongst the great administrative statesmen of Ts'i. The half-barbarous King of Ts'u concocted with his obsequious courtiers a nice little scheme for humiliating the northern envoy by indicating to him the small door provided for his entry into the presence, such as the Grand Seigneurs in their hey-day used to provide for the Christian ambassadors to Turkey. Yen-tsz, of course, at once saw through this contemptible insult and said: "My master had his own reasons for selecting so unworthy an individual as myself for this mission; yet if he had sent me on a mission to a dog-court, I should have obeyed orders and entered by a dog-gate: however, it so happens that I am here on a mission to the King of Ts'u, and of course I expect to enter by a gate befitting the status of that ruler." Still another prank was tried by the foolish king: a "variety entertainment" was got up, in which one scene represented a famished wretch who was being belaboured for some reason. Naturally every one asked: "What is that?" The answer was: "A Ts'i man who has been detected in thieving." Yen-tsz said: "I understand that the best fruits come from Ts'u, and they say we northern men cannot come near the quality of their peaches. We are honest simpletons, too, and do not look natural on the variety stage as thieves. The true rogue, like the true peach, is a southern speciality. I did see rogues on the stage, it is true, but none of them looked like a Ts'i man; hence I asked, 'What is it?'" The king laughed sheepishly, and, for a time at least, gave up taking liberties with Yen-tsz.

In 545, when Ts'u for the moment had the predominant say over CHÊNG's political action, it was insisted that the ruler of CHÊNG should come in person to pay his respects: this was after a great Peace Conference, held at Sung, on which occasion Tsin and Ts'u arranged a modus operandi for their respective subordinate or allied vassals. There was no help for it, and the Earl accordingly went. The minister in attendance was Tsz-ch'an-a very great name indeed in Chinese history; he was a lawyer, statesman, "democratic conservative," sceptic, and philosopher, deeply lamented on his death alike by the people of CHÊNG, and by his friend or correspondent Confucius of Lu state. The Chinese diplomats then, as now, had the most roundabout ways of pointing a moral or delicately insinuating an innuendo. On arrival at the outskirts of the capital, instead of building the usual daïs for formalities and sacrifices, Tsz-ch'an threw up a mean hut for the accommodation of his mission, saying: "Altars are built by great states when they visit small ones as a symbol of benefits accorded, and by way of exhortation to continue in virtuous ways." Four years later Ts'u sent a mission of menacing size to CHÊNG, ostensibly to complete the carrying out of a marriage agreed upon by treaty between Ts'u and CHÊNG. Tsz-ch'an insisted that the bows and arrows carried by the escort should be left outside the city walls, adding: "Our poor state is too small to bear the full honour of such an escort; erect your altar daïs outside the wall for the service of the ancestral sacrifices, and we will there await your commands about the marriage."

In 538, when Ts'u was, for the first time, holding a durbar as recognized Protector, being at the time, however, on hostile terms with her former vassal, Wu, the King of Ts'u committed the gross outrage of seizing the ruler of a petty state, who was then present at the durbar, because that ruler had married (being himself of eastern barbarian descent) a princess of Wu. The following year, when two very distinguished statesmen from the territory of his secular enemy Tsin came on a political mission, the King of Ts'u consulted his premier about the advisability of castrating the one for a harem eunuch, and cutting off the feet of the other for a door-porter. "Your Majesty can do it, certainly," was the reply, "but how about the consequences?" This was the occasion, mentioned in Chapter VI., on which the king was reminded how many great private families there were in Tsin quite capable of raising a hundred chariots apiece.

It appears that envoys, at least in Lu, were hereditary in some families, just as other families provided successive generations of ministers. A Lu envoy to Tsin, who carried a very valuable gem- studded girdle with him, had very great pressure put upon him by a covetous Tsin minister who wanted the girdle. The envoy offered to give some silk instead, but he said that not even to save his life would he give up the girdle. The Tsin magnate thought better of it; but it is remarkable how many cases of sordid greed of this kind are recorded, all pointing to the comparative absence of commercial exchanges, or standards of value between the feudal states.

Ts'u seems to have thoroughly deserved Yen-tsz's imputations of treachery and roguery. At the great Peace Conference held outside the Sung capital in 546, the Ts'u escort was detected wearing cuirasses underneath their clothing. One of the greatest of the Tsin statesmen, Shuh Hiang (a personal friend of Yen-tsz, Confucius, and Tsz-ch'an) managed diplomatically to keep down the rising indignation of the other powers and representatives present by pooh-poohing the clumsy artifice on the ground that by such treachery Ts'u simply injured her own reputation in the federation to the manifest advantage of Tsin: it did not suit Tsin to continue the struggle with Ts'u just then. Then there was a squabble as to precedence at the same Peace Conference; that is, whether Tsin or Ts'u had the first right to smear lips with the blood of sacrifice: here again Shuh Hiang tactfully gave way, and by his conciliatory conduct succeeded in inducing the federal princes to sign a sort of disarmament agreement. This is one of the numerous instances in which Confucius as an annalist tries to menager the true facts in the interests of orthodoxy.

Even the more fully civilized state of Ts'i attempted an act of gross treachery, when in 500 B.C. the ruler of Lu, accompanied by Confucius as his minister in attendance, went to pay his respects. But Confucius was just as sharp as Yen-tsz and Tsz-ch'an, his friends, neighbours, and colleagues: he at once saw through the menacing appearance of the barbarian "dances" (introduced here, again, as a "variety entertainment"), and by his firm behaviour not only saved the person of his prince, but shamed the ruler of Ts'i into disclaiming and disavowing his obsequious fellow- practical jokers. Yen-tsz was actually present at the time, in attendance upon his own marquis; but it is nowhere alleged that he was responsible for the disgraceful manoeuvre. As a result T'si was obliged to restore to Lu several cities and districts wrongfully annexed some years before, and Lu promised to assist Ts'i in her wars.

CHAPTER X.THE SECOND PROTECTOR

We must now go back a little. The first of the so-called Five Tyrants, or the Five successive Protectors of orthodox China, had died in 643, his philosopher and friend, Kwan-tsz, having departed this life a little before him. Their joint title to fame lies in the fact that "they saved China from becoming a Tartar province," and even Confucius admits the truth of this—a most important factor in enabling us to understand the motive springs of Chinese policy. Under these circumstances the Duke of Sung, who, as we have seen, had special moral pretensions to leadership on account of his being the direct lineal representative of the Shang dynasty which perished in 1122 B.C., immediately put forward a claim to the hegemony. He rather prejudiced his reputation, however, by committing the serious ritual offence of "warring upon Ts'i's mourning," that is, of engaging the allies in hostilities with the late Protector's own country whilst his body lay unburied, and his sons were still wrangling over the question of succession. The Tartars, however, came to the rescue of, and made a treaty with, Ts'i—this is only one of innumerable instances which show how the northern Chinese princes of those early days were in permanent political touch with the horse-riding nomads. The orthodox Duke of Sung, dressed in his little brief authority as Protector, had the temerity to "send for" the ruler of Ts'u to attend his first durbar. (It must be remembered that the "king" in his own dominions was only "viscount" in the orthodox peerage of ruling princes.) The result was that the King unceremoniously took his would-be protector into custody at the durbar, and put in a claim to be Protector himself. During the military operations connected with this political manoeuvre, the Duke of Sung was guilty of the most ridiculous piece of ritual chivalry; highly approved, it is true, by the literary pedants of all subsequent ages, but ruinous to his own worldly cause. The Ts'u army was crossing a difficult ford, and the Duke's advisers recommended a prompt attack. "It is not honourable," said the Duke, "to take advantage even of an enemy in distress." "But," said his first adviser, "war is war, and its only object is to punish the foe as severely and promptly as possible, so as to gain the upper hand, and establish what you are fighting for."

Meanwhile important events had been going on in the marquisate of Tsin, which, during the thirty-five years' hegemony of Ts'i, had been engaged in extending its territory in all directions, in fighting Ts'in, and in annexing bordering Tartar tribes. At its greatest development Tsin practically comprised all between the Yellow River in its turns south, east, and north; but, though probably half its population was Tartar, it never ceased to be "orthodox" in administrative principle. The energetic but licentious ruler of Tsin had married a Tartar wife in addition to his more legitimate spouse (daughter of the late Protector, Marquess of Ts'i); or, rather, he took two wives, the one being sister of the other, but the younger sister brought him no children. Before this he had already married two sisters of quite a different Tartar tribe, and each of his earlier wives had brought him a son. His last pair of Tartar lady-loves gained such a strong hold upon his affections that he was induced by the mother, being the elder sister of the two, to nominate her own son as his heir to the exclusion of the three elder brethren, who were sent on various flimsy pretexts to defend the northern frontiers against the more hostile Tartars. To complicate matters, the Marquess's legitimate or first spouse, the Ts'i princess, besides bearing a son, had also given him a daughter, who had married the powerful ruler of Ts'in to the west. Thus not only were Ts'in and Tsin both half-Tartar in origin and sympathy, but at this period three out of four of the Tsin possible heirs were actually sons of Tartar women. The legitimate heir, whose mother was of Ts'i origin, and, who himself was a man of very high character, ended the question so far as he was concerned, by committing dutiful suicide; the three sons by Tartar mothers succeeded to the throne one after the other, but in the inverse order of their respective ages. The story of the wanderings of the eldest brother, who did not come to the throne until he was sixty-two years of age, is one of the most interesting and romantic episodes in the whole history of China; and, even with the unfamiliar proper names, would make a capital romantic novel, so graphically and naturally are some of the scenes depicted. First he threw himself heart and soul into Tartar life, joined the rugged horsemen in their internecine wars, married a Tartar wife, and gave her sister to his most faithful henchman; then, hearing of the death of the Ts'i premier, Kwan- tsz, he vowed he would go to Ts'i and try to act as political adviser in his place. Hospitably received by the Marquess of Ts'i, he was presented with a charming and sensible Ts'i princess, who for five years exercised so enervating an influence upon his virility, ambition, and warlike ardour, that he had to be surreptitiously smuggled away from the gay Ts'i capital whilst drunk, by his Tartar father-in-law and by his chief Chinese henchman and brother-in-law. Then he commenced a series of visits to the petty orthodox courts which separated Ts'i from Ts'u. Several of them were rude and neglectful to this unfortunate prince in distress; but Sung was an exception, for Sung ambition, as above narrated, had been roughly checked by Ts'u, and Sung now wished to make overtures to Tsin instead, and to conciliate a prince who was as likely as not to come to the throne of Tsin. In 637 the prince reached the court of Ts'u, whose ruler had quite recently begun to take formal and official rank as a "civilized" federal prince. Meanwhile, news came that his brother (by his own mother's younger sister) was dead; this younger brother had taken refuge in Ts'in during the reign of his youngest brother (the one born of the last Tartar favourite), and had, after that brother's death, been most generously assisted to the throne in turn by the ruler of Ts'in, on the understanding, however, that Tsin should cede to Ts'in all territory on the right bank of the Yellow River, i.e. in the modern province of Shen Si: but the new Tsin ruler had been persuaded by his courtiers to go back on this humiliating bargain, in consequence of which war had been declared by Ts'in upon Tsin, and the faithless ruler of Tsin had been for some time a prisoner of war in Ts'in; but, regaining his throne through the influence of his half-sister, the wife of the Ts'in ruler, had died in harness in 637 B.C. This deceased ruler's young son was not popular, and Ts'in was now instrumental in welcoming the refugee back from Ts'u, and in leading him in triumph, after nineteen years of adventurous wandering, to his own ancestral throne; his rival and nephew was killed.

All orthodox China seemed to feel now that the interesting wanderer, after all his experiences of war, travel, Tartars, Chinese, barbarians, and politics, was the right man to be Protector. But it was first necessary for Tsin to defeat Ts'u in a decisive battle; a war had arisen between Tsin and Ts'u out of an attempt on the part of CHÊNG (one of the orthodox Chinese states that had been uncivil to the wanderer), to drag in the preponderant power of Ts'u by way of shielding itself from punishment at Tsin's hands for past rude behaviour. The Emperor sent his own son to confer the status of "my uncle" upon him,—which is practically another way of saying "Protector" to a kinsman,—and in the year 632 accordingly a grand durbar was held, in which the Emperor himself took part. The Tsin ruler, who had summoned the durbar, and had even "commanded the presence" of the Emperor, was the guiding spirit of the meeting in every respect, except in the nominal and ritualistic aspect of it; nevertheless, he was prudent and careful enough scrupulously to observe all external marks of deference, and to make it appear that he was merely acting as mouthpiece to the puppet Emperor; he even went the length of dutifully offering to the Emperor some Ts'u prisoners, and the Emperor in turn "graciously ceded" to Tsin the imperial possessions north of the Yellow River. Thus Ts'in and Tsin each in turn clipped the wings of the Autocrat of All the Chinas, so styled.

During these few unsettled years between the death of the first real Protector in 643 and the formal nomination by the Emperor of the second in 632, Ts'u and Sung had, as we have seen, both attempted to assert their rival claims. A triangular war had also been going on for some time between Ts'i and Ts'u, the bone of contention being some territory of which Ts'i had stripped Lu; and there was war also between Tsin and Ts'i, Tsin and Ts'in, and Tsin and Ts'u, which latter state always tried to secure the assistance of Ts'in when possible. From first to last, there never was, during the period covered by Confucius' history, any serious war between Tartar Ts'in and barbarian Ts'u; rather were they natural allies against orthodox China, upon which intermediate territory they both learned to fix covetous eyes.

The situation is too involved, in view of the uncouthness of strange names and the absence of definite frontiers—changing as they did with the result of each few years' campaigning—to make it possible to give a full, or even approximately intelligible, explanation of each move. But the following main features are incontestable:—Ts'in, Tsin, Ts'i, and Ts'u were growing, progressive, and aggressive states, all of them strongly tinged with foreign blood, which foreign blood was naturally assimilated the more readily in proportion to the power, wealth, and culture of the assimilating orthodox nucleus. The imperial domain was an extinct political volcano, belching occasional fumes of threatening, sometimes noxious, but not ever fatally suffocating smoke, always without fire. "The Hia," that is, the federation of princes belonging to pure Hia, or (as we now say) "Chinese" stock, were evidently unwarlike in proportion to the absence of foreign blood in their veins; but they were all of them equally rusés, and all of them past-masters in casuistic diplomacy. Trade, agriculture, literature, and even law, were now quite active, and (as we shall gradually see in these short chapters) China was undoubtedly beginning to move, as, after 2500 years of a second "ritual" sleep, she is again now moving, at the beginning of the

CHAPTER XI.RELIGION

All through these five centuries of struggle, between the flight of the Emperor with the transfer of the metropolis in 771 B.C., and the total destruction of the feudal system by the First August Emperor of Ts'in in 221 B.C., it is of supreme interest to note that religion in our Western sense was not only non-existent throughout China, but had not yet even been conceived of as an abstract notion; apart, that is to say, from government, public law, family law, and class ritual. No word for "religion" was known to the language; the notion of Church or Temple served by a priestly caste had not entered men's minds. Offences against "the gods" or "the spirits," in a vague sense, were often spoken of; but, on the other hand, too much belief in their power was regarded as superstition. "Sin" was only conceivable in the sense of infraction of nature's general laws, as symbolized and specialized by imperial commands; direct, or delegated to vassal princes; in both cases as representatives, supreme or local, of Heaven, or of the Emperor Above, whose Son the dynastic central ruler for the time being was figuratively supposed to be. No vassal prince ever presumed to style himself "Son of Heaven," though nearly all the barbarous vassals called themselves "King" (the only other title the Chou monarchs took) in their own dominions. "In the Heaven there can only be one Sun; on Earth there can only be one Emperor"; this was the maxim, and, ever since the Chou conquest in 1122 B.C., the word "King" had done duty for the more ancient "Emperor," which, in remote times had apparently not been sharply distinguished in men's minds from God, or the "Emperor on High."

Prayer was common enough, as we shall frequently see, and sacrifice was universal; in fact, the blood of a victim was almost inseparable from solemn function or record of any kind. But such ideas as conscience, fear of God, mortal sin, repentance, absolution, alms-giving, self-mortification, charity, sackcloth and ashes, devout piety, praise and glorification,—in a word, what the Jews, Christians, Mussulmans, and even Buddhists have each in turn conceived to be religious duty, had no well-defined existence at all. There are some traces of local or barbarous gods in the semi-Turkish nation of Ts'in, before it was raised to the status of full feudal vassal; and also in the semi-Annamese nation of Ts'u (with its dependencies Wu and Yiieh); but the orthodox Chinese proper of those times never had any religion such as we now conceive it, whatever notions their remote ancestors may have conceived.

Notwithstanding this, the minds of the governing classes at least were powerfully restrained by family and ancestral feeling, and, if there were no temples or priests for public worship, there were invariably shrines dedicated to the ancestors, with appropriate rites duly carried out by professional clerks or reciters. Whenever a ruler of any kind undertook any important expedition or possible duty, he was careful first to consult the oracles in order to ascertain the will of Heaven, and then to report the fact to the manes of his forefathers, who were likewise notified of any great victory, political change, or piece of good fortune. There is a distinction (not easy to master) between the loss of a state and the loss of a dynasty; in the latter case the population remain comparatively unaffected, and it is only the reigning family whose sacrifices to the gods of the place and of the harvest are interrupted. Thus in 567, when one of the very small vassals (of whom the ruler of Lu was mesne lord) crushed the other, it is explained that the spirits will not spiritually eat the sacrifices (i.e. accept the worship) of one who does not belong to the same family name, and that in this case the annihilating state was only a cousin through sisters: "when the country is 'lost,' it means that the strange surname succeeds to power; but, when a strange surname becomes spiritual heir, we say 'annihilated.'" We have seen in the ninth chapter how the

Shang dynasty lost the empire, but was sacrificially maintained in Sung. From the remotest times there seems to have been a tender unwillingness to "cut off all sacrifices" entirely, probably out of a feeling that retribution in like form might at some future date occur to the ruthless condemner of others. There is another reason, which is, nearly all ruling families hailed from the same remote semi-mythical emperors, or from their ministers, or from their wives of inferior birth. Thus, although the body of the last tyrannical monarch of the Shang dynasty just cited was pierced through and through by the triumphant Chou monarch, that monarch's brother (acting as regent on behalf of the son and successor) conferred the principality of Sung upon the tyrant's elder half- brother by an inferior wife, "in order that the dynastic sacrifices might not be cut off"; and to the very last the Duke of Sung was the only ruling satrap under the Chou dynasty who permanently enjoyed the full title of "duke." His neighbour, the Marquess of Wei (imperial clan), was, it is true, made "duke" in 770 B.C. for services in connection with the Emperor's flight; but the title seems to have been tacitly abandoned, and at durbars he is always styled "marquess." Of the Shang tyrant himself it is recorded: "thus in 1122 B.C. he lost all in a single day, without even leaving posterity." Of course his elder brother could not possibly be his spiritual heir. In 597 B.C., when Ts'u, in its struggle with Tsin for the possession of CHÊNG, got the ruling Earl of CHÊNG in its power, the latter referred appealingly to his imperial ancestors (the first earl, in 806, was son of the Emperor who fled from his capital north in 842), and said: "Let me continue their sacrifices." There are, at least, a score of similar instances: the ancestral sacrifices seem to refer rather to posterity, whilst those to gods of the land and grain appear more connected with rights as feoffee.

Prayer is mentioned from the earliest times. For instance Shun, the active ploughman monarch (not hereditary) who preceded the three dynasties of Hia (2205-1767), Shang (1766-1123), and Chou (1122-249), prayed at a certain mountain in the centre of modern Hu Nan province, where his grave still is, (a fact which points to the possibility of the orthodox Chinese having worked their way northwards from the south-west). When the Chou conqueror, posthumously called the Martial King, fell ill, his brother, the Duke of Chou (later regent for the Martial King's son), prayed to Heaven for his brother's recovery, and offered himself as a substitute; the clerk was instructed to commit the offer to writing, and this solemn document was securely locked up. The same man, when regent, again offered himself to Heaven for his sick nephew, cutting his nails off and throwing them into the river, as a symbol of his willingness to give up his own body. The Emperor K'ang-hi of the present Manchu dynasty, perhaps in imitation of the Duke of Chou, offered himself to Heaven in place of his sick Mongol grandmother. A very curious instance of prayer occurs in connection with the succession to the Tsin throne; it will be remembered that the legitimate heir committed dutiful suicide, and two other half-brothers (and, for a few months, one of these brother's sons) reigned before the second Protector secured his ancestral rights. The suicide's ghost appears to his usurping brother, and says: "I have prayed to the Emperor (God), who will soon deliver over Tsin into Ts'in's hands, so that Ts'in will perform the sacrifices due to me." The reply to the ghost was: "But the spirits will only eat the offerings if they come from the same family stock." The ghost said: "Very good; then I will pray again. . . . God now says my half-brother will be overthrown at the battle of Han" (the pass where the philosopher Lao-tsz is supposed to have written his book 150 years later). In 645 the ruler of Tsin was in fact captured in battle by his brother-in-law of Ts'in, who was indeed about to sacrifice to the Emperor on High as successor of Tsin; but he was dissuaded by his orthodox wife (the Tsin princess, daughter of a Ts'i princess as explained on page 51).

In 575 Tsin is recorded as "invoking the spirits and requesting a victory." A little later one of the

Tsin generals, after a defeat, issued a general order by way of concealing his weakness: to deceive the enemy he suggested that the army should amongst other things make a great show of praying for victory. There are many other similar analogous instances of undoubted prayer. Much later, in the year 210 B.C., when the King (as he had been) of Ts'in had conquered all China and given himself the name, for the first time in history, of August Emperor (the present title), he consulted his soothsayers about an unpleasant dream he had had. He was advised to pray, and to worship (or to sacrifice, for the two are practically one) with special ardour if he wished to bring things round to a favourable conclusion: and this is a monarch, too, who was steeped in Lao-tsz's philosophy.

CHAPTER XII.ANCESTRAL WORSHIP

We have just seen that, when a military expedition started out, the event was notified, with sacrifice, to the ancestors of the person most concerned: it was also the practice to carry to battle, on a special chariot, the tablet of the last ancestor removed from the ancestral hall, in order that, under his aegis so to speak, the tactics of the battle might be successful. Ancestral halls varied according to rank, the Emperor alone having seven shrines; vassal rulers five; and first-class ministers three; courtiers or second-class ministers had only two; that is to say, no one beyond the living subject's grandfather was in these last cases worshipped at all. From this we may assume that the ordinary folk could not pretend to any shrine, unless perhaps the house- altar, which one may see still any day in the streets of Canton. In 645 B.C. a first-class minister's temple was struck by lightning, and the commentator observes: "Thus we see that all, from the Emperor down to the courtiers, had ancestral shrines",—a statement which proves that already at the beginning of our Christian era such matters had to be explained to the general public. The shrines were disposed in the following fashion:—To the left (on entrance) was the shrine of the living subject's father; to the right his grandfather; above these two, to the left and right again, the great-grandfather and great-great- grandfather; opposite, in the centre, was that of the founder, whose tablet or effigy was never moved; but as each living individual died, his successor of course regarded him in the light of father, and, five being the maximum allowed, one tablet had to be removed at each decease, and it was placed in the more general ancestral hall belonging to the clan or gens rather than to the specific family: it was therefore the, tablet or effigy of the great-great-grandfather that was usually carried about in war. The Emperor alone had two special chapels beyond the five shrines, each chapel containing the odds (left) and evens (right) of those higher up in ascent than the great and great-great-grandfathers respectively. The King of Ts'u who died in 560 B.C. said on his death-bed: "I now take my place in the ancestral temple to receive sacrifices in the spring and autumn of each year." In the year 597, after a great victory over Tsin, the King of Ts'u had been advised to build a trophy over the collected corpses of the enemy; but, being apparently rather a high-minded man, after a little reflection, he said: "No! I will simply erect there a temple to my ancestors, thanking them for the success." After the death in 210 B.C. of the First August Emperor, a discussion arose as to what honours should be paid to his temple shrine: it was explained that "for a thousand years without any change the rule has been seven shrines for the Son of Heaven, five for vassal princes, and three for ministers." In the year 253, after the conquest of the miserable Chou Emperor's limited territory, the same Ts'in conqueror "personally laid the matter before the Emperor Above in the suburb sacrifice";— which means that he took over charge of the world as Vicar of God. The Temple of Heaven (outside the Peking South Gate), occupied in 1900 by the British troops, is practically the "suburb sacrifice" place of ancient times. It was not until the year 221 B.C. that the King of Ts'in, after that date First August Emperor, formally annexed the whole empire: "thanks to the shrines in the ancestral temple," or "thanks to the spiritual help of my ancestors' shrines the Under-Heaven (i.e. Empire) is now first settled." These expressions have been perpetuated dynasty by dynasty, and were indeed again used but yesterday in the various announcements of victory made to Heaven and his ancestors by the Japanese Tenshi, or Mikado; that is by the "Son of Heaven," or T'ien-tsz of the ancient Chinese, from whom the Japanese Shinto ritual was borrowed in whole or in part.

In the year 572 B.C., on the accession of a Tsin ruler after various irregular interruptions in the lineal succession, he says: "Thanks to the supernatural assistance of my ancestors—and to your assistance, my lords—I can now carry out the Tsin sacrifices." In the year 548 the wretched ruler of Ts'i, victim of a palace intrigue, begged the eunuch who was charged with the task of assassinating him at least "to grant me permission to commit suicide in my ancestral hall." The wooden tablet representing the ancestor is defined as being "that on which the spirit reclines"; and the temple "that place where the ancestral spiritual consciousness doth dwell." Each tablet was placed on its own altar: the tablet was square, with a hole in the centre, "in order to leave free access on all four sides." The Emperor's was twelve inches, those of vassal princes one foot (i.e. ten inches) in length, and no doubt the inscription was daubed on in varnish (before writing on silk became general, and before the hair-brush and ink came into use about 200 B.C.). The rulers of Lu, being lineal descendants of the Duke of Chou, brother of the first Emperor of the Chou dynasty (1122 B.C.) had special privileges in sacrificial matters, such as the right to use the imperial music of all past dynasties; the right to sacrifice to the father of the Duke of Chou and the founder; the right to imperial rites, to suburban sacrifice, and so on; besides the custody of certain ancient symbolic objects presented by the first Chou Emperors, and mentioned on page 22.

Of course no punishment could be spiritually greater than the destruction of ancestral temples: thus on two occasions, notably in 575 B.C. when a first-class minister traitorously fled his country, his prince, the Marquess of Lu, as a special act of grace, simply "swept his ancestral temple, but did not cut off the sacrifices." The second instance was also in Lu, in 550: the Wei friend with whom Confucius lived seventy years later, when wandering in Wei, retrospectively gave his ritual opinion on the case—a proof of the solidarity in sympathy that existed between the statesmen of the orthodox principalities. In the bloodthirsty wars between the semi-barbarous southern states of Wu and Ts'u, the capital of the latter was taken by storm in the year 506, the ancestral temple of Ts'u was totally destroyed, and the renegade Ts'u ministers who accompanied the Wu armies even flogged the corpse of the previous Ts'u king, their former master, against whom they had a grievance. This mutilation of the dead (in cases where the guilty rulers have contravened the laws of nature and heaven) was practised even in imperial China; for (see page 57) the founder of the dynasty, on taking possession of the last Shang Emperor's palace, deliberately fired several arrows into the body of the suicide Emperor. Decapitating corpses and desecrating tombs of great criminals have frequently been practised by the existing Manchu government, in criticizing whom we must not forget the treatment of Cromwell's body at the Restoration. In the year 285 B.C., when the Ts'i capital was taken possession of by the allied royal powers then united against Ts'i, the ancestral temple was burnt. In 249 B.C. Ts'u extinguished the state of Lu, "which thus witnessed the interruption of its ancestral sacrifices." Frequent instances occur, throughout this troublous period, of the Emperor's sending presents of meat used in ancestral sacrifices to the vassal princes; this was intended as a special mark of honour, something akin to the "orders" or decorations distributed in Europe. Thus in 671 the new

King of Ts'u who had just murdered his predecessor, which predecessor had for the first time set the bad example of annexing petty orthodox Chinese principalities, received this compliment of sacrificial meat from the Emperor, together with a mild hint to "attack the barbarians such as Yiieh, but always to let the Chinese princes alone." Ts'i, Lu, Ts'in, and Yiieh on different occasions between that date and the fourth century B.C. received similar donations, usually, evidently, more propitiatory than patronizing. In 472 the barbarous King of Yiieh was even nominated Protector along with his present of meat; this was after his total destruction of Wu, when he was marching north to threaten North China. Presents of private family sacrificial meat are still in vogue between friends in China.

Fasting and purification were necessary before undertaking solemn sacrifice of any kind. Thus the King of Ts'u in 690 B.C. did this before announcing a proposed war to his ancestors; and an envoy starting from Ts'u to Lu in 618 reported the circumstance to his own particular ancestors, who may or may not have been (as many high officers were) of the reigning caste. On another occasion the ruler of Lu was assassinated whilst purifying himself in the enclosure dedicated to the god of the soil, previous to sacrificing to the manes of an individual who had once saved his life. Practically all this is maintained in modern Chinese usage.

A curious distinction is mentioned in connection with official mourning tidings in the highly ritual state of Lu. If the deceased were of a totally different family name, the Marquess of Lu wept outside his capital, turning towards deceased's native place, or place of death; if of the same name, then in the ancestral temple: if the deceased was a descendant of the same founder, then in the founder's temple; if of the same family branch, then in the paternal temple. All these refinements are naturally tedious and obscure to us Westerners; but it is only by collating specific facts that we can arrive at any general principle or rule.

CHAPTER XIII.ANCIENT DOCUMENTS FOUND

The reign of the Tsin marquess (628-635), second of the Five Protectors, only lasted eight years, and nothing is recorded to have happened during this period at all commensurate with his picturesque figure in history while yet a mere wanderer. But it is very interesting to note that the Bamboo Annals or Books, i.e. the History of Tsin from 784 B.C., and incidentally also of China from 1500 years before that date, are one of the corroborative authorities we now possess upon the accuracy of Confucius' history from 722 B.C., as expanded by his three commentators; and it is satisfactory to know that the oldest of the three commentaries, that usually called the Tso Chwan, or "Commentary of Tso K'iu-ming," a junior contemporary of Confucius, and official historiographer at the Lu Court, is the most accurate as well as the most interesting of the three. These Bamboo Books were only discovered in the year 281 A.D., after having been buried in a tomb ever since the year 299 B.C. The character in which they were written, upon slips of bamboo, had already become so obsolete that the sustained work of antiquarians was absolutely necessary in order to reduce it to the current script of the day; or, in other words, of to-day. Another interesting fact is, that whilst the Chou dynasty, and consequently Confucius of Lu (which state was intimately connected by blood with the Chou family), had introduced a new calendar, making the year begin one (Shang) or two (Hia) months sooner than before, Tsin had continued to compute (see page 27) the year according to the system of the Hia dynasty: in other words, the intercalary moons, or massed fractions of time periodically introduced in order to bring the solar and lunar years into line, had during the millennium so accumulated (at the rate apparently of, roughly, sixty days in 360,000, or, say, three half-seconds a day) that the Chou dynasty found it necessary to call the Hia eleventh moon the first and the Hia first moon the third of the year. A parallel distinction is observable in modern times when the Russian year (until a few years ago twelve days later than ours), was declared thirteen days later; and when we ourselves in 1900 (and in three-fourths of all future years making up a net hundred), omit the intercalary day of the 29th February, which otherwise occurs every fourth year of even numbers divisible by four. Thus the very discrepancies in the dates of the Bamboo Books (where the later editors, in attempting to accommodate all dates to later calendars, have accidentally left a Tsin date unchanged) and in the dates of Confucius' expanded history, pointed out and explained as they are by the Chinese commentators themselves, are at once a guarantee of fact, and of good faith in recording that fact.

But the neighbour and brother-in-law of the Tsin marquess (himself three parts Turkish), the Earl of Ts'in, who reigned from 659 to 621 B.C., and during that reign quietly laid the foundations of a powerful state which was destined to achieve the future conquest of all China, was himself a remarkable man; and there is some reason to believe that he, even at this period, also possessed a special calendar of his own, as his successors certainly did 400 years later, when they imposed their own calendar reckoning upon China. We have already seen (page 52) what powerful influence he exercised in bringing the semi-Tartar Tsin brethren to the Tsin throne in turn. He had invited several distinguished men from the neighbouring petty, but very ancient, Chinese principalities to settle in his capital as advisers; he was too far off to attend the durbars held by the, First Protector, but he sent one of these Chinese advisers as his representative, He is usually himself counted as one of the Five Protectors; but, although he was certainly very influential, and for that reason was certainly one of the Five Tyrants, or Five Predominating Powers, it is certain that he never succeeded in obtaining the Emperor's formal sanction to act as such over the orthodox principalities, nor did he ever preside at a durbar of Chinese federal princes. Long and bloody wars with his neighbour of Tsin were the chief feature of his reign so far as orthodox China was concerned; but his chief glory lies in his great Tartar conquests, and in his enormous extensions to the west. These extensions, however, must not be exaggerated, and there is no reason to suppose that they ever reached farther than Kwa Chou and Tun-hwang (long. 95ø, lat. 40ø), two very ancient places which still appear under those names on the most modern maps of China, and from which roads (recently examined by Major Bruce) branch off to Turkestan and Lob Nor respectively.

Most Emperors and vassal princes are spoken of in history by their posthumous names, that is by the names voted to them after death, with the view of tersely expressing by that name the essential features (good or bad) of the deceased's personal character; just as we say in Europe, officially or unofficially, Louis le Bienaimé, Albert the Good, or Charles the Fat. The posthumous name of this Ts'in earl was "the Duke Muh" (no matter whether duke, marquess, earl, viscount, or baron when living, it was customary to say "duke" when the ruler was dead), and the posthumous name of the Emperor who died in 947 B.C. was "the King Muh"; for, as already stated, the Chou dynasty of Sons of Heaven were called "King," and not "Emperor" though their supreme position was as fully imperial as that of previous dynastic monarchs, and they were, in fact, "Emperors" as we now understand that word in Europe. At the same time that the Bamboo Annals were unearthed, there were also found copies of some of the old "classics" or "Scripture," and a hitherto unknown book called "the Story of the Son of Heaven Muh," all, of course, written in the same ancient script. This Son of Heaven (a term applied to all the Emperors of China, no matter whether they styled themselves Emperor, King, or August Emperor) was supposed to have travelled far west, and to have had interviews with a foreign prince, who, as his land too, was transcribed as Siwangmu. The subject will be touched upon more in detail in another chapter; but, for the present, it will be useful to say that, in the opinion of one very learned sinologist, all evidence points clearly to this expedition having been undertaken by Duke Muh of Ts'in, installed as he was in the old appanage of the emperors lost to the Tartars (as we have explained) in 771, and made over at the same time by the Emperor involved to the ancestors of Duke Muh. This view of the case is supported by the fact that in 664 B.C. Ts'in and Tsin, for some unknown reason, forced the Tartars of Kwa Chou to migrate into China, which migration was subsequently alluded to by a Tartar chief (when attending a Chinese durbar in 559 B.C.) as a well- known historical fact. It was undoubtedly the practice of semi-Chinese states, such as Ts'u, Wu, Yueh, and Shuh (the last is the modern Sz Ch'wan province, and its history was only discovered long after Confucius' time), to call themselves "Kings," "Emperors," and "Sons of Heaven," in their own country (just as the tributary King of Annam always did until the French assumed a protectorate over him; and just as the tributary Japanese did before they officially announced the fact to China in the seventh century A.D.); and there are many indications that Ts'in did, or at least might have done and would like to have done, the same thing. Hence, when the story of Muh was discovered, the literary manipulators—even if they did not really believe that it positively must refer to the Emperor Muh-might well have honestly doubted whether the story referred to Ts'in or to the Emperor; or might well have decided to incorporate it with orthodox history, as a strengthening factor in support of the theory of one single and indivisible imperial dignity; just as, again, in the seventh century and eighth century A.D., the Japanese manipulators of their traditional history incorporated hundreds, not to say thousands of Chinese historical facts and speeches, and worked them into their own historical episodes and into their own emperors' mouths, for the honour and glory of Dai Nippon (Great Japan).

After the death of the Second Protector in 628 B.C., there was a continuous struggle between Tsin and Ts'in on the one hand, and between Tsin and Ts'u on the other. Meanwhile Ts'i had all its own work cut out in order to keep the Tartars off the right bank of the Yellow River in its lower course, and in order to protect the orthodox Chinese states, Lu, Sung, Wei, etc., from their attacks; but Ts'i never again after this date put in a formal claim to be Protector, although in 610 she led a coalition of princes against an offending member, and thus practically acted as Protector.

In addition to the Chinese adviser at the disposal of Ts'in, in the year 626 the King (or a king) of the Tartars supplied Duke Muh with a very able Tartar adviser of Tsin descent; i.e. his ancestors had in past times migrated to Tartarland, though he himself still "spoke the Tsin dialect," and must have had considerable literary capacity, as he was an author. Ts'in was now, in addition to being, if only informally, a federal Chinese state, also supreme suzerain over all the Tartar principalities within reach; well supplied, moreover, with expert advisers for both classes of work. All this is important in view of the pre- eminence of Ts'in when the time came, 400 years later, to abolish the meticulous feudal system altogether.

CHAPTER XIV.MORE ON PROTECTORS

The Five Tyrants, or Protectors, are usually considered to be the five personages we have mentioned; to wit, in order of succession, the Marquess of Ts'i (679-643), under whose reign the great economist, statesman, and philosopher Kwan-tsz raised this far eastern part of China to a hitherto unheard-of pitch of material prosperity; the Marquess of Tsin (632-628), a romantic prince, more Turkish than Chinese, who was the first vassal prince openly to treat the Emperor as a puppet; the Duke of Sung (died 637), representing the imperial Shang dynasty ejected by the Chou family in 1122, whose ridiculous chivalry failed, however, to secure him the effective support of the other Chinese princes; the Earl of Ts'in (died 621) who was, as we see, quietly creating a great Tartar dominion, and assimilating it to Chinese ways in the west; and the King of Ts'u (died 591), who, besides taking his place amongst the recognized federal princes, and annexing innumerable petty Chinese principalities in the Han River and Hwai River basins, had been for several generations quietly extending his dominions at the expense of what we now call the provinces of Sz Ch'wan, Kiang Si, Hu Kwang-perhaps even Yun Nan and Kwei Chou; Certainly Kiang Su and Cheh Kiang, and possibly in a loose way the coast regions of modern Fuh Kien and the Two Kwang; but it cannot be too often repeated that if any thing intimate was known of the Yang-tsz basin, it was only Ts'u (in its double character of independent local empire as well as Chinese federal prince) that knew, or could have known, any thing about it; just as, if any thing specific was known of the Far West, Turkestan, the Tarim valley, and the Desert, it was only Ts'in (in its double character of independent Tartar empire as well as Chinese federal prince) that knew, or could know, any thing about them. Ts'i and Tsin were also Tartar powers, at least in the sense that they knew how to keep off the particular Tartars known to them, and how to make friendly alliances with them, thus availing themselves, on the one hand, of Tartar virility, and faithful on the other to orthodox Chinese culture. So that, with the exception of the pedantic Duke of Sung, who was summarily snuffed out after a year or two of brief light by the lusty King of Ts'u, all the nominal Five Protectors of China were either half-barbarian rulers or had passed through the crucible of barbarian ordeals. Finally, so vague were the claims and services of Sung, Ts'u, and Ts'in, from a protector point of view, that for the purposes of this work, we only really recognize two, the First Protector (of Ts'i) and, after a struggle, the Second Protector (of Tsin): at most a third,—Ts'u.

But although the Chinese historians thus loosely confine the Five- Protector period to less than a century of time, it is a fact that Ts'u and Tsin went on obstinately struggling for the hegemony, or for practical predominance, for at least another 200 years; besides, Ts'in, Ts'u, and Sung were never formally nominated by the Emperor as Protectors, nor were they ever accepted as such by the Chinese federal princes in the permanent and definite way that Ts'i and Tsin had been and were accepted. Moreover, the barbarian states of Wu and Yüeh each in turn acted very effectively as Protector, and are never included in the Five-Great-Power series. The fact is, the Chinese have never grasped the idea of principles in history: their annals are mere diaries of events; and when once an apparently definite "period" is named by an annalist, they go on using it, quite regardless of its inconsistency when confronted with facts adverse to a logical acceptance of it.

The situation was this: Tsin and Ts'u were at perpetual loggerheads about the small Chinese states that lay between them, more especially about the state of Cheng, which, though small, was of quite recent imperial stock, and was, moreover, well supplied with brains. Tsin and Ts'in were at perpetual loggerheads about the old Tsin possessions on the west bank of the Yellow River, which, running from the north to the south, lay between them; and about their rival claims to influence the various nomadic Tartar tribes living along both the banks, Tsin and Ts'i were often engaged in disputes about Lu, Wei, and other orthodox states situated in the Lower Yellow River valley running from the west to the east and north-east; also in questions concerning eastern barbarian states inhabiting the whole coast region, and concerning the petty Chinese states which had degenerated, and whose manners savoured of barbarian ways. Thus Ts'in and Ts'u, and also to some extent Ts'i and Ts'u, had a regular tendency to ally themselves against Tsin's flanks, and it was therefore always Tsin's policy as the "middle man" to obstruct communications between Ts'in and Ts'u, and between Ts'i and Ts'u. In 580 Tsin devised a means of playing off a similar flanking game upon Ts'u: negotiations were opened with Wu, which completely barbarous state only begins to appear in history at all at about this period, all the kings having manifestly phonetic barbarian names, which mean absolutely nothing (beyond conveying the sound) as expressed in Chinese, Wu was taught the art of war, as we have seen, by (page 34) a Ts'u traitor who had fled to Tsin and taken service there; and the King of Wu soon made things so uncomfortable for Ts'u that the latter in turn tried by every means to block the way between Tsin and Wu. Within a single generation Wu was so civilized that one of the royal princes was sent the rounds of the Chinese states as special ambassador, charged, under the convenient cloak of seeking for civilization, ritual, and music, with the duty of acquiring political and strategical knowledge. This prince so favourably impressed the orthodox statesmen of Ts'i, Lu, Tsin, and Wei (the ruling family of this state, like that of Sung, was, until it revolted in 1106 B.C. against the new Chou dynasty, of Shang dynasty origin, and the Yellow River ran through it northwards), that he was everywhere deferentially received as an equal: his tomb is still in existence, about ten miles from the treaty- port of Chinkiang, and the inscription upon it, in ancient characters, was written by Confucius himself, who, though a boy of eight when the Wu prince visited Lu in 544, may well have seen the prince in the flesh elsewhere, for the latter lived to prevent a war with Ts'u in 485; i.e. he lived to within six years of Confucius' death: he is known, too, to have visited Tsin on a spying mission in 515 B.C. The original descent of the first voluntarily barbarous Wu princes from the same grandfather as the Chou emperors would afford ample basis for the full recognition of a Wu prince by the orthodox as their equal, especially when his manners were softened by rites and music. It was like an oriental prince being feted and invested in Europe, so long as he should conform to the conventional dress and mannerisms of "society."

Just as Wu had been quietly submissive to Ts'u until the opportunity came to revolt, so did the still more barbarous state of Yueh, lying to the south-east of and tributary to Wu as her mesne lord, eagerly seize the opportunity of attacking Wu when the common suzerain, Ts'u, required it. The wars of Wu and Yueh are almost entirely naval, and, so far as the last-named state is concerned, it is never reported as having used war-chariots at all. Wu adopted the Chinese chariot as rapidly as it had re- adopted the Chinese civilization, abandoned by the first colonist princes in 1200 B.C.; but of course these chariots were only for war in China, on the flat Chinese plains; they were totally impracticable in mountainous countries, except along the main routes, and useless (as Major Bruce shows) in regions cut up by gulleys; even now no one ever sees a two-wheeled vehicle in the Shanghai-Ningpo region. It must, therefore, always be remembered that Wu, though barbarous in its population, was, in its origin as an organized system of rule, a colony created by certain ancestors of the founder of the Chou dynasty, who had voluntarily gone off to carve out an appanage in the Jungle; i.e. in the vague unknown dominion later called Ts'u, of which dominion all coast regions were a part, so far as they could be reduced to submission. This gave the Kings of Wu, though barbarian, a pretext for claiming equality with, and even seniority over Tsin, the first Chou-born prince of which was junior in descent to most of the other enfeoffed vassals of the imperial clan-name. In 502 Wu armies even threatened the northern state of Ts'i, and asserted in China generally a brief authority akin to that of Protector. Ts'i was obliged to buy itself off by marrying a princess of the blood to the heir-apparent of Wu, an act which two centuries later excited the disgust of the philosopher Mencius. The great Ts'i statesman and writer Yen-tsz, whom we have already mentioned more than once, died in 500, and earlier in that year Confucius had become chief counsellor of Lu, which state, on account of Confucius' skill as a diplomat, nearly obtained the Protectorate. It was owing to the fear of this that the assassination of the Lu prince was attempted that year, as narrated in Chapter IX. In order to understand how Wu succeeded in reaching Lu and Ts'i, it must be recollected that the river Sz, which still runs from east to west past Confucius's birthplace, and now simply feeds the Grand Canal, then flowed south-east along the line of the present canal and entered the Hwai River near Sü-chou. Moreover, there was at times boat- communication between the Sz and the Yellow River, though the precise channel is not now known. Consequently, the Wu fleets had no difficulty in sailing northwards first by sea and then up the Hwai and Sz Rivers. Besides, in 485, the King of Wu began what we now call the Grand Canal by joining as a beginning the Yang-tsz River with the Hwai River, and then carrying the canal beyond the Hwai to the state of Sung, which state was then disputing with Lu the possession of territory on the east bank of the Sz, whilst Ts'u was pushing her annexations up to the west bank of the same river. There were in all twelve minor orthodox states between the Sz and the Hwai. In 482 the all-powerful King of Wu held a genuine durbar as Protector, at a place in modern Ho Nan province, north of the Yellow River as it now runs, but at that time a good distance to the south-east of it. This is one of the most celebrated meetings in Chinese history, partly because Wu successfully asserted political pre-eminence over Tsin; partly because Confucius falsifies the true facts out of shame (as we have seen he did when Ts'u similarly seized the first place over Tsin); and partly owing to the shrewd diplomacy of the King of Wu, who had learnt by express messenger that the King of Ytieh was marching on his capital, and who had the difficult double task to accomplish of carrying out a "bluff," and operating a retreat without showing his weak hand to either side, or losing his army exposed between two foes.

In 473, after long and desperate fighting, Wu was, however, at last annihilated by Yiieh, which state was now unanimously voted Protector, Vae victis! The Yueh capital was promptly removed from near the modern Shao-hing (west of Ningpo) far away north to what is now practically the German colony of Kiao Chou; but, though a maritime power of very great-strength, Yiieh never succeeded in establishing any real land influence in the Hwai Valley. During her short protectorate she rectified the River Sz question by forcing Sung to make over to Lu the land on the east bank of the River Sz.

CHAPTER XV.STATE INTERCOURSE

Whatever may be the reason why details of interstate movement are lacking up to 842 B.C., it is certain that, from the date of the Emperor's flight eastwards in 771, the utmost activity prevailed between state and state within the narrow area to which, as we have seen, the federated Chinese empire was confined. Confucius' history, covering the 250-year period subsequent to 722, consists largely of statements that this duke visited that country, or returned from it, or drew up a treaty with it, or negotiated a marriage with it. "Society," in a political sense, consisted of the four great powers, Ts'in, Tsin, Ts'i, and Ts'u, surrounding the purely Chinese enclave; and of the innumerable petty Chinese states, mostly of noble and ancient lineage, only half a dozen of them of any size, which formed the enclave in question, and were surrounded by Ts'in, Tsin, Ts'i, and Ts'u, to the west, north, east, and south. Secondary states in extent and in military power, like Lu, CHÊNG, and Wei, whilst having orthodox and in some cases barbarian sub-vassals of their own, were themselves, if not vassals to, at all events under the predominant influence of, one or the other of the four great powers. Thus Lu was at first nearly always a handmaid of Ts'i, but later fell under the influence of Tsin, Ts'u, and Wu; Cheng always coquetted between Tsin and Ts'u, not out of love for either, but in order to protect her own independence; and so on with the rest. If we inquire what a really small state meant in those days, the answer is that the modern walled city, with its district of several hundred square miles lying around it, was (and usually still is) the equivalent of the ancient principality; and proof of that lies in the fact that one of the literary designations of what we now term a "district magistrate" is still "city marquess." Another proof is that in ancient times "your state" was a recognized way of saying "your capital town"; and "my poor town" was the polite way of saying "our country"; both expressions still used in elegant diplomatic composition.

This being so, and it having besides been the practice for a visiting duke always to take along with him a "minister in attendance," small wonder that prominent Chinese statesmen from the orthodox states were all personal friends, or at least correspondents and acquaintances, who had thus frequent opportunity of comparing political notes. To this day there are no serious dialect differences whatever in the ancient central area described in the first chapter, nor is there any reason to suppose that the statesmen and scholars who thus often met in conclave had any difficulty in making themselves mutually understood. The "dialects'" of which we hear so much in modern times (which, none the less, are all of them pure Chinese, except that the syllables differ, just as _coeur, cuore, and corazon, coraçao, differ from cor), all belong to the southern coasts, which were practically unknown to imperial China in Confucius' time. The Chinese word which we translate "mandarin" also means "public" or "common," and "mandarin dialect" really means "current" or "common speech," such as is, and was, spoken with no very serious modifications all over the enclave; and also in those parts of Ts'in, Tsin, Ts'i, and Ts'u, which immediately impinged upon the enclave, in the ratio of their proximity. Finally, Shen Si, Shan Si, Shan Tung, and Hu Kwang are still called Ts'in, Tsin, Ts'i, and Ts'u in high-class official correspondence; and so with all other place-names. China has never lost touch with antiquity. There is record for nearly every thing: the only difficulty is to separate what is relevant from what is irrelevant in the mass of confused data.

Another matter must be considered. Although the Chinese never had a caste system in the Hindoo sense, there is, as we have stated once before, every reason to believe that the ruling classes and the educated classes were nearly all nobles, in the sense that they were all lineal or branch descendants, whether by first- class wife or by concubine, of either the ruling dynastic family or of some previous imperial dynastic family. Some families were by custom destined for hereditary ministers, others for hereditary envoys, others again for hereditary soldiers; not, it is true, by strict rule, but because the ancient social idea favoured the descent of office, or land, or trade, or craft from father to son. This, indeed, was part of the celebrated Kwan-tsz's economic philosophy. Thus generation after generation of statesmen and scholars kept in steady touch with one another, exactly as our modern scientists of the first rank, each as a link, form an unbroken intimate chain from Newton down to Lord Kelvin, outside which pale the ordinary layman stands a comparative stranger to the arcana within.

Kwan-tsz, the statesman-philosopher of Ts'i, and in a sense the founder of Chinese economic science, was himself a scion of the imperial Chou clan; every writer on political economy subsequent to 643 B.C. quotes his writings, precisely as every European philosophical writer cites Bacon. Quite a galaxy of brilliant statesmen and writers, a century after Kwan-tsz, shed lustre upon the Confucian age (550-480), and nearly all of them were personal friends either of Confucius or of each other, or of both. Thus Tsz-ch'an of CHÊNG, senior to Confucius, but beloved and admired by him, was son of a reigning duke, and a prince of the ducal CHÊNG family, which again was descended from a son of the Emperor who fled in 842 B.C.

If Tsz-ch'an had written works on philosophy and politics, it is possible that he might have been China's greatest man in the place of Confucius; for he based his ideas of government, as did Confucius, who probably copied much from him, entirely upon "fitting conduct," or "natural propriety"; in addition to which he was a great lawyer, entirely free from superstition and hypocrisy; a kind, just, and considerate ruler; a consummate diplomat; and a bold, original statesman, economist, and administrator. The anecdotes and sayings of Tsz-ch'an are as numerous and as practical as those about Julius Caesar or Marcus Aurelius.

Another great pillar of the state praised by Confucius was Shuh Hiang of Tsin, whose reputation as a sort of Chinese Cicero is not far below that of Tsz-ch'an. He belonged to one of the great private families of Tsin, of whom it was said in Ts'u that "any of them could bring 100 war-chariots into the field." Nothing could be more interesting than the interviews and letters (see Appendix No. 1) between these two friends and their colleagues of Ts'i, Ts'u, Lu, and Sung. Yen-tsz of Ts'i almost ranks with Kwan-tsz as an administrator, philosopher, economist, author, and statesman. Confucius has a good word for him too, though Yen-tsz's own opinion of Confucius' merits was by no means so high. The two men had to "spar" with each other behind their respective rulers like Bismarck and Gortschakoff did. Yen-tsz's interview with Shuh Hiang, when the pair discussed the vices of their respective dukes, is almost as amusing as a "patter" scene in the pantomime, a sort of by-play which takes place whilst the curtain is down in preparation for the next formal act (see Appendix No. 2).

Confucius himself had descended in the direct line from the ducal family of Sung; but Sung, like the other states, was cursed with the "great family" nuisance, and one of his ancestors, having incurred a grandee's hostility, had met with his death in a palace intrigue, in consequence of which the Confucian family, despairing of justice, had migrated to Lu. When we read of Confucius' extensive wanderings (which are treated of more at length in a subsequent chapter), the matter takes a very different complexion from what is usually supposed, especially if it be recollected what a limited area was really covered. He never got even so far as Tsin, though part of Tsin touched the Lu frontier, and it is doubtful if he was ever 300 miles, as the crow flies, from his own house in Lu; true, he visited the fringe of Ts'u, but it must be remembered that the place he visited was only in modern Ho Nan province, and was one of the recent conquests of Ts'u, belonging to the Hwai River system. As we explained in the last chapter, Ts'u's policy then was to work up eastwards to the river Sz; that is, to the Grand Canal of to-day. Confucius, it is plain, was no mere pedant; for we have seen how, in the year 500, when he first enjoyed high political power, he displayed conspicuously great strategical and diplomatic ability in defeating the treacherous schemes of the ruler of Ts'i, who had been endeavouring to filch Lu territory, and who was dreadfully afraid lest Lu should, through Wu's favour, acquire the hegemony or protectorship. He could even be humorous, for when the barbarian King of Wu put in a demand for a "handsome hat," Confucius contemptuously observed that the gorgeousness of a hat's trimmings appealed to this ignorant monarch more than the emblem of rank distinguishing one hat from another.

Sung provided one distinguished statesman in Hiang Suh, whose fame is bound up with a kind of Hague Disarmament or Peace Conference, which he successfully engineered in 546 B.C. (see Appendix No. 3). In the year 558 he had been sent on a marriage mission to Lu. Ki- chah of Wu, who died at the ripe age of 90, was quite entitled to be king of that country, but he repeatedly waived his claims in favour of his brothers. K'ü-pêh-yüh of Wei, is mentioned in the Book of Rites, and in many other works. With him Confucius lodged on the two occasions of long sojourn in Wei: he is the man mentioned in Chapter XII who gave his authoritative "ritual" opinion about traitors. Ts'in never seems to have produced a native literary statesman on its own soil. During this 500-year period of isolated development, and also during the later period of conquest in the third century B.C., all its statesmen were borrowed from Tsin, or from some orthodox state of China proper; in military genius, however, Ts'in was unrivalled, and a special chapter will be devoted to her huge battues. The literary reputation of Ts'u was high at a comparatively early date, and even now the "Elegies of Ts'u" include some of the very finest of the Chinese poems and belles lettres; but in Confucius' time no Ts'u man, except possibly Lao-tsz, had any reputation at all; and Lao-tsz, being a mere archive keeper, not entrusted with any influential office, naturally lacked opportunity to emerge from the chrysalis stage. Moreover, the imperial dynasty, which Lao-tsz served, had no political influence at all: it was an ironical saying of the times; "the best civilians are Ts'u's, but they all serve other states," (meaning that the Ts'u rule was too capricious to attract talent). Hence, apart from the fact that Confucius doubted the wisdom of Lao-tsz's novel philosophy, Confucius had no occasion whatever to mention the secluded, self- contained old man in his political history, or, rather, in his bald annals of royal-movements.

CHAPTER XVI.LAND AND PEOPLE

What sort of folk were the masses of China, upon whom the ruling classes depended, then as now, for their support? In the year 594 B.C. the model state of Lu for the first time imposed a tax of ten per cent, upon each Chinese "acre" of land, being about one-sixth of an English acre: as the tax was one-tenth, it matters not what size the acre was. Each cultivator under the old system had an allotment of 100 such acres for himself, his parents, his wife, and his children; and in the centre of this allotment were 10 acres of "public land," the produce of which, being the result of his labour, went to the State; there was no further taxation. A "mile," being about one-third of an English mile, and, therefore, in square measure one-ninth of an English square mile, consisted of 300 fathoms (taking the fathom roughly), and its superficies contained 900 "acres" of which 80 were public under the above arrangement, 820 remaining for the eight families owning this "well-field"—so called because the ideograph for a "well" represents nine squares: a four-sided square in the centre, four three-sided squares impinging on it; and four two-sided squares at the corners; i.e. 100 "acres" each, plus 2-1/2 "acres" each for "homestead and onions"; or 20 of these last in all. Nine cultivators in one "well," multiplied by four, formed a township, and four townships formed a "cuirass" of 144 armed warriors; but this was under a modified system introduced four years later (590). It will be observed that the arithmetic seems confused, if not faulty; but that does not seriously affect the genuineness of the picture, and may be ignored as mere detail.

The ancient classification of people was into four groups. The scholar people employed themselves in studying tao and the sciences, from which we plainly see that the doctrine of tao, or "the way," existed long before Lao-tsz, in Confucius' time, superadded a mystic cosmogony upon it, and made of it a socialist or radical instead of an imperialist or conservative doctrine. The second class were the trading people, who dealt in "produce from the four quarters"; there is evidence that this meant chiefly cattle, grain, silk, horses, leather, and gems. The third class were the cultivators, and in those days tea and cotton, amongst other important products of to-day, were totally unknown. The fourth class consisted of handicraftsmen, who naturally made all things they could sell, or knew how to make.

Another classification of men is the following, which was given to the King of Ts'u by a sage adviser, presumably an importation from orthodox China. He divided people into ten classes, each inferior class owing obedience to its superior, and the highest of all owing obedience only to the gods or spirits. First, the Emperor; secondly, the "inner" dukes, or grandees of estates within the imperial domain: these grandees were dukes proper, not dukes by posthumous courtesy like the vassal princes after decease, and the Emperor used to send them on service, when required, to the vassal states; they were, in fact, like the "princes of the Church" or cardinals, who surround the Pope. Thirdly, "the marquesses," that is the semi-independent vassal states, no matter whether duke, marquess, earl, viscount, or baron; this term seems also to include the reigning lords of very small states which did not possess even the rank of baron, and which were usually attached to a larger state as clients, under protectorate; in fact, the recognized stereotyped way of saying "the vassal rulers" was "the marquesses." Then came what we should call the "middle classes," or bourgeoisie, followed by the artisans and cultivators: it will be noticed that the artisans are here given rank over the cultivators, which is not in accord with either very ancient or very modern practice; this, indeed, places cultivators before both traders and artisans. Lastly came the police, the carriers of burdens, the eunuchs, and the slaves. By "police" are meant the runners attached to public offices, whose work too often involves "squeezing" and terrorizing, torturing, flogging, etc. To the present day police, barbers, and slaves require three generations of purifying, or living down, before their descendants can enter for the public examinations; or, to use the official expression, their "three generations" must be "clear"; at least so it was until the old Confucian examination system was abolished as a test for official capacity a few years ago. Of eunuchs we shall have more to say shortly; but very little indeed is heard of private slaves, who probably then, as now, were indistinguishable from the ordinary people, and were treated kindly. The callous Greek and still more brutal Roman system, not to mention the infinitely more cowardly and shocking African slavery abuses of eighteenth-century Europe and nineteenth-century America, have never been known in China: no such thing as a slave revolt has ever been heard of there.

In the year 548 the kingdom of Ts'u ordered a cadastral survey, and also a general stock-taking of arms, chariots, and horses. Records were made of the extent and value of the land in each parish, the extent of the mountains and forests, and the resources they might furnish. Observation was also made of lakes and marshes suitable for sport, and it was forbidden to fill these in. Note was taken of such hills and mounds as might be available for tombs—a detail which shows that modern graves in China differ little if at all from the ancient ones; in fact in Canton "my hill," or "mountain," is synonymous with "my cemetery." In order to fix the taxes at a just figure, stock was taken of the salt- flats, the unproductive lands, and the tracts liable to periodical inundation. Areas rescued from the waters were protected by dykes, and subdivided for allotment by sloping banks, but without introducing the rigid nine-square system. Good lands, however, were divided according to the method introduced by the Chou dynasty; that is to say, six feet formed a "fathom," 100 fathoms an "acre," 100 "acres" the allotment of one family; these English terms are, of course, only approximately correct. Nine families still formed a hamlet or "well," and they cultivated together 1000 "acres," the central hundred going to pay the imposts. Taxes, direct and indirect, were fixed with exactitude, and also the number of war-chariots that each parish had to furnish; the number of horses; their value, age, and colour; the number of armoured troopers and foot soldiers, with a return of their cuirasses and shields. Regarding this colour classification, of the horses, it may be mentioned that the Tartars, in the second century B.C., were in the habit of equipping whole regiments of cavalry on mounts of the same colour, and it is, therefore, possible that this practice may have been imitated in South China; but Ts'u never once herself engaged in warfare with the Tartars; at all events with Tartars other than Tartars brought into Chinese settlements.

Long before this, the philosopher-statesman Kwan-tsz of Ts'i had so developed the agriculture, fisheries, trade, and salt gabelle, and had governed the country in such a way that his State, hitherto of minor importance, soon took the lead amongst the Chinese powers for wealth and for military influence. His classification of the people was into scholars, artisans, traders, and agriculturalists. He is generally credited with having introduced the "Babylonian woman" into the Ts'i metropolis, in order that traders, having sold their goods there, might leave as much as possible of their money behind in the houses of pleasure. There are many accounts of the luxury of this populous city, where "every woman possessed one long and one short needle," and where a premium levied upon currency, fish, and salt was applied to the relief of the poor and (!) to the rewarding of virtue. Kwan-tsz also maintained a standing army, or perhaps a militia force, of 30,000 men; but he was careful so to husband his strength that Ts'i should not have the external appearance of dominating; his aim was that she should rather hold her power in reserve, and only use it indirectly: as we have seen, his master was, in consequence of Kwan-tsz's able administration, raised to the high position of the first of the Five Protectors.

From this it will be plain that there was considerable commercial activity in China even before the time of Confucius: there was quite a string of fairs or market towns extending from the imperial reserve eastwards along the Yellow River to Choh-thou (still so called, south of Peking), which was then the most northernly of them: apparently each considerable state possessed one of these fairs. The headwaters of the River Hwai system were served by the great mart (now called Yii Chou) belonging to the state of Cheng. As with our own histories, Chinese annals consist chiefly of the record of what kings and grandees did, and mention of the people is only occasional; and, even then, only in connection with the policy of their leaders.

As soon as the second of the Protectors, the Marquess of Tsin, was seated on his ancestral throne (637), his first act was to reduce the tolls and make the roads safer; to facilitate trade, and to encourage agriculture. Also to "make friends of the eleven great families" (already mentioned twice in preceding pages), whose development, however, in time led to the collapse of this princely power, and to its division between three of the "great families." A century after this, a minister of the Ts'u state praised very highly the efficiency of the Tsin administration. "The common people are devoted to agriculture; the merchants, artisans, and menials are all dutiful." For the conveyance of grain between the Ts'in and the Tsin capitals, both carts and boats were requisitioned, from which we must assume that there were practicable roads of some sort for two-wheeled vehicles. In the year 546, when some important reserves were made by Tsin at the Peace Conference, an express messenger was sent from Sung to the Ts'u capital to take the king's pleasure: this means an overland journey from the sources of the Hwai to the modern treaty port of Sha-shr above Hankow.

It may be added that, five centuries before Kwan-tsz existed, the founder of the Ts'i state, as a vassal to the new Chou dynasty, had already distinguished himself by encouraging trade, manufactures, fisheries, and the salt production; so that Kwan-tsz was an improver rather than an inventor.

Thus we see that, from very early times, China was by no means a sleepy country of ignorant husbandmen, but was a place full of multifarious activities; and that her local rulers, at least from the time when the patriarchal power of the Emperors decayed in 771, were often men of considerable sagacity, quite alive to the necessity of developing their resources and encouraging their people: this helps us to understand their restlessness under the yoke of "ritual."

CHAPTER XVII.EDUCATION AND LITERARY

There is singularly little mention of writing or education in ancient times, and it seems likely that written records were at first confined to castings or engravings upon metal, and carvings upon stone. In the days when the written character was cumbrous, there would be no great encouragement to use it for daily household purposes. It is a striking fact, not only that writings upon soft clay, afterwards baked, were not only non-existent in China, but have never once been mentioned or conceived of as being a possibility. This fact effectually disposes of the allegation that Persian and Babylonian literary civilization made its way to China, for it is unreasonable to suppose that an invention so well suited to the clayey soil (of loess mud with cementing properties) in which the Chinese princes dwelt could have been ignored by them, if ever the slightest inkling of it had been obtained.

In 770 B.C., when the Emperor, having moved his capital to the east, ceded his ancestral lands in the west to Ts'in on condition that Ts'in should recover them permanently from the Tartars, the document of cession was engraved upon a metal vase. Fifteen hundred years before this, the Nine Tripods of the founder of the Hia dynasty, representing tributes of metal brought to the Emperor by outlying tribes, were inscribed with records of the various productions of China: these tripods were ever afterwards regarded as an attribute of imperial authority; and even Ts'u, when it began to presume upon the Chou Emperor's weakness, put in a claim (probably based upon his ancestors' own ancient Chinese descent, as explained in Chapter IV.) to possess them. In distributing the fiefs amongst relatives and friends, the first Chou emperors "composed orders" conferring rights upon their new vassals; but it is not stated what written form these orders took. Written prayers for the recovery of the first Emperor's health are mentioned, but here again we are ignorant of the material on which the prayers were written by the precentor. Four hundred years later, in 65, when Ts'in had assisted to the throne his neighbour the Marquess of Tsin, the latter gave a promise in writing to Ts'in that he would cede to her all the territory lying to the west of the Yellow River. The next ruler of Tsin, the celebrated wanderer who afterwards became the second Protector, is distinctly stated to have had an adviser who taught him to read; it is added that the same marquess also consulted this adviser about a suitable teacher for his son and heir. About the same time one of the Marquess's friends, objecting to take office, took to flight: his friends, as a protest, hung up "a writing" at the palace gate. In 584 a Ts'u refugee in Tsin sends a writing to the leading general of Ts'u, threatening to be a thorn in his side. It is presumed that in all these cases the writing was on wood. The text of a declaration of war against Ts'u by Ts'in in 313 B.C., at a time when these two powers had ceased to be allies, and were competing for empire, refers to an agreement made three centuries earlier between the King of Ts'u and the Earl of Ts'in; this declaration was carved upon several stone tablets; but it does not appear upon what material the older agreement was carved. In 538, at a durbar held by Ts'u, Hiang Suh, the learned man of Sung, who has already been mentioned in Chapter XV. as the inventor of Peace Conferences in 546, and as one of the Confucian group of friends, remarked: "What I know of the diplomatic forms to be observed is only obtained from books." A few years later, when the population of one of the small orthodox Chinese states was moved for political convenience by Ts'u away to another district, they were allowed to take with them "their maps, cadastral survey, and census records."

There is an interesting statement in the Kwoh Yü, an ancillary history of these times, but touching more upon personal matters, usually considered to have been written by the same man that first expanded Confucius' annals, to the effect that in 489 B.C. (when Confucius was wandering about on his travels, a disappointed and disgusted man) the King of Wu inflicted a crushing defeat upon Ts'i at a spot not far from the Lu frontier, and that he captured "the national books, 800 leather chariots, and 3000 cuirasses and shields." If this translation be perfectly accurate, it is interesting as showing that Ts'i did possess Kwoh-shu, or "a State library," or archives. But unfortunately two other histories mention the capture of a Ts'i general named Kwoh Hia, alias Kwoh Hwei-tsz, so that there seems to be a doubt whether, in transcribing ancient texts, one character (shu) may not have been substituted for the other (hia). Two years later the barbarian king in question entered Lu, and made a treaty with that state upon equal terms.

Shortly after this date, the Chinese adviser who brought about the conquest of Wu by the equally barbarous Yiieh, had occasion to send a "closed letter" to a man living in Ts'u. When we come to later times, subsequent to the death of Confucius, we find written communications more commonly spoken of. Thus, in 313, Ts'i, enraged at the supposed faithlessness of Ts'u, "broke in two the Ts'u tally" and attached herself to Ts'in instead. This can only refer to a wooden "indenture" of which each party preserved a copy, each fitting 'in, "dog's teeth like," as the Chinese still say, closely to the other. A few years later we find letters from Ts'i to Ts'u, holding forth the tempting project of a joint attack upon Ts'in; and also a letter from Ts'in to Ts'u, alluding to the escape of a hostage and the cause of a war. In the year 227, when Ts'in was rapidly conquering the whole empire, the northernmost state of Yen (Peking plain), dreading annexation, conceived the plan of assassinating the King of Ts'in; and, in order to give the assassin a plausible ground for gaining admittance to the tyrant's presence, sent a map of Yen, so that the roads available for troops might be explained to the ambitious conqueror, who would fall into the trap. He barely escaped.

All these matters put together point to the clear conclusion that such states as Ts'in, Tsin, Ts'i, Yen, and Ts'u (none of which belonged, so far as the bulk of their population was concerned, to the purely Chinese group concentrated in the limited area described in the first chapter) were able to communicate by letter freely with each other: á fortiori, therefore, must the orthodox states, whose civilization they had all borrowed or shared, have been able to communicate with them, and with each other. Besides, there is the question of the innumerable treaties made at the durbars, and evidently equally legible by all the dozen or so of representatives present; and the written prayers, already instanced, which were probably offered to the gods at most sacrifices. A special chapter will be devoted to treaties.

In the year 523 the following passage occurs, or rather it occurs in one of the expanded Confucian histories having retrospective reference to matters of 523 B.C:—"It is the father's fault if, at the binding up of the hair (eight years of age), boys do not go to the teacher, though it may be the mother's fault if, before that age, they do not escape the dangers of fire and water: it is their own fault if, having gone to the teacher, they make no progress: it is their friends' fault if they make progress but get no repute for it: it is the executive's fault if they obtain repute but no recommendation to office: it is the prince's fault if they are recommended for office but not appointed." Here we have in effect the nucleus at least of the examination system as it was until a year or two ago, together with an inferential statement that education was only meant for the governing classes.

It is rather remarkable that the invention of the "greater seal" character in 827 B.C. practically coincides with the first signs of imperial decadence; this is only another piece of evidence in favour of the proposition that enlightenment and patriarchal rule could not exist comfortably together. When Ts'in conquered the whole of modern China 600 years later, unified weights and measures, the breadth of axles, and written script, and remedied other irregularities that had hitherto prevailed in the rival states, it is evident that the need of a more intelligible script was then found quite as urgent as the need of roads suitable for all carts, and of measures by which those carts could bring definite quantities of metal and grain tribute to the capital. Accordingly the First August Emperor's prime minister did at once set to work to invent the "lesser seal" character, in which (so late as A.D. 200) the first Chinese dictionary was written; this "lesser seal" is still fairly readable after a little practice, but for daily use it has long been and is impracticable and obsolete. If we reflect how difficult it is for us to decipher the old engrossed charters and written letters of the English kings, we may all the more easily imagine how even a slight change in the form of "letters," or strokes, will make easy reading of Chinese impossible. It is a mistake to suppose that the Chinese have to "spell their way" laboriously through the written character so familiar to them: it is just as easy to "skim over" a Chinese newspaper in a few minutes as it is to "take in" the leading features of the Times in the same limited time; and volumes of Chinese history or literature in general can be "gutted" quite easily, owing to the facility with which the so-called pictographs, once familiar, lend themselves to "skipping." The Bamboo Books, dug up in A.D. 281, the copies of the classics concealed in the walls of Confucius' house, the copy of Lao-tsz's philosophical work recorded to have been in the possession of a Chinese empress in 150 B.C.—all these were written in the "greater seal," and the painstaking industry of Chinese specialists was already necessary when the Christian era began, in order to reduce the ancient characters to more modern forms. Since then the written character has been much clarified and simplified, and it is just as easy to express sentiments in written Chinese as in any other language; but, of course, when totally new ideas are introduced, totally new characters must be invented; and inventions, both of individual characters and of expressions, are going on now.

CHAPTER XVIII.TREATIES AND VOWS

Treaties were always very solemn functions, invariably accompanied by the sacrifice of a victim. A part of the victim, or of its blood, was thrown into a ditch, in order that the Spirit of the Earth might bear witness to the deed; the rest of the blood was rubbed upon the lips of the parties concerned, and also scattered upon the documents, by way of imprecation; sometimes, however, the imprecations, instead of being uttered, were specially written at the end of the treaty. Just as we now say "the ink was scarcely dry before, etc., etc.," the Chinese used to say "the blood of the victim was scarcely dry on their lips, before, etc., etc." When the barbarian King of Wu succeeded for a short period in "durbaring" the federal Chinese princes, a dispute took place (as narrated in Chapter XIV.) between Tsin and Wu as to who should rub the lips with blood first— in other words, have precedence. In the year 541 B.C., sixty years before the above event, Tsin and Ts'u had agreed to waive the ceremony of smearing the lips with blood, to choose a victim in common, and to lay the text of the treaty upon the victim after a solemn reading of its contents. This modification was evidently made in consequence of the disagreement between Tsin and Ts'u at the Peace Conference of 546, when a dispute had arisen (page 47), as to which should smear the lips first. This was the occasion on which the famous Tsin statesman, Shuh Hiang, in the face of seventeen states' representatives, all present, had the courage to ignore Ts'u's treachery in concealing cuirasses under the soldiers' clothes. He said: "Tsin holds her pre-eminent position as Protector by her innate good qualities, which will always command the adhesion of other states; why need we care if Ts'u smears first, or if she injures herself by being detected in treachery?" It has already been mentioned that Confucius glosses over or falsifies both the above cases, and gives the victory in each instance to Tsin. Though these little historical peccadilloes on the part of the saint homme are considered even by orthodox critics to be objectionable, it must be remembered that it was very risky work writing history at all in those despotic times: even in comparatively democratic days (100 B.C.), the "father of Chinese history" was castrated for criticizing the reigning Emperor in the course of issuing his great work; and so late as the fifth century A.D. an almost equally great historian was put to death "with his three generations" for composing a "true history" of the Tartars then ruling as Emperors of North China; i.e. for disclosing their obscure and barbarous origin, Moreover, foreigners who fix upon these trifling specific and admitted discrepancies, in order to discredit the general truth of all Chinese history, must remember that the Chinese critics, from the very beginning, have always, even when manifestly biased, been careful to expose errors; the very discrepancies themselves, indeed, tend to prove the substantial truth of the events recorded; and the fact that admittedly erroneous texts still stand unaltered proves the reverent care of the Chinese as a nation to preserve their defective annals, with all faults, in their original condition.

At this treaty conference of 546 B.C., held at the Sung capital, the host alone had no vote, being held superior (as host) to all; and, further, out of respect for his independence, the treaty had to be signed outside his gates: the existence of the Emperor was totally ignored.

A generation before this (579) another important treaty between the two great rivals, Tsin and Ts'u, had been signed by the high contracting parties outside the walls of Sung. The articles provided for community of interest in success or failure; mutual aid in every thing, more especially in war; free use of roads so long as relations remained peaceful; joint action in face of menace from other powers; punishment of those neglecting to come to court. The imprecation ran: "Of him who breaks this, let the armies be dispersed and the kingdom be lost; moreover, let the spirits chastise him." Although both orthodox powers professed their anxiety to "protect" the imperial throne, yet, seeing that the Emperor was quietly shelved in all these conventions, the reference to "court duty" probably refers to the duty of Cheng and the other small orthodox states to render homage to Tsin or Ts'u (as the case might be) as settled by this and previous treaties. In fact, at the Peace Conference of 546, it was agreed between the two mesne lords that the vassals of Ts'u should pay their respects to Tsin, and vice versa. But, during the negotiations, a zealous Tsin representative went on to propose that the informal allies of the chief contracting powers should also be dragged in: "If Ts'in will pay us a visit, I will try and induce Ts'i to visit T'su." These two powers had ententes, Ts'i with Tsin, and Ts'u with Ts'in, but recognized no one's hegemony over them. It was this surprise sprung upon the Ts'u delegates that necessitated an express messenger to the king, as recounted at the end of Chapter XVI. The King of Ts'u sent word: "Let Ts'in and Ts'i alone; let the others visit our respective capitals." Accordingly it was understood that Tsin and Ts'u should both be Protectors, but that neither Ts'in nor Ts'i should recognize their status to the point of subordinating themselves to the joint hegemons. This was Ts'u's first appearance as effective hegemon, but her official debut alone did not take place till 538. Ts'i and Ts'in had both approved, in principle, the terms of peace, but Ts'in sent no representative, whilst Ts'i sent two. It is very remarkable that Sz-ma Ts'ien (the great historian of 100 B.C., who was castrated) does not mention this important meeting in his great work, either under the heading of Ts'i, or of Tsin, or under the headings of Sung and Ts'u. It seems, however, really to have had good effect for several generations; but there was some thing behind it which shows that love for humanity was not the leading motive of the chief parties. Two years later it was that the philosophical brother of the King of Wu went his rounds among the Chinese princes, and it is evident that Ts'u only desired peace with North China whilst she tackled this formidable new enemy on the coast. Tsin, on the other hand, was in trouble with the "six great families" (the survivors of the "eleven great families" conciliated by the Second Protector), who were gradually undermining the princely authority in Tsin to their own private aggrandisement. In 572 B.C., when the legitimate ruler of Tsin, who had been superseded by irregular successors, was fetched back from the Emperor's court, to which he had gone for a quiet asylum, he drew up a treaty of conditions with his own ministers, and immolated a chicken as sanction; this idea is still occasionally perpetuated in British courts of justice, where Chinese, probably without knowing it, draw upon ancient history when asked by the court how they are accustomed to sanction an oath; cocks are often also carried about by modern Chinese boatmen for purposes of sacrifice. In the year 504, after Wu had captured the Ts'u capital, one of the petty orthodox Chinese states taken by Ts'u— the first to be so taken by barbarians—in 684, but left by Ts'u internally independent, declined to render any assistance to Wu, unless she could prove her competence to hold permanently the Ts'u territory thus conquered. The King of Ts'u was so grateful for this that he drew some blood from the breast of his own half- brother, and on the spot made a treaty with the vassal prince. It 662, even in a love vow, the ruler of Lu cut his own arm and exchanged drops of blood with his lady-love. In 481 the people of Wei (the small orthodox state on the middle Yellow River between Tsin and Lu) forced one of their politicians to swear allegiance to the desired successor under the sanction of a sacrificial pig.

The great Kwan-tsz insisted on his prince carrying out a treaty which had been extorted in times of stress; but, as a rule, the most opportunistic principles were laid down, even by Confucius himself when he was placed under personal stress: "Treaties obtained by force are of no value, as the spirits could not then have really been present." In 589 Ts'u invaded the state of Wei, just mentioned, and menaced the adjoining state of Lu, compelling the execution of a treaty. Confucius, who once broke a treaty himself, naturally retrospectively considered this ducal treaty of no effect, and he even goes so far as to avoid mentioning in his annals some of the important persons who were present; he especially "burkes" two Chinese ruling princes, who were shameless enough to ride in the same chariot with the King of Ts'u, under whose predominancy they were, and who were therefore themselves under a kind of stress. In 482 one of Confucius' pupils made the following casuistical reply to the government of Wu on their application for renewal of a treaty with her: "It is only fidelity that gives solidity to treaties; they are determined by mutual consent, and it is with sacrifices that they are laid before our ancestors; the written words give expression to them, and the spirits guarantee them. A treaty once concluded cannot be changed: otherwise it were vain to make a new one. Remember the proverb: "What needs warming up more may just as well be eaten cold." The ordinary rough-and-ready form of oath or vow between individuals was: "If I break this, may I be as this river"; or, "may the river god be witness." There were many other similar forms, and it was often customary to throw something valuable into the river as a symbol.

CHAPTER XIX.CONFUCIUS AND LITERATURE

Let us return for a moment to the history of China's development. Confucius was born in the autumn of 551, B.C., and he died in 479. If we survey the condition of the empire during these seventy years, we may begin to understand better the secret of his teachings, and of his influence in later times. When he was a boy of seven or eight years, the presence in Lu of Ki-chah, the learned and virtuous brother of the barbarian King of Wu, must have opened his eyes widely to the ominous rise, of a democratic and mixed China. Lu, like Tsin, was now beginning to suffer from the "powerful family" plague; in other words, the story of King John and his barons was being rehearsed in China. Tsin and Ts'u had patched up ancient enmities at the Peace

Conference; Tsin during the next twenty years administered snub after snub to the obsequious ruler of Lu, who was always turned back at the Yellow River whenever he started west to pay his respects. Lu, on the other hand, declined to attend the Ts'u durbar of 538, held by Ts'u alone only after the approval of Tsin had been obtained. In 522 the philosopher Yen-tsz, of Ts'i, accompanied his own marquess to Lu in order to study the rites there: this fact alone proves that Ts'i, though orthodox and advanced, had not the same lofty spiritual status that was the pride of Lu. In 517 the Marquess of Lu was driven from his throne, and Ts'i took the opportunity to invade Lu under pretext of assisting him; however, the fugitive preferred Tsin as a refuge, and for many years was quartered at a town near the common frontier. But the powerful families (all branches of the same family as the duke himself) proved too strong for him; they bribed the Tsin statesmen, and the Lu ruler died in exile in the year 510. In the year 500 Confucius became chief counsellor to the new marquess, and by his energetic action drove into exile in Tsin a very formidable agitator belonging to one of the powerful family cliques. In 488 the King of Wu, after marching on Ts'i, summoned Lu to furnish "one hundred sets of victims" as a mark of compliancy; the king and the marquess had an interview; the next year the king came in person, and a treaty was made with him under the very walls of K'üh-fu, the Lu capital (this shameful fact is concealed by Confucius, who simply says: "Wu made war on us"). In 486 Lu somewhat basely joined Wu in an attack upon orthodox Ts'i. In 484-483 Confucius, who had meanwhile been travelling abroad for some years in disgust, was urgently sent for; four years later he died, a broken and disappointed man.

Now, it is one thing to be told in general terms that Confucius represented conservative forces, disapproved of the quarrelsome wars of his day, and wished in theory to restore the good old "rules of propriety"; but quite another thing to understand in a human, matter-of-fact sort of way what he really did in definite sets of circumstances, and what practical objects he had in view. The average European reader, not having specific facts and places under his eye, can only conceive from this rough generalization, and from the usual anecdotal tit-bits told about him, that Confucius was an exceedingly timid, prudent, benevolent, and obsequious old gentleman who, as indeed his rival Lao-tsz hinted to him, was something like a superior dancing-master or court usher, But when the disjointed apothegms of his "Analects" (put together, not by himself, but by his disciples) are placed alongside the real human actions baldly touched upon in his own "Springs and Autumns," and as expanded by his three commentators, one of them, at least, being a contemporary of his own, things assume quite a different complexion, Moreover, this last-mentioned or earliest in date of the expanders (see p. 91) also composed a chatty, anecdotal, and intimately descriptive account of Lu, Ts'i, Tsin, CHÊNG, Ts'u, Wu, and Yiieh (of no other states except quite incidentally); and we have also the Bamboo Books dug up in 281 A.D., being the Annals of Tsin and a sketch of general history down to 299 B.C. Finally, the "father of history," in about go B.C., published, or issued ready for publication, a resumé of all the above (except what was in the Bamboo Books, which were then, of course, unknown to him); so that we are able to compare dates, errors, misprints, concealments, and so on; not to mention the advantage of reading all that the successive generations of commentators have had to say.

The matter may be compendiously stated as follows. Without attempting to go backward beyond the conquest by the Chou principality and the founding of a Chou dynasty in 122 B.C. (though there is really no reason to doubt the substantial accuracy of the vague "history" of patriarchal times, at least so far back beyond that as to cover the 1000 years or more of the two previous dynasties' reigns), we may state that, whilst in general the principles and ritual of the two previous dynasties were maintained, a good many new ideas were introduced at this Chou conquest, and amongst other things, a compendious and all- pervading practical ritual government, which not only marked off the distinctions between classes, and laid down ceremonious rules for ancestral sacrifice, social deportment, family duties, cultivation, finance, punishment, and so on, but endeavoured to bring all human actions whatsoever into practical harmony with supposed natural laws; that is to say, to make them as regular, as comprehensible, as beneficent, and as workable, as the perfectly manifest but totally unexplained celestial movements were; as were the rotation of seasons, the balancing of forces, the growth and waning of matter, male and female reproduction, light and darkness; and, in short, to make human actions as harmonious as were all the forces of nature, which never fail or go wrong except under (presumed) provocation, human or other. The Emperor, as Vicar of God, was the ultimate judge of what was tao, or the "right way."

Now this simple faith, when the whole of the Chinese Empire consisted of about 50,000 square miles of level plain, inhabited probably by not more than 2,000,000 or 3,000,000 homogeneous people, was admirably suited for the patriarchal rule of a central chief (the King or Emperor), receiving simple tribute of metals, hemp, cattle, sacrificial supplies, etc.; entertaining his relatives and princely friends when they came to do annual homage and to share in periodical sacrifice; declaring the penal laws (there were no other laws) for all his vassals; compassionating and conciliating the border tribes living beyond those vassals. But this peaceful bucolic life, in the course of time and nature, naturally produced a gradual increase in the population; the Chinese cultivators spread themselves over the expanse of loess formed by the Yellow River and Desert deposits and by aeons of decayed vegetation in the low-lying lands; no other nation or tribe within their ken having the faintest notion of written character, there was consequently no political cohesion of any sort amongst the non-Chinese tribes; the position was akin to that of the European powers grafting themselves for centuries upon the still primitive African tribes, comparatively few of which have seen fit to turn the art of writing to the practical purpose of keeping records and cementing their own power. Wherever a Chinese adventurer went, there he became founder of a state; to this day we see enterprising Chinamen founding petty "dynasties" in the Siamese Malay Peninsula; or, for instance, an Englishman like Rajah Brooke founding a private dynasty in Borneo.

Some of these frontier tribes, notably the Tartars, were of altogether too tough a material to be assimilated. They even endeavoured to check the Chinese advance beyond the Yellow River, and carried fire and sword themselves into the federal conclave. Where resistance was nil or slight, as, for instance, among some of the barbarians to the east, there the Chinese adventurers, either adopting native ways, or persuading the autochthones to adopt their ways, by levelling up or levelling down, developed strong cohesive power; besides (owing to the difficulties of inter-communication) creating a feeling of independence and a disinclination to obey the central power. The emperors who used in the good old days to summon the vassals—a matter of a week or two in that small area—to chastise the wicked tribes on their frontiers, gradually found themselves unable to cope with the more distant Tartar hordes, the eastern barbarians of the coast, the Annamese, Shans, and other unidentified tribes south of the Yang- tsz, as they had so easily done with nearer tribes when the Chinese had not pushed out so far. Moreover, new-Chinese, Chinese- veneered, and half-Chinese states, recognizing their own responsibilities, now interposed themselves as "buffers" or barriers between the Emperor and the unadulterated barbarians; these hybrid states themselves were quite as formidable to the imperial power as the displaced barbarians had formerly been. Hence, as we have seen, the pitiful flight from his metropolis of one Emperor after the other; the rise of great and wealthy persons outside the former limited sacred circle; the pretence of protecting the Emperor, advanced by these rising powers, partly in order to gain prestige by using his imperial name in support of their local ambitions, and partly because—as during the Middle Ages in the case of the Papacy—no one cared to brave the moral odium of annihilating a venerable spiritual power, even though gradually shorn of its temporal rights and influence.

Lu was almost on a par with the imperial capital in all that concerns learning, ritual, music, sacrifice, deportment, and spiritual prestige. Confucius, in his zeal for the recovery of imperial rights, was really no more of a stickler for mere form than were Tsz-ch'an of Cheng, Ki-chah of Wu, Hiang Suh of Sung, Shuh Hiang of Tsin, and others already enumerated; the only distinguishing feature in his case was that he was not a high or influential official in his earlier days; besides, he was a Sung man by descent, and all the great families were of the Lu princely caste. Thus, for want of better means to assert his own views, he took to teaching and reading, to collecting historical facts, to pointing morals and adorning tales. As a youth he was so clever, that one of the Lu grandees, on his death-bed, foretold his greatness. It was a great bitterness for him to see his successive princely masters first the humble servants of Ts'i, then buffeted between Tsin and Ts'u, finally invaded and humiliated by barbarian Wu, only to receive the final touches of charity at the hands of savage Yiieh. His first act, when he at last obtained high office, was to checkmate Ts'i, the man behind the ruler of which jealous state feared that Lu might, under Confucius' able rule, succeed in obtaining the Protectorate, and thus defeat his own insidious design to dethrone the legitimate Ts'i house. The wily Marquess of Ts'i thereupon—of course at the instigation of the intriguing "great families"—tried another tack, and succeeded at last in corrupting the vacillating Lu prince with presents of horses, racing chariots, and dancing women. Then it was (497) that Confucius set out disheartened on his travels. Recalled thirteen years later, he soon afterwards began to devote his remaining powers to the Annals so frequently referred to above, and it was whilst engaged in finishing this task that he had presentiments of his coming end; he does not appear to have been able to exercise much political or advisory power after his return to Lu.

During his thirteen years of travel (a more detailed account of which will be given in a subsequent chapter), he found time to revise and edit the books which appear to have formed the common stock-in-trade for all China; one of his ideas was to eliminate from these all sentiments of an anti-imperial nature. They were not then called "classics," but simply "The Book" (of History), "The Poems" (still known by heart all over China), "The Rites" (as improved by the Chou family), "The Changes" (a sort of cosmogony combined with soothsaying), and "Music."

CHAPTER XX.LAW

Let us now consider the notions of law as they existed in the primitive Chinese mind. As all government was supposed to be based on the natural laws of the universe, of which universal law or order of things, the Emperor, as "Son of Heaven," was (subject to his own obedience to it) the supreme mouthpiece or expression, there lay upon him no duty to define that manifest law; when it was broken, it was for him to say that it was broken, and to punish the breach. Nature's bounty is the spring, and therefore rewards are conferred in spring; nature's fall is in the autumn, which is the time for decreeing punishments; these are carried out in winter, when death steals over nature. A generous table accompanies the dispensing of rewards, a frugal table and no music accompanies the allotment of punishments; hence the imperial feasts and fasts. Thus punishment rather than command is what was first understood by Law, and it is interesting to observe that "making war" and "putting to death" head the list of imperial chastisements, war being thus regarded as the Emperor's rod in the shape of a posse of punitory police, rather than as an expression of statecraft, ambitious greed, or vainglorious self-assertion. Then followed, in order of severity, castration, cutting off the feet or the knee-cap, branding, and flogging. The Emperor, or his vassals, or the executive officers of each in the ruler's name, declared the law, i.e. they declared the punishment in each case of breach as it occurred. Thus from the very beginning the legislative, judicial, and executive functions have never been clearly separated in the Chinese system of thought; new words have had to be coined within the last two years in order to express this distinction for purposes of law reform. Mercantile Law, Family Law, Fishery Laws—in a word, all the mass of what we call Commercial and Civil Jurisprudence,—no more concerned the Government, so far as individual rights were concerned, than Agricultural Custom, Bankers' Custom, Butchers' Weights, and such like petty matters; whenever these, or analogous matters, were touched by the State, it was for commonwealth purposes, and not for the maintenance of private rights. Each paterfamilias was absolutely master of his own family; merchants managed their own business freely; and so on with the rest. It was only when public safety, Government interests, or the general weal was involved that punishment-law stepped in and said,—always with tao, "propriety," or nature's law in ultimate view: "you merchants may not wear silk clothes"; "you usurers must not ruin the agriculturalists"; "you butchers must not irritate the gods of grain by killing cattle":— these are mere examples taken at random from much later times. The Emperor Muh, whose energies we have already seen displayed in Tartar conquests and exploring excursions nearly a millennium before our era, was the first of the Chou dynasty to decide that law reform was necessary in order to maintain order among the "hundred families" (still one of the expressions meaning "the Chinese people"). A full translation of this code is given in Dr. Legge's Chinese classics, where a special chapter of The Book is devoted to it: in charging his officer to prepare it, the Emperor only uses the words "revise the punishments," and the code itself is only known as the "Punishments" (of the marquess who drew it up); although it also prescribes many judicial forms, and lays down precepts which are by no means all castigatory. The mere fact of its doing so is illustrative of reformed ideas in the embryo. There is good ground to suppose that the Chinese Emperor's "laws," such as they were at any given time, were solemnly and periodically proclaimed, in each vassal kingdom; but, subject to these general imperial directions, the themis, diké or inspired decision of the magistrate, was the sole deciding factor; and, of course, the ruler's arbitrary pleasure, whether that ruler were supreme or vassal, often ran riot when he found himself strong enough to be unjust. For instance, in 894 B.C., the Emperor boiled alive one of the Ts'i rulers, an act that was revenged by Ts'i 200 years later, as has been mentioned in previous chapters.

In 796 B.C. a ruler of Lu was selected, or rather recommended to the Emperor for selection, in preference to his elder brother, because "when he inflicted chastisement he never failed to ascertain the exact instructions left by the ancient emperors." This same Emperor had already, in 817, nominated one younger brother to the throne of Lu, because he was considered the most attractive in appearance on an occasion when the brethren did homage at the imperial court. For this caprice the Emperor's counsellor had censured him, saying: "If orders be not executed, there is no government; if they be executed, but contrary to established rule, the people begin to despise their superiors."

In 746 B.C. the state of Ts'in, which had just then recently emerged from Tartar barbarism, and had settled down permanently in the old imperial domain, first introduced the "three stock" law, under which the three generations, or the three family connections of a criminal were executed for his crime as well as himself. In 596 and 550 Tsin (which thus seems to have taken the hint from Ts'in) exterminated the families of two political refugees who had fled to the Tartars and to Ts'i respectively. Even in Ts'u the relatives of the man who first taught war to Wu were massacred in 585, and any one succouring the fugitive King of Ts'u was threatened with "three clan penalties"; this last case was in the year 529. The laws of Ts'u seem to have been particularly harsh; in 55 the premier was cut into four for corruption, and one quarter was sent in each direction, as a warning to the local districts. About 650 B.C. a distinguished Lu statesman, named Tsang Wen-chung, seems to have drawn up a special code, for one of Confucius' pupils (two centuries later) denounced it as being too severe when compared with Tsz-ch'an's mild laws—to be soon mentioned. Confucius himself also described the man as being "too showy." This Lu statesman, about twenty years later, made some significant and informing observations to the ruler of Lu when report came that Tsin (the Second Protector) was endeavouring to get the Emperor to poison a federal refugee from Wei, about whose succession the powers were at the moment quarrelling. He said: "There are only five recognized punishments: warlike arms, the axe, the knife or the saw, the branding instruments, the whip or the bastinado; there are no surreptitious ones like this now proposed." The result was that Lu, being of the same clan as the Emperor, easily succeeded in bribing the imperial officials to let the refugee prince go. The grateful prince eagerly offered Tsang W&n-chung a reward; but the statesman declined to receive it, on the ground that "a subject's sayings are not supposed to be known beyond his own master's frontier." About, a century later a distinguished Tsin statesman, asking what "immortality" meant, was told: "When a man dies, but when his words live; like the words of this distinguished man, Tsang W&n-chung, of Lu state." This same Tsin statesman is said to have engraved some laws on iron (513), an act highly disapproved by Confucius. It is only by thus piecing together fragmentary allusions that we can arrive at the conclusion that "there were judges in those days." Mention has been several times made in previous chapters of Tsz-ch'an, whose consummate diplomacy maintained the independence and even the federal influence of the otherwise obscure state of Cheng during a whole generation. In the year 536 B.C. he decided to cast the laws in metal for the information of the people: this course was bitterly distasteful to his colleague, Shuh Hiang of Tsin (see Appendix I.), and possibly the Tsin "laws on iron" just mentioned were suggested by this experiment, for it must be remembered that Tsin, Lu, Wei, and Cheng were all of the same imperial clan. Confucius, who had otherwise a genuine admiration for Tsz-ch'an, disapproved of this particular feature in his career. In a minor degree the same question of definition and publication has also caused differences of opinion between English lawyers, so far as the so-called "judge-made law" is concerned; it is still considered to be better practice to have it declared as circumstances arise, than to have it set forth beforehand in a code. The arguments are the same; in both cases the judges profess to "interpret" the law as it already exists; that is, the Chinese judge interprets the law of nature, and the English judge the common and statute laws; but neither wishes to hamper himself by trying to publish in advance a scheme contrived to fit all future hypothetical cases.

About 680 B.C. the King of Ts'u is recorded to have passed a law against harbouring criminals, under which the harbourer was liable to the same penalty as the thief; and at the same time reference is made by his advisers to an ancient law or command of the imperial dynasty, made before it came to power in 1122 B.C.-"If any of your men takes to flight, let every effort be made to find him." Thus it would seem that other ruling classes, besides those of the Chou clan, accepted the general imperial laws, Chou- ordained or otherwise. Although it is thus manifest that the vassal states, at least after imperial decadence set in, in 771 B.C., drew up and published laws of their own, yet, at the great durbar of princes held by the First Protector in 651 B.C., it is recorded that the "Son of Heaven's Prohibitions" were read over the sacrificial victim. They are quite patriarchal in their laconic style, and for that reason recall that of the Roman Twelve Tables. They run: "Do not block springs!" "Do not hoard grain!" "Do not displace legitimate heirs!" "Do not make wives of your concubines!" "Do not let women meddle with State affairs!" From the Chinese point of view, all these are merely assertions of what is Nature's law. In the year 640, the state of Lu applied the term "Law Gate" to the South Gate, "because both Emperor and vassal princes face south when they rule, and because that is, accordingly, the gate through which all commands and laws do pass." It is always possible, however, that this "facing south" of the ancient ruler points to the direction whence some of his people came, and towards which, as their guide and leader, he had to look in order to govern them.

In the year 594 there is an instance cited where two dignitaries were killed by direct specific order of the Emperor. In explaining this exceptional case, the commentator says: "The lord of all below Heaven is Heaven, and Heaven's continuer or successor is the Prince; whilst that which the Prince holds fast is the Sanction, which no subject can resist."

Not very long after Confucius' death in 479 B.C., the powerful and orthodox state of Tsin, which had so long held its own against Ts'in, Ts'i, and Ts'u, tottered visibly under the disintegrating effects of the "great family" intrigues: of the six great families which had, as representatives of the earlier eleven, latterly monopolized power, three only survived internecine conflicts, and at last the surviving three split up into the independent states of Han, Wei, and Chao, those names being eponymous, as being their sub-fiefs, and, therefore, their "surnames," or family names. In the year 403 the Emperor formally recognized them as separate, independent vassaldoms. Wei is otherwise known as Liang, owing to the capital city having borne that name, and the kings of Liang are celebrated for their conversations with the peripatetic philosopher, Mencius, in the fourth century B.C. In order to distinguish this state from that of Wei (imperial clan) adjoining Lu and Sung, we shall henceforth call it Ngwei, as, in fact, it originally was pronounced, and as it still is in some modern dialects. The first of the Ngwei sovereigns had in his employ a statesman named Li K'wei, who introduced, for taxation purposes, a new system of land laws, and also new penal laws. These last were in six books, or main heads, and, it is said, represented all that was best in the laws of the different feudal states, mostly in reference to robbery: the minor offences were roguery, getting over city walls, gambling, borrowing, dishonesty, lewdness, extravagance, and transgressing the ruler's commands—their exact terms are now unknown. This code was afterwards styled the "Law Classic," and its influence can be plainly traced, dynasty by dynasty, down to modern times; in fact, until a year or two ago, the principles of Chinese law have never radically changed; each successive ruling family has simply taken what it found; modifying what existed, in its own supposed interest, according to time, place, and circumstance. Li K'wei's land laws singularly resembled those recommended to the Manchu Government by Sir Robert Hart four years ago.

CHAPTER XXI. PUBLIC WORKS

It is difficult to guess how much truth there is in the ancient traditions that the water-courses of the empire were improved through gigantic engineering works undertaken by the ancient Emperors of China. There is one gorge, well known to travellers, above Ich'ang, on the River Yang-tsz, on the way to Ch'ung-k'ing, where the precipitous rocks on each side have the appearance and hardness of iron, and for a mile or more—perhaps several miles— stand perpendicularly like walls on both sides of the rapid Yang- tsz River: the most curious feature about them is that from below the water-level, right up to the top, or as far as the eye can reach, the stone looks as though it had been chipped away with powerful cheese-scoops: it seems almost impossible that any operation of nature can have fashioned rocks in this way; on the other hand, what tools of sufficient hardness, driven by what great force, could hollow out a passage of such length, at such a depth, and such a height? It is certain that after Ts'in conquered the hitherto almost unknown kingdoms of Pa and Shuh (Eastern and Western Sz Ch'wan) a Chinese engineer named Li Ping worked wonders in the canalization of the so-called CH'ÊNg-tu plain, or the rich level region lying around the capital city of Sz Ch'wan province, which was so long as Shuh endured also the metropolis of Shuh. The consular officers of his Britannic Majesty have made a special study of these sluices, which are still in full working order, and they seem almost unchanged in principle from the period (280 B.C.) when Li Ping lived. The Chinese still regard this branch of the Great River as the source; or at least they did so until the Jesuit surveys of two centuries ago proved otherwise; it was quite natural that they should do so in ancient times, for the true upper course, and also Yiin Nan and Tibet through which that course runs, were totally unknown to them, and unheard of by name; even now the so-called Lolo country of Sz Ch'wan and Yiin Nan is mostly unexplored, and the mountain Lolos are quite independent of China. The fact that they have whitish skins and a written script of their own (manifestly inspired by the form of Chinese characters) makes them a specially interesting people. Li Ping's engineering feats also included the region around Ya-thou and Kia- ting, as marked on the modern maps. The founder of the Hia dynasty (2205 B.C.) is supposed to have liberated the stagnant waters of the Yellow River and sent them to the sea; as this is precisely what all succeeding dynasties have tried to do, and have been obliged to try, and what in our own times the late Li Hung-chang was ordered to do just before his death, there seems no good reason for suspecting the accuracy of the tradition; the more especially as we see that the founder of the Chou dynasty sent his chief political adviser and his two most distinguished relatives to settle along this troublesome river's lower course, as rulers of Ts'i, Yen, and Lu; the other considerable vassals were all ranged along the middle course.

The original Chinese founder of the barbarian colony of Wu belonged, as already explained, to the same clan or family as the founder of the Chou dynasty, and in one respect even took ancestral or spiritual precedence of him, because the emigrant had voluntarily retired into obscurity with his brother in order to make way for a third and more brilliant younger brother, whose grandson it was that afterwards, in 1122 B.C., conquered China, and turned the Chou principality, hitherto vassal to the Shang dynasty, into the Chou dynasty, to which the surviving Shang princes then became vassals in the Sung state and elsewhere. Even though the founder of Wu may have adopted barbarian ways, such as tattooing, hair-cutting, and the like, he must have possessed considerable administrative power, for he made a canal (running past his capital) for a distance of thirty English miles along the new "British" railway from Wu-sih to Ch'ang-shuh, as marked on present maps; his idea was to facilitate boat-travelling, and to assist cultivators with water supplies for irrigation.

In the year 485 B.C. the King of Wu, who was then in the hey-day of his success, and by way of becoming Protector of China, erected a wall and fortifications round the well-known modern city of Yangchow (where Marco Polo 1700 years later acted as governor); he next proceeded for the first time in history to establish water communication between the Yang-tsz River and the River Hwai; this canal was then (483-481) continued farther north, so as to give communication with the southern and central parts of modern Shan Tung province.

His object was to facilitate the conveyance of stores for his armies, then engaged in bringing pressure upon Ts'i (North Shan Tung) and Lu (South Shan Tung). He succeeded in getting his boats to the River Tsi, running past Tsi-nan Fu, and to the River I, running past I-thou Fu, thus dominating the whole Shan Tung region; for these two were then the only navigable rivers in Shan Tung besides the Sz. The River Tsi is now taken possession of by the Yellow River, which, as we have shown, then ran a parallel course much to the westward of it; and the River I then ran south into the River Sz, which, as already explained, has in its lower course, in comparatively modern times, been taken possession of permanently by the Grand Canal; but the upper course of the Sz, now, as then, ran past Confucius' town, the Lu metropolis, of K'üh-fu. In 483 B.C. the same king cast his faithful adviser (of Ts'u origin) into the canal by which the waters of lake T'ai Hu now run to modern Soochow, and thence to Hangchow. Ever since that date the unfortunate man in question has been a popular "god of the waters" in those parts. It follows, therefore, that the Wu founder's modest canal must have been from time to time extended, at least in an easterly direction. It was only after the conquest of China by Ts'in, 250 years later, that the First August Emperor extended this system of canals northwards and westwards, from Ch'ang-thou Fu to Tan-yang and Chinkiang, as marked on the modern maps. Thus the barbarian kings of Wu have found the true alignment of our "British", railway for us; and, so far as the northern canal is concerned, have really achieved the task for which credit is usually given to Kublai Khan, the Mongol patron of Marco Polo. Kublai merely improved the old work. The ancient Wu capital was 10 English miles south-east of Wu-sih, and 17 miles north of Soochow, to which place the capital was transferred in the year 513 B.C., as it was more suitable than the old capital for the arsenals and ship-building yards then, for the first time, being built on an extensive scale by the King of Wu.

The first bridge over the Yellow River was constructed by the kingdom of Ts'in in 257 B.C., on what is still the high-road between T'ung-thou Fu and P'u-chou Fu. Previous to that date armies had to cross the Yellow River at the fords; and, as an instance of this, it may be stated that the founder of the Chou dynasty in 1122 B.C. summoned his vassals to meet him at the Ford of Mêng, a place still so marked on the maps, and lying on the high-road between the two modern cities of Ho-nan Fu and Hwai- k'ing Fu; thus there was no excuse for the feudal princes failing to arrive at the rendezvous. It was not far from the same place, but on the north bank of the river, that Tsin in 632 B.C. held the great durbar as Second Protector, on the notorious occasion when the puppet Emperor was "sent for" by the Tsin dictator. To conceal this outrage on "the rites," Confucius says: "The Son of Heaven went in camp north of the river." To go on hunt, or in camp, is still a vague historical expression for "go on fief inspection," and it was so used in 1858, when the Manchu Emperor Hien-fêng took refuge from the allied troops at Jêhol in Tartary.

The first thing Ts'in did when it united the empire in 221 B.C. was to occupy all the fords and narrow passes, and to put them in working order for the passage of armies. As even now the lower Yellow River is only navigable for large craft for 20 miles from its mouth (now in Shan Tung), it is easy to imagine how many fords there must have been in its shallow waters, and also how it came to pass that boats were so little used to convey large bodies of troops with their stores.

The great wall of China of 217 B.C. was by no means the first of its kind. A century before that date Ts'in built a long wall to keep off the Tartars; and, half a century before that again, Ngwei (one of the three powerful families of Tsin, all made independent princes in 403) had built a wall to keep off its western neighbour Ts'in; both these walls seem to have been in the north part of the modern Shen Si region, and they were possibly portions of the later continuous great wall of the August Emperor, which occupied the forced energies of 700,000 men. There is a statement that the same Emperor set 700,000 eunuchs to work on the palaces and the tomb he was constructing for himself at his new metropolis (moved since 350 B.C. to the city of Hien-yang, north of the river Wei, opposite the present Si-ngan Fu). This probably means, not that eunuchs were common in those times as palace employés, but that castration still was the usual punishment inflicted throughout China for grave offences not calling for the penalty of death, or for the more serious forms of maiming, such as foot- chopping or knee-slicing; and that all the prisoners of that degree were told off to do productive work: although humiliatingly deformed, they were still available for the common purposes of native life, and their defenceless and forlorn plight would probably make it an easier matter to handle them in gangs than to handle sound males; and if they died off under the rough treatment of task-masters, they would have no families to mourn or avenge them in accordance with family duty; for a eunuch has no name and no family. The palaces in question were joined by a magnificent bridge on the high-road between Hien-yang and Si-ngan. This very year a German firm has contracted to build an iron bridge over the Yellow River at Lan-thou Fu, where crossed by Major Bruce.

CHAPTER XXII.CITIES AND TOWNS

There are singularly few descriptions of cities in ancient Chinese history, but here again we may safely assume that most of them were in principle, if only on a small scale, very much what they are now, mere inartistic, badly built collections of hovels. Sõul, the quaint capital of Corea, as it appeared in its virgin condition to its European discoverers twenty-five years ago, probably then closely resembled an ancient vassal Chinese prince's capital of the very best kind. Modern trade is responsible for the wealthy commercial streets now to be found in all large Chinese cities; but a small hien city in the interior—and it must be remembered that a hien circuit or district corresponds to an old marquisate or feudal principality of the vassal unit type—is often a poor, dusty, dirty, depressing, ramshackle agglomeration of villages or hamlets, surrounded by a disproportionately pretentious wall, the cubic contents of which wall alone would more than suffice to build in superior style the whole mud city within; for half the area of the interior is apt to be waste land or stagnant puddles: it was so even in Peking forty years ago, and possibly is so still except in the "Legation quarter."

In 745 B.C., when the Tsin marquess foolishly divided his patrimony with a collateral branch, the capital town of this subdivided state is stated to have been a greater place than the old capital. They are both of them still in existence as insignificant towns, situated quite close together on the same branch of the River Fên (the only navigable river) in South Shan Si; marked with their old names, too; that is to say, K'iih-wuh and Yih-CH'ÊNg. It was only after the younger branch annexed the elder in 679 that Tsin became powerful and began to expand; and it was only when a policy of "home rule" and disintegration set in, involving the splitting up of Tsin's orthodox power into three royal states of doubtful orthodoxy, that China fell a prey to Ts'in ambition. Absit omen to us.

In 560, when the deformed philosopher Yen-tsz visited Ts'u, and entertained that semi-barbarous court with his witticisms, he took the opportunity boastfully to enlarge upon the magnificence of Lin-tsz (still so marked), the capital of Ts'i. "It is," said he, "surrounded by a hundred villages; the parasols of the walkers obscure the sky, whose perspiration runs in such streams as to cause rain; their shoulders and heels touch together, so closely are they packed." The assembled Ts'u court, with mouths open, but inclined for sport at the cost of their visitor, said: "If it is such a grand place, why do they select you?" Yen-tsz played a trump card when he replied: "Because I am such a mean-looking fellow,"—meaning, as explained in Chapter IX., that "any pitiful rascal is good enough to send to Ts'u." Exaggerations apart, however, there is every reason to believe that the statesman- philosopher Kwan-tsz, a century before that date, had really organized a magnificent city. A full description of how he reconstructed the economic life of both city and people is given in the Kwoh-yü (see Chapter XVII.), the authenticity of which work, though not free from question, is, after all, only subject to the same class of criticism as Rénan lavishes upon one or two of the Gospels, the general tenor of which, be says, must none the less be accepted, with all faults, as the bonâfide attempt of some one, more or less contemporary, to represent what was then generally supposed to be the truth.

Ts'u itself must have had something considerable to show in the way of public buildings, for in the year 542 B.C. after paying a visit to that country in accordance with the provisions of the Peace Conference of 546, the ruler of Lu built himself a palace in imitation of one he saw there. The original capital of Wu (see Chapter VII.) was a poor place, and is described as having consisted of low houses in narrow streets, with a vulgar palace; this was in 523. In 513 a new king moved to the site now occupied by Soochow, and he seems to have made of it the magnificent city it has remained ever since—the place, of course it will be remembered, where General Gordon and Li Hung-chang had their celebrated quarrel about decapitating surrendered rebels. There were eight gates, besides eight water-gates for boats; it was eight English miles in circuit, and contained the palace, several towers (pagodas, being Buddhist, were then naturally unknown), kiosks, ponds, and duck preserves. The extensive arsenal and ship- yard was quite separate from the main town. No city in the orthodox part of China is so closely described as this one, nor is it likely that there were many of them so vast in extent.

Judging by the frequency with which Ts'in moved its capitals (but always within a limited area in the Wei valley, between that river and its tributary the K'ien), they cannot have been very important or substantial places; in fact, there are no descriptions of early Ts'in economic life at all; and, for all we know to the contrary, the headquarters of Duke Muh, when he entered upon his reforms in the seventh century B.C., may have resembled a Tartar encampment. The Kwoh-yü has no chapter devoted to Ts'in, which (as indeed stated) for 500 years lived a quite isolated life of its own. In later times, especially after the reforms introduced by the celebrated Chinese princely adventurer, Wei Yang, during the period 360—340, the land administration was reconstituted, the capital was finally moved to Hien-yang, and every effort was made to develop all the resources of the country. Ts'in then possessed 41 hien, those with a population of under 10,000 having a governor with a lower title than the governors of the larger towns, Probably the total population of Ts'in by this time reached 3,000,000. A century later, when the First August Emperor was conquering China, armies of half a million men on each side were not at all uncommon. When his conquests were complete, he set about building palaces on both banks of the Wei in most lavish style, as narrated in the last chapter. It is said of him that, "as he conquered each vassal prince, he had a sketch made of his palace buildings," and, with these before him as models, he lined the river with rows of beautiful edifices,—evidently, from the description given, much resembling those lying along the Golden Horn at Constantinople; if not in quality, at least in general spectacular arrangement.

As to the minor orthodox states grouped along the Yellow River, they seem to have shifted their capitals on very slight provocation; scarcely one of them remained from first to last in the same place. To take one as an instance, the state of Hu, an orthodox state belonging to the same clan name as Ts'i. The history of this petty principality or barony is only exactly known from the time when Confucius' history begins, and it was continually being oppressed by Cheng and Ts'u, its more powerful neighbours; in 576, 533, 524 and onwards from that, there were incessant removals, so that even the native commentators say: "it was just like shifting a village, so superficial an affair was it." The accepted belles lettres style (see p. 78) of saying "my country" is still the ancient pi-yih or "unworthy village": the Empress of China once (about 190 B.C.) used this expression, even after the whole of China had been united, in order to reject politely the offer of marriage conveyed to her by a powerful Tartar king. The expression is particularly interesting, inasmuch as it recalls, as we have already pointed out, a time when the "country" of each feudal chief was simply his mud village and the few square miles of fields around it, which were naturally divided off from the next chief's territory by hills and streams. On the Burmo-Chinese frontier there are at this moment many Kakhyen "kings" of this kind, each of them ruling over his mountain or valley, and supreme in his own domain.

That there were walled cities in China (apart from the Emperor's, which, of course, would be "the city" par excellence) is plain from the language used at durbars, which were always held "outside the walls." In the loess plains there could not have been any stone whatever for building purposes, and there is little, if any, specific mention of brick. Probably the walls were of adobe, i.e. of mud, beaten down between two rigid planks, removed higher as the wall dries below. This is the way most of the houses are still built in modern Peking, and perhaps also in most parts of China, at least where stone (or brick) is not cheaper; the "barbarian" parts of China are still the best built; for instance, CH'ÊNg-tu in Sz Ch'wan, Canton in the south. Hankow (Ts'u) is a comparatively poor place; Peking the dingiest of all. Chinkiang is a purely loess country.

At the time of the unification of China, during the middle of the third century B.C., the Ts'in armies found it necessary to flood Ta-liang or "Great Liang," the capital of Ngwei (otherwise called Liang), corresponding to the modern K'ai-fêng Fu, the Jewish centre in Ho Nan province: the waters of the Yellow River were allowed to flood the country (this was again done by the Tai-p'ing rebels fifty years ago, when the Jews suffered like other people, and lost their synagogue), the walls of which collapsed. It is evident that the ancient city walls could not have been such solid, brick-faced walls as we now see round Peking and Nanking, but simply mud ramparts.

CHAPTER XXIII.BREAK-UP OF CHINA

We must turn to unorthodox China once more, and see how it fared after Confucius' death. After only a short century of international existence, the vigorous state of Wu perished once for all in the year 473 B.C., and the remains of the ruling caste escaped eastwards in boats. When for the first time embassies between the Japanese and the Chinese became fairly regular, in the second and third centuries of our era, there began to be persistent statements made in standard Chinese history that the then ruling powers in Japan considered themselves in some way lineally connected with a Chinese Emperor of 2100 B.C., and with his descendants, their ancestors, who, it was said, escaped from Wu to China. This is the reason why, in Chapter VII., we have suggested, not that the population of Japan came from China, but that some of the semi-barbarous descendants of those ancient Chinese princes who first colonized the then purely barbarous Wu, finding their power destroyed in 473 B.C. by the neighbouring barbarous power of Yüeh, settled in Japan, and continued their civilizing mission in quite a new sphere. Many years ago I endeavoured, in various papers published in China and Japan, to show that, apart from Chinese words adopted into Japanese ever since A.D. 1 from the two separate sources of North China by land and Central China by sea, there is clear reason to detect, in the supposed pure Japanese language, as it was anterior to those importations, an admixture of Chinese words adopted much earlier than A.D. 1, and incorporated into the current tongue at a time when there was no means or thought of "nailing the sounds down" by any phonetic system of writing. There is much other very sound Chinese historical evidence in favour of the migration view, and it has been best summarized in an excellent little work in German, by Rev. A. Tschepe, S.J., published in the interior of Shan Tung province only last year.

The ancient native names for Wu and Yiieh, according to the clumsy Confucian way of writing them, were something like Keu-ngu and O-viet (see Chapter VII.); but it is quite hopeless to attempt reconstruction of the exact sounds intended then to be expressed by syllables which, in Chinese itself, have quite changed in power. The power of Yüeh was supreme after 473; its king was voted Protector by the federal princes, and in 472 he held a grand durbar at the "Lang-ya Terrace," which place is no longer exactly identifiable, but is probably nothing more than the German settlement at Kiao Chou; in 468 he transferred his capital thither, and it remained there for over a century, till 379: but his power, it seems, was almost purely maritime, and he never succeeded in obtaining a sure footing north of or even in the Hwai valley, the greater part of which he subsequently returned to Ts'u. It must be remembered that the Hwai then had a free course to the sea, and of a part of it, the now extinct Sui valley, the Yellow River took possession for several centuries up to 1851 A.D. He also returned to Sung the territory Wu had taken from her, and made over to Lu 100 li square (30 miles) to the east of the River Sz; to understand this it must be remembered, at the cost of a little iteration, that Sung and Lu were the two chief powers of the middle and lower Sz valley, which is now entirely monopolized by the Grand Canal.

The imperial dynasty went from bad to worse; in 440 there were family intrigues, assassinations, and divisions. The imperial metropolis, which was towards the end about all the Emperors had left to them, was divided into two, each half ruled by an Eastern and a Western Emperor respectively; unfortunately, no literature has survived which might depict for us the life of the inhabitants during those wretched days. Meanwhile, the ambitious great families of Tsin very nearly fell under the dictatorship of one of their number; in 452 he was himself annihilated by a combination of the others, and the upshot of it was that next year the three families that had crushed the dictator and, emerged victorious, divided up the realm of Tsin into three separate and practically independent states, called respectively Wei or Ngwei (the Shan Si parts), Han (the Ho Nan parts), and Chao (the Chih Li parts). The other ancient and more orthodox state of Wei, occupying the Yellow River valley to the west of Sung and Lu, was now a mere vassal to these three Tsin powers, which had not quite yet declared themselves independent, and which had for the present left the old Tsin capital to the direct administration of the legitimate prince. It was only in the year 403 that the Emperor's administration formally declared them to be feudal princes. This year is really the next great turning-point in Chinese history, in order of date, after the flight of the Emperors from their old capital in 771 B.C.; and it is, in fact, with this year that the great modern historical work of Sz-ma Kwang begins; it was published A.D. 1084, and brings Chinese events down to a century previous to that date.

As to the state of Ts'i, it also had fallen into evil ways. So early as 539 B.C., when the two philosophers Yen-tsz and Shuh Hiang had confided to each other their mutual sorrows (see Appendix No. 2), the former had predicted that the powerful local family of T'ien or Ch'en was slowly but surely undermining the legitimate princely house, and would certainly end by seizing the throne; one of the methods adopted by the supplanting family was to lend money to the people on very favourable terms, and so to manipulate the grain measures that the taxes due to the prince were made lighter to bear; in this ingenious and indirect way, all the odium of taxation was thrown upon the extravagant princes who habitually squandered their resources, whilst the credit for generosity was turned towards this powerful tax-farming family, which thus took care of its own financial interests, and at the same time secured the affections of the people. In 481 the ambitious T'ien Hêng, alias CH'ÊN Ch'ang, then acting as hereditary maire du palais to the legitimate house, assassinated the ruling prince, an act so shocking from the orthodox point of view that Confucius was quite heartbroken on learning of it, notwithstanding that his own prince had narrowly escaped assassination at the hands of the murdered man's grandfather. It was not until the year 391, however, that the T'ien, or CH'ÊN, family, after setting up and deposing princes at their pleasure for nearly a century, at last openly threw off the mask and usurped the Ts'i throne: their title was officially recognized by the Son of Heaven in the year 378.

As to Ts'in ambitions, for a couple of centuries past there had been no further advance of conquest, at least in China. The hitherto almost unheard of state of Shuh (Sz Ch'wan) now begins to come prominently forward, and to contest with Ts'in mastery of the upper course of the Yang-tsz River. After being for 260 years in unchallenged possession of all territory west of the Yellow River, Ts'in once more lost this to Tsin (i.e. to Ngwei) in 385. It was not until the other state of Wei, lower down the Yellow River, lost its individuality as an independent country that the celebrated Prince Wei Yang (see Chapter XXII.), having no career at home, offered his services to Ts'in, and that this latter state, availing itself to the full of his knowledge, suddenly shot forth in the light of real progress. We have seen in Chapter XX. that an eminent lawyer and statesman of Ngwei, Ts'in's immediate rival on the east, had inaugurated a new legal code and an economic land system. This man's work had fallen under the cognizance of Wei Yang, who carried it with him to Ts'in, where it was immediately utilized to such advantage that Ts'in a century later was enabled to organize her resources thoroughly, and thus conquered the whole empire,

We have now arrived at what is usually called the Six Kingdom Period, or, if we include Ts'in, against whose menacing power the six states were often in alliance, the period of the Seven Kingdoms. These were the three equally powerful states of Ngwei, Han, and Chao (this last very Tartar in spirit, owing to its having absorbed nearly all the Turko-Tartar tribes west of the Yellow River mouth); the northernmost state of Yen, which seems in the same way to have absorbed or to have exercised a strong controlling influence over the Manchu-Corean group of tribes extending from the Liao River to the Chao frontier; Ts'u, which now had the whole south of China entirely to itself, and managed even to amalgamate the coast states of Yiich in 334; and finally Ts'i. In other words, the orthodox Chinese princes, whose comparatively petty principalities in modern Ho Nan province had for several centuries formed a sort of cock-pit in which Ts'in, Tsin, Ts'i, and Ts'u fought out their rivalries, had totally disappeared as independent and even as influential powers, and had been either absorbed by those four great powers (of which Tsin and Ts'i were in reconstituted form), or had become mere obedient vassals to one or the other of them. In former times Tsin had been kinsman and defender; but now Tsin, broken up into three of strange clans, herself afforded an easy prey to Ts'in ambition; the orthodox states were in the defenceless position of the Greek states after Alexander had exhausted Macedon in his Persian wars, and when their last hope, Pyrrhus, had taught the Romans the art of war: they had only escaped Persia to fall into the jaws of Rome.

In the middle of the fourth century B.C. all six powers began to style themselves wang, or "king," which, as explained before, was the title borne by the Emperors of the Chou dynasty. Military, political, and literary activities were very great after this at the different emulous royal courts, and, however much the literary pedants of the day may have bewailed the decay of the good old times, there can be no doubt that life was now much more varied, more occupied, and more interesting than in the sleepy, respectable, patriarchal days of old. The "Fighting State"

Period, as expounded in the Chan-Kwoh Ts'eh, or "Fighting State Records," is the true period of Chinese chivalry, or knight- errantry.

CHAPTER XXIV.KINGS AND NOBLES

The emperors of the dynasty of Chou, which came formally into power in 1122 B.C., we have seen took no other title than that of wang, which is usually considered by Europeans to mean "king"; in modern times it is applied to the rulers of (what until recently were) tributary states, such as Loochoo, Annam, and Corea; to foreign rulers (unless they insist on a higher title); and to Manchu and Mongol princes of the blood, and mediatized princes. Confucius in his history at first always alludes to the Emperor whilst living as t'ien-wang, or "the heavenly king"; it is not until in speaking of the year 583 that he uses the old term t'ien-tsz, or "Son of Heaven," in alluding to the reigning Emperor. After an emperor's death he is spoken of by his posthumous name; as, for instance, Wu Wang, the "Warrior King," and so on: these posthumous names were only introduced (as a regular system) by the Chou dynasty.

The monarchs of the two dynasties Hia (2205-1767) and Shang (1766- 1123) which preceded that of Chou, and also the somewhat mythical rulers who preceded those two dynasties, were called Ti, a word commonly translated by Western nations as "Emperor." For many generations past the Japanese, in order better to assert vis-á- vis of China their international rank, have accordingly made use of the hybrid expression "Ti-state," by which they seek to convey the European idea of an "empire," or a state ruled over by a monarch in some way superior to a mere king, which is the highest title China has ever willingly accorded to a foreign prince; this royal functionary in her eyes is, or was, almost synonymous with "tributary prince." Curiously enough, this "dog- Chinese" (Japanese) expression is now being reimported into Chinese political literature, together with many other excruciating combinations, a few of European, but mostly of Japanese manufacture, intended to represent such Western ideas as "executive and legislative," "constitutional," "ministerial responsibility," "party," "political view," and so on. But we ourselves must not forget, in dealing with the particular word "imperial," that the Romans first extended the military title of imperator to the permanent holder of the "command," simply because the ancient and haughty word of "king" was, after the expulsion of the kings, viewed with such jealousy by the people of Rome that even of Caesar it is said that he did thrice refuse the title, So the ancient Chinese Ti, standing alone, was at first applied both to Shang Ti or "God" and to his Vicar on Earth, the Ti or Supreme Ruler of the Chinese world. Even Lao-tsz (sixth century B.C.), in his revolutionary philosophy, considers the "king" or "emperor" as one of the moral forces of nature, on a par with "heaven," "earth," and "Tao (or Providence)." When we reflect what petty "worlds" the Assyrian, Egyptian, and Greek worlds were, we can hardly blame the Chinese, who had probably been settled in Ho Nan just as long as the Western ruling races had been in Assyria and Egypt respectively, for imagining that they, the sole recorders of events amongst surrounding inferiors, were the world; and that the incoherent tribes rushing aimlessly from all sides to attack them, were the unreclaimed fringe of the world.

It does not appear clearly why the Chou dynasty took the new title of wang, which does not seem to occur in any titular sense previous to their accession: the Chinese attempts to furnish etymological explanation are too crude to be worth discussing. No feudal Chinese prince presumed to use it during the Chou régime and if the semi-barbarous rulers of Ts'u, Wu, and Yiieh did so in their own dominions (as the Hwang Ti, or "august emperor," of Annam was in recent times tacitly allowed to do), their federal title in orthodox China never went beyond that of viscount. When in the fourth century B.C. all the powers styled themselves wang, and were recognized as such by the insignificant emperors, the situation was very much the same as that produced in Europe when first local Caesars, who, to begin with, had been "associates" of the Augustus (or two rival Augusti), asserted their independence of the feeble central Augustus, and then set themselves up as Augusti pure and simple, until at last the only "Roman Emperor" left in Rome was the Emperor of Germany.

It is not explained precisely on what grounds, when the first Chou emperors distributed their fiefs, some of the feudal rulers, as explained in Chapter VII., were made dukes; others marquesses, earls, viscounts, and barons. Of course these translated terms are mere makeshifts, simply because the Chinese had five ranks, and so have we. In creating their new nobility, the Japanese have again made use of the five old Chinese titles, except that for some reason they call Duke Ito and Duke Yamagata "Prince" in English. The size of the fiefs had something to do with it in China; the pedigree of the feoffees probably more; imperial clandom perhaps most of all. The sole state ruled by a duke in his own intrinsic right from the first was Sung, a small principality on the northernmost head-waters of the River Hwai, corresponding to the modern Kwei-t&h Fu: probably it was because this duke fulfilled the sacrificial and continuity duties of the destroyed dynasty of Shang that he received extraordinary rank; just as, in very much later days, the Confucius family was the only non-Manchu to possess "ducal" rank, or, as the Japanese seem to hold in German style, "princely" rank. But it must be remembered that the Chou emperors had imperial dukes within their own appanage, precisely as cardinals, or "princes of the Church," are as common around Rome as they are scarce among the spiritually "feudal" princes of Europe; for feudal they once practically were.

Confucius' petty state of Lu was founded by the Duke of Chou, brother of the founder posthumously called the Wu Wang, or the "Warrior King": for many generations those Dukes of Lu seem to have resided at or near the metropolis, and to have assisted the Emperors with their advice as counsellors on the spot, as well as to have visited at intervals and ruled their own distant state, which was separated from Sung by the River Sz and by the marsh or lakes through which that river ran. Yet Lu as a state had only the rank of a marquisate ruled by a marquess. Another close and influential relative of the founder or "Warrior King" was the Duke of Shao, who was infeoffed in Yen (the Peking plain), and whose descendants, like those of the Duke of Chou, seem to have done double duty at the metropolis and in their own feudal appanage. Confucius' history scarcely records anything of an international kind about Yen, which was a petty, feeble region, dovetailed in between Tsin and Ts'i, quite isolated, and occupied in civilizing some of the various Tartar and Corean barbarians; but it must have gradually increased in wealth and resources like all the other Chinese states; for, as we have seen in the last chapter, the Earls of Yen blossomed out into Kings at the beginning of the fourth century B.C., and the philosopher Mencius, when advising the King of Ts'i, even strongly recommended him to make war on the rising Yen power. The founder of Ts'i was the chief adviser of the Chou founder, but was not of his family name; his ancestors—also the ancestors later on claimed by certain Tartar rulers of China—go back to one of the ultra-mythical Emperors of China; his descendants bore, under the Chou dynasty, the dignity of marquess, and reigned without a break until, as already related, the T'ien or Ch'en family, emanating from the orthodox state of Ch'en, usurped the throne. Ts'i was always a powerful and highly civilized state; on one occasion, in 589 B.C., as mentioned in Chapter VI., its capital was desecrated by Tsin; and on another, a century later, the overbearing King of Wu invaded the country. After the title of king was taken in 378 B.C., the court of Ts'i became quite a fashionable centre, and the gay resort of literary men, scientists, and philosophers of all kinds, Taoists included.

Tsin, like Ts'i, was of marquess rank, and though its ruling family was occasionally largely impregnated with Tartar blood by marriage, it was not much more so than the imperial family itself had sometimes been, The Chinese have never objected to Tartars quâ Tartars, except as persons who "let their hair fly," "button their coats on the wrong side," and do not practise the orthodox rites; so soon as these defects are remedied, they are eligible for citizenship on equal terms. There has never been any race question or colour question in China, perhaps because the skin is yellow in whichever direction you turn; but it is difficult to conceive of the African races being clothed with Chinese citizenship.

Wei was a small state lying between the Yellow River as it now is and the same river as it then was: it was given to a brother of the founder of the Chou dynasty, and his subjects, like those of the Sung duke, consisted largely of the remains of the Shang dynasty; from which circumstance we may conclude that the so- called "dynasties," including that of Chou, were simply different ruling clans of one and the same people, very much like the different Jewish tribes, of which the tribe of Levi was the most "spiritual": that peculiarity may account for the universal unreadiness to cut off sacrifices and destroy tombs, an outrage we only hear of between barbarians, as, for instance, when Wu sacked the capital of Ts'u. We have seen in Chapter XII. that a reigning duke even respected at least some of the sacrificial rights of a traitor subject.

The important state of CHÊNG, lying to the eastward of the imperial reserve, was only founded in the ninth century B.C. by one of the then Emperor's sons; to get across to each other, the great states north and south of the orthodox nucleus had usually to "beg road" of CHÊNG, which territory, therefore, became a favourite fighting-ground; the rulers were earls. Ts'ao (earls) and Ts'ai (marquesses) were small states to the north and south of CHÊNG, both of the imperial family name. The state of CH'ÊN was ruled by the descendants of the Emperor Shun, the monarch who preceded the Hia dynasty, and who, as stated before, is supposed to have been buried in the (modern) province of Hu Nan, south of the Yang-tsz River: they were marquesses. These three last-named states were always bones of contention between Tsin and Ts'u, on the one hand, and between Ts'i and Ts'u on the other. The remaining feudal states are scarcely worth special mention as active participators in the story of how China fought her way from feudalism to centralization; most of their rulers were viscounts or barons in status, and seem to have owed, or at least been obliged to pay, more duty to the nearest great feudatory than direct to the Emperor.

No matter what the rank of the ruler, so soon as he had been supplied with a posthumous name (expressing, in guarded style, his personal character) he was known to history as "the Duke So- and- So." Even one of the Rings of Ts'u, is courteously called "the Duke Chwang" after his death, because as a federal prince he had done honour to the courtesy title of viscount. Princes or rulers not enjoying any of the five ranks were, if orthodox sovereign princes over never so small a tract, still called posthumously, "the Duke X."

Hence Western writers, in describing Confucius' master and the rulers of other feudal states, often speak of "the Duke of Lu," or "of Tsin"; but this is only an accurate form of speech when taken subject to the above reserves.

CHAPTER XXV.VASSALS AND EMPEROR

The relations which existed between Emperor and feudal princes are best seen and understood from specific cases involving mutual relations. The Chou dynasty had about 1800 nominal vassals in all, of whom 400 were already waiting at the ford of the Yellow River for the rendezvous appointed by the conquering "Warrior King"; thus the great majority must already have existed as such before the Chou family took power; in other words, they were the vassals of the Shang dynasty, and perhaps, of the distant Hia dynasty too. The new Emperor enfeoffed fifteen "brother" states, and forty more having the same clan-name as himself: these fifty-five were presumably all new states, enjoying mesne-lord or semi-suzerain privileges over the host of insignificant principalities; and it might as well be mentioned here that this imperial clan name of Ki was that of all the ultra-ancient emperors, from 2700 B.C. down to the beginning of the Hia dynasty in 2205 B.C. Fiefs were conferred by the Chou conqueror upon all deserving ministers and advisers as well as upon kinsmen. The more distant princes they enfeoffed possessed, in addition to their distant satrapies, a village in the neighbourhood of the imperial court, where they resided, as at an hotel or town house, during court functions; more especially in the spring, when, if the world was at peace, they were supposed to pay their formal respects to the Emperor. The tribute brought by the different feudal states was, perhaps euphemistically, associated with offerings due to the gods, apparently on the same ground that the Emperor was vaguely associated with God. The Protectors, when the Emperors degenerated, made a great show always of chastising or threatening the other vassals on account of their neglect to honour the Emperor. Thus in 656 the First Protector (Ts'i) made war upon Ts'u for not sending the usual tribute of sedge to the Emperor, for use in clarifying the sacrificial wine. Previously, in 663, after assisting the state of Yen against the Tartars, Ts'i had requested Yen "to go on paying tribute, as was done during the reigns of the two first Chou Emperors, and to continue the wise government of the Duke of Shao." In 581, when Wu's pretensions were rising in a menacing degree, the King of Wu said: "The Emperor complains to me that not a single Ki (i.e. not a single closely-related state) will come to his assistance or send him tribute, and thus his Majesty has nothing to offer to the Emperor Above, or to the Ghosts and Spirits."

Land thus received in vassalage from the Emperor could not, or ought not to, be alienated without imperial sanction. Thus in 711 B.C. two states (both of the Ki surname, and thus both such as ought to have known better) effected an exchange of territory; one giving away his accommodation village, or hotel, at the capital; and the other giving in exchange a place where the Emperor used to stop on his way to Ts'i when he visited Mount T'ai-shan, then, as now, the sacred resort of pilgrims in Shan Tung. Even the Emperor could not give away a fief in joke. This, indeed, was how the second Chou Emperor conferred the (extinct or forfeited) fief of Tsin upon a relative. But just as

Une reine d'Espagne ne regarde pas par la fenêtre,

so an Emperor of China cannot jest in vain. An attentive scribe standing by said: "When the Son of Heaven speaks, the clerk takes down his words in writing; they are sung to music, and the rites are fulfilled." When, in 665 B.C., Ts'i had driven back the Tartars on behalf of Yen, the Prince of Yen accompanied the Prince of Ts'i back into Ts'i territory. The Prince of Ts'i at once ceded to Yen the territory trodden by the Prince of Yen, on the ground that "only the Emperor can, when accompanying a ruling prince, advance beyond the limits of his own domain." This rule probably refers only to war, for feudal princes frequently visited each other. The rule was that "the Emperor can never go out," i.e. he can never leave or quit any part of China, for all China belongs to him. It is like our "the King can do no wrong."

The Emperor could thus neither leave nor enter his own particular territory, as all his vassals' territory is equally his. Hence his "mere motion" or pleasure makes an Empress, who needs no formal reception into his separate appanage by him. If the Emperor gives a daughter or a sister in marriage, he deputes a ruling prince of the Ki surname to "manage" the affair; hence to this day the only name for an imperial princess is "a publicly managed one." A feudal prince must go and welcome his wife, but the Emperor simply deputes one of his appanage dukes to do it for him. In the same way, these dukes are sent on mission to convey the Emperor's pleasure to vassals. Thus, in 651 B.C., a duke was sent by the Emperor to assist Ts'in and Ts'i in setting one of the four Tartar-begotten brethren on the Tsin throne (see Chapter X.). In 649 two dukes (one being the hereditary Duke of Shao, supposed to be descended from the same ancestor as the Earl reigning in the distant state of Yen) were sent to confer the formal patent and sceptre of investiture on Tsin. The rule was that imperial envoys passing through the vassal territory should be welcomed on the frontier, fed, and housed; but in 716 the fact that Wei attacked an imperial envoy on his way to Lu proves how low the imperial power had already sunk.

The greater powers undoubtedly had, nearly all of them, clusters of vassals and clients, and it is presumed that the total of 1800, belonging, at least nominally, to the Emperor, covered all these indirect vassals. Possibly, before the dawn of truly historical times, they all went in person to the imperial court; but after the débâcle of 771 B.C., the Emperor seems to have been left severely alone by all the vassals who dared do so. So early as 704 B.C. a reunion of princelets vassal to Ts'u is mentioned; and in the year 622 Ts'u annexed a region styled "the six states," admittedly descended from the most ancient ministerial stock, because they had presumed to ally themselves with the eastern barbarians; this was when Ts'u was working her way eastwards, down from the southernmost headwaters of the Hwai River, in the extreme south of Ho Nan. It was in 684 that Ts'u first began to annex the petty orthodox states in (modern) Hu Pêh province, and very soon nearly all those lying between the River Han and the River Yang-tsz were swallowed up by the semi-barbarian power. Ts'u's relation to China was very much like that of Macedon to Greece. Both of the latter were more or less equally descended from the ancient and somewhat nebulous Pelasgi; but Macedon, though imbued with a portion of Greek civilization, was more rude and warlike, with a strong barbarian strain in addition. Ts'u was never in any way "subject" to the Chou dynasty, except in so far as it may have suited her to be so for some interested purpose of her own. In the year 595 Ts'u even treated Sung and Cheng (two federal states of the highest possible orthodox imperial rank) as her own vassals, by marching armies through without asking their permission. As an illustration of what was the correct course to follow may be taken the case of Tsin in 632, when a Tsin army was marching on a punitory expedition against the imperial clan state of Ts'ao; the most direct way ran through Wei, but this latter state declined to allow the Tsin army to pass; it was therefore obliged to cross the Yellow River at a point south of Wei-hwei Fu (as marked on modern maps), near the capital of Wei, past which the Yellow River then ran.

Lu, though itself a small state, had, in 697, and again in 615, quite a large number of vassals of its own; several are plainly styled "subordinate countries," with viscounts and even earls to rule them. Some of these sub-vassals to the feudal states seem from the first never to have had the right of direct communication with the Emperor at all; in such cases they were called fu-yung, or "adjunct-functions," like the client colonies attached to the colonial municipia of the Romans. A fu-yung was only about fifteen English miles in extent (according to Mencius); and from 850 B.C. to 771 BC. even the great future state of Ts'in had only been a fu-yung,—it is not said to what mesne lord. Sung is distinctly stated to have had a number of these fu-yung. CH'ÊN is also credited with suzerainty over at least two sub-vassal states. In 661 Tsin annexed a number of orthodox petty states, evidently with the view of ultimately seizing that part of the Emperor's appanage which lay north of the Yellow River (west Ho Nan); it was afterwards obtained by "voluntary cession." The word "viscount," besides being applied complimentarily to barbarian "kings" when they showed themselves in China, had another special use. When an orthodox successor was in mourning, he was not entitled forthwith to use the hereditary rank allotted to his state; thus, until the funeral obsequies of their predecessors were over, the new rulers of Ch'en and Ts'ai were called "the viscount," or "son" (same word).

The Emperor used to call himself "I, the one Man," like the Spanish "Yo, el Rey." Feudal princes styled themselves to each other, or to the ministers of each other, "The Scanty Man." Ministers, speaking (to foreign ministers or princes) of their own prince said, "The Scanty Prince"; of the prince's wife, "The Scanty Lesser Prince"; of their own ministers, "The Scanty Minister." It was polite to avoid the second person in addressing a foreign prince, who was consequently often styled "your government" by foreign envoys particularly anxious not to offend. The diplomatic forms were all obsequiously polite; but the stock phrases, such as, "our vile village" (our country), "your condescending to instruct" (your words), "I dare not obey your commands" (we will not do what you ask), probably involved nothing more in the way of humility than the terms of our own gingerly worded diplomatic notes, each term of which may, nevertheless, offend if it be coarsely or carelessly expressed.

In some cases a petty vassal was neither a sub-kingdom nor an adjunct-function to another greater vassal, but was simply a political hanger-on; like, for instance, Hawaii was to the United States, or Cuba now is; or like Monaco is to France, Nepaul to India. Thus Lu, through assiduously cultivating the good graces of Ts'i, became in 591 a sort of henchman to Ts'i; and, as we have seen, at the Peace Conference of 546, the henchmen of the two rival Protectors agreed to pay "cross respects" to each other's Protector. It seems to have been the rule that the offerings of feudal states to the Emperor should be voluntary, at least in form: for instance, in the year 697, the Emperor or his agents begged a gift of chariots from Lu, and in 618 again applied for some supplies of gold; both these cases are censured by the historians as being undignified. On the other hand, the Emperor's complimentary presents to the vassals were highly valued. Thus in the year 530, when Ts'u began to realize its own capacity for empire, a claim was put in for the Nine Tripods, and for a share of the same honorific gifts that were bestowed by the founders upon Ts'i, Tsin, Lu, and Wei at the beginning of the Chou dynasty. In the year 606 Ts'u had already "inquired" at the imperial court about these same Tripods, and 300 years later (281 B.C.), when struggling with Ts'in for the mastery of China, Ts'u endeavoured to get the state of Han to support her demand for the Tripods, which eventually fell to Ts'in; it will be remembered that the Duke of Chou had taken them to the branch capital laid out by him, but which was not really occupied by the Emperor until 771 B.C.

In 632, after the great Tsin victory over Ts'u, the Emperor "accepted some Ts'u prisoners," conferred upon Tsin the Protectorate, ceded to Tsin that part of the imperial territory referred to on page 53, and presented to the Tsin ruler a chariot, a red bow with 1000 arrows, a black bow with 1000 arrows, a jar of scented wine, a jade cup with handle, and 300 "tiger" body-guards. In 679, when Old Tsin had been amalgamated by New Tsin (both of them then tiny principalities), the Emperor had already accepted valuable loot from the capture of Old Tsin. In a word, the Emperor nearly always sided with the strongest, accepted faits accomplis, and took what he could get. This has also been China's usual policy in later times.

CHAPTER XXVI.FIGHTING STATE PERIOD

The period of political development covered by Confucius' history— the object of which history, it must be remembered, was to read to the restless age a series of solemn warnings—was immediately succeeded by the most active and bloodthirsty period in the Chinese annals, that of the Fighting States, or the Six Countries; sometimes they (including Ts'in) were called the

"Seven Males," i.e. the Seven Great Masculine Powers. Tsin had been already practically divided up between the three surviving great families of the original eleven in 424 B.C.; but these three families of Ngwei, Han, and Chao were not recognized by the Emperor until 403; nor did they extinguish the legitimate ruler until 376, about three years after the sacrifices of the legitimate Ts'i kings were stopped. Accordingly we hear the original name Tsin, or "the three Tsin," still used concurrently with the names Han, Ngwei, and Chao, as that of Ts'u's chief enemy in the north for some time after the division into three had taken place.

Tsin's great rival to the west, Ts'in, now found occupation in extending her territory to the south-west at the expense of Shuh, a vast dominion corresponding to the modern Sz Ch'wan, up to then almost unheard of by orthodox China, but which, it then first transpired, had had three kings and ten "emperors" of its own, nine of these latter bearing the same appellation. Even now, the rapids and gorges of the Yang-tsz River form the only great commercial avenue from China into Sz Ch'wan, and it is therefore not hard to understand how in ancient times, the tribes of "cave barbarians" (whose dwellings are still observable all over that huge province) effectively blocked traffic along such subsidiary mountain-roads as may have existed then, as they exist now, for the use of enterprising hawkers.

The Chinese historians have no statistics, indulge in fen (few?) remarks about economic or popular development, describe no popular life, and make no general reflections upon history; they confine themselves to narrating the bald and usually unconnected facts which took place on fixed dates, occasionally describing some particularly heroic or daring individual act, or even sketching the personal appearance and striking conduct of an exceptionally remarkable king, general, or other leading personality: hence there is little to guide us to an intelligent survey of causes and effects, of motives and consequences; it is only by carefully piecing together and collating a jumble of isolated events that it is possible to obtain any general coup d'oeil at all: the wood is often invisible on account of the trees.

But there can be no doubt that populations had been rapidly increasing; that improved means had been found to convey accumulated stores and equipments; that generals had learnt how to hurl bodies of troops rapidly from one point to the other; and that rulers knew the way either to interest large populations in war, or to force them to take an active part in it. The marches, durbars, and gigantic canal works, undertaken by the barbarous King of Wu, as described in Chapter XXI., prove this in the case of one country. Chinese states always became great in the same way: first Kwan-tsz developed, on behalf of his master the First Protector, the commerce, the army, and the agriculture of Ts'i. He was imitated at the same time by Duke Muh of Ts'in and King Chwang of Ts'u, both of which rulers (seventh century B.C.) set to work vigorously in developing their resources. Then Tsz-ch'an raised Cheng to a great pitch of diplomatic influence, if not also of military power. His friend Shuh Hiang did the same thing for Tsin; and both of them were models for Confucius in Lu, who had, moreover, to defend his own master's interests against the policy of the philosopher Yen-tsz of Ts'i. After his first defeat by the King of Wu, the barbarian King of Yueh devoted himself for some years to the most strenuous life, with the ultimate object of amassing resources for the annihilation of Wu; the interesting steps he took to increase the population will be described at length in a later chapter. In 361, as we have explained in Chapter XXII., a scion of Wei went as adviser to Ts'in, and within a generation of his arrival the whole face of affairs was changed in that western state hitherto so isolated; the new position, from a military point of view, was almost exactly that of Prussia during the period between the tyranny of the first Napoleon, together with the humiliation experienced at his hands, and the patient gathering of force for the final explosion of 1870, involving the crushing of the second (reigning) Napoleon.

Very often the term "perpendicular and horizontal" period is applied to the fourth century B.C. That is, Ts'u's object was to weld together a chain of north and south alliances, so as to bring the power of Ts'i and Tsin to bear together with her own upon Ts'in; and Ts'in's great object was, on the other hand, to make a similar string of east and west alliances, so as to bring the same two powers to bear upon Ts'u. The object of both Ts'in and Ts'u was to dictate terms to each unit of; and ultimately to possess, the whole Empire, merely utilizing the other powers as catspaws to hook the chestnuts out of the furnace. No other state had any rival pretensions, for, by this time, Ts'in and Ts'u each really did possess one-third part of China as we now understand it, whilst the other third was divided between Ts'i and the three Tsin. In 343 B.C. the Chou Emperor declared Ts'in Protector, and from 292 to 288 B.C., Tsin and Ts'i took for a few years the ancient title of Ti or "Emperor" of the West and East respectively: in the year 240 the Chou Emperor even proceeded to Ts'in to do homage there. Tsin might have been in the running for universal empire had she held together instead of dividing herself into three. Yen was altogether too far away north,—though, curiously enough, Yen (Peking) has been the political centre of North China for 900 years past,—and Ts'i was too far away east. Moreover, Ts'i was discredited for having cut off the sacrifices of the legitimate house. Ts'u was now master of not only her old vassals, Wu and Yiieh, but also of most of the totally unknown territory down to the south sea, of which no one except the Ts'u people at that time knew so much as the bare local names; it bore the same relation to Ts'u that the Scandinavian tribes did to the Romanized Germans. Ts'in had become not only owner of Sz Ch'wan— at first as suzerain protector, not as direct administrator—but had extended her power down to the south-west towards Yiin Nan and Tibet, and also far away to the north-west in Tartarland, but not farther than to where the Great Wall now extends. It is in the year 318 B.C. that we first hear the name Hiung-nu (ancestors of the Huns and Turks), a body of whom allied themselves in that year with the five other Chinese powers then in arms against the menacing attitude of Ts'in; something remarkable must have taken place in Tartarland to account for this sudden change of name, The only remains of old federal China consisted of about ten petty states such as Sung, Lu, etc., all situated between the Rivers Sz and Hwai, and all waiting, hands folded, to be swallowed up at leisure by this or that universal conqueror.

Ts'in s'en va t'en guerre seriously in the year 364, and began her slashing career by cutting off 60,000 "Tsin" heads; (the legitimate Tsin sacrifices had been cut off in 376, so this "Tsin" must mean "Ngwei," or that part of old Tsin which was coterminous with Ts'in); in 331, in a battle with Ngwei, 80,000 more heads were taken off. 'In 318 the Hiung-nu combination just mentioned lost 82,000 heads between them; in 314 Han lost 10,000; in 312 Ts'u lost 80,000; in 307 Han lost 60,000; and in 304 Ts'u lost 80,000. In the year 293 the celebrated Ts'in general, Pêh K'i, who has left behind him a reputation as one of the greatest manipulators of vast armies in Eastern history, cut off 240,000 Han heads in one single battle; in 275, 40,000 Ngwei heads; and in 264, 50,000 Han heads. "Enfin je vais me mesurer avec ce Vilainton" said the King of Chao, when his two western friends of Han and Ngwei had been hammered out of existence. In the year 260 the Chao forces came to terrible grief; General Pêh K'i managed completely to surround their army of 400,000 men he accepted their surrender, guaranteed their safety, and then proceeded methodically to massacre the whole of them to a man. In 257 "Tsin" (presumably Han or Ngwei) lost 6,000 killed and 20,000 drowned; in 256 Han lost 40,000 heads, and in 247 her last 30,000, whilst also in 256 Chao her last 90,000. These terrible details have been put together from the isolated statements; but there can be no mistake about them, for the historian Sz-ma Ts'ien, writing in 100 B.C., says: "The allies with territory ten times the extent of the Ts'in dominions dashed a million men against her in vain; she always had her reserves in hand ready, and from first to last a million corpses bit the dust."

No such battles as these are even hinted at in more ancient times; nor, strange to say, are the ancient chariots now mentioned any more. Ts'in had evidently been practising herself in fighting with the Turks and Tartars for some generations, and had begun to perceive what was still only half understood in China, the advantage of manoeuvring large bodies of horsemen; but, curiously enough, nothing is said of horses either; yet all these battles seem to have been fought on the flat lands of old federal China, suitable for either chariots or horses. The first specific mention of cavalry manoeuvres on a large scale was in the year 198 B.C. when the new Han Emperor of China in person, with a straggling army of 320,000 men, mostly infantry, was surrounded by four bodies of horsemen led by the Supreme Khan, in white, grey, black, and chestnut divisions, numbering 300,000 cavalry in all: his name was Megh-dun (? the Turkish Baghatur).

Whilst all this was going on, Mencius, the Confucian philosopher, and the two celebrated diplomatists (of Taoist principles), Su Ts'in and Chang I, were flying to and fro all over orthodox China with a view of offering sage political advice; this was the time par excellence when the rival Taoist and Confucian prophets were howling in the wilderness of war and greed: but Ts'in cared not much for talkers: generals did her practical business better: in 308 she began to cast covetous eyes on the Emperor's poor remaining appanage. In 301 she was called upon to quell a revolt in Shuh; then she materially reduced the pretensions of her great rival Ts'u; and finally rested a while, whilst gathering more strength for the supreme effort-the conquest of China.

CHAPTER XXVII.FOREIGN BLOOD

The history of China may be for our present purposes accordingly summed up as follows. The pure Chinese race from time immemorial had been confined to the flat lands of the Yellow River, and its one tributary on the south, the River Loh, the Tartars possessing most of the left bank from the Desert to the sea. However, from the beginning of really historical times the Chinese had been in unmistakable part-possession of the valleys of the Yellow River's two great tributaries towards the west and north, the Wei (in Shen Si) and the Fen (in Shan Si). Little, if any, Chinese colonizing was done much before the Ts'in conquests in any other parts of Tartarland; none in Sz Ch'wan that we know of; little, if any, along the coasts, except perhaps from Ts'i and Lu (in Shan Tung), both of which states seem to have always been open to the sea, though many barbarian coast tribes still required gathering into the Chinese fold. The advance of Chinese civilization had been first down the Yellow River; then down the River Han towards the Middle Yang-tsz; and lastly, down the canals and the Hwai network of streams to the Shanghai coast. Old colonies of Chinese had, many centuries before the conquest of China by the Chou dynasty, evidently set out to subdue or to conciliate the southern tribes: these adventurous leaders had naturally taken Chinese ideas with them, but had usually found it easier for their own safety and success to adopt barbarian customs in whole or in part. These mixed or semi-Chinese states of the navigable Yang-tsz Valley, from the Ich'ang gorges to the sea, had generally developed in isolation and obscurity, and only appeared in force as formidable competitors with orthodox Chinese when the imperial power began to collapse after 771 B.C. The isolation of half-Roman Britain for several centuries after the first Roman conquest, and the departure of the last Roman legions, may be fitly compared with the position of the half-Chinese states. Ts'u, Wu, and Yüeh all had pedigrees, more or less genuine, vying in antiquity with the pedigree of the imperial Chou family; and therefore they did not see why they also should not aspire to the overlordship when it appeared to be going a-begging. Even orthodox Tsin and Ts'i in the north and north-east were in a sense colonial extensions, inasmuch as they were governed by new families appointed thereto by the Chou dynasty in 1122 B.C., in place of the old races of rulers, presumably more or less barbarian, who had previously to 1122 B.C. been vassal—in name at least—to the earlier imperial Hia and Shang dynasties: but these two great states were never considered barbarian under Chou sway; and, indeed, some of the most ancient mythological Chinese emperors anterior to the Hia dynasty had their capitals in Tsin and Lu, on the River Fên and the River Sz.

It is not easy to define the exact amount of "foreignness" in Ts'u. One unmistakable non-Chinese expression is given; that is kou-u-du, or "suckled by a tigress." Then, again, the syllable ngao occurs phonetically in many titles and in native personal names, such as jo-ngao, tu-ngao, kia-ngao, mo-ngao. There are no Ts'u songs in the Odes as edited by Confucius, and the Ts'u music is historically spoken of as being "in the southern sound"; which may refer, it is true, to the accent, but also possibly to a strange language. The Ts'u name for "Annals," or history, was quite different from the terms used in Tsin and Lu, respectively; and the Ts'u word for a peculiar form of lameness, or locomotor ataxy, is said to differ from the expressions used in either Wei and Ts'i. So far aspossible, all Ts'u dignities were kept in the royal family, and the king's uncle was usually premier. The premier of Ts'u was called Zing-yin, a term unknown to federal China; and Ts'u considered the left-hand side more honourable than the right, which at that time was not the case in China proper, though it is now. The "Borough-English" rule of succession in Ts'u was to give it to one of the younger sons; this statement is repeated in positive terms by Shuh Hiang, the luminous statesman of Tsin, and will be further illustrated when we come to treat of that subject specially. The Lu rule was "son after father; or, if none, then younger after eldest brother; if the legitimate heir dies, then next son by the same mother; failing which, the eldest son by any mother; if equal claims, then the wisest; if equally wise, cast lots": Lu rules would probably hold good for all federal China, because the Duke of Chou, founder of Lu, was the chief moral force in the original Chou administration. In the year 587 Lu, when coquetting between Tsin and Ts'u, was at last persuaded not to abandon Tsin for Ts'u, "who is not of our family, and can never have any real affection." Once in Tsin it was asked, about a prisoner: "Who is that southernhatted fellow?" It was explained that he was a Ts'u man. They then handed him a guitar, and made him sing some "national songs." In 597 a Ts'u envoy to the Tsin military durbar said: "My prince is not formed for the fine and delicate manners of the Chinese": here is distinct evidence of social if not ethnological cleaving. The Ts'u men had beards, whilst those of Wu were not hirsute: this statement proves that the two barbarian populations differed between themselves. In 635 the King of Ts'u spoke of himself as "the unvirtuous" and the "royal old man"—designations both appropriate only to barbarians under Chinese ritual. In 880 B.C., when the imperial power was already waning, and the first really historical King of Ts'u was beginning to bring under his authority the people between the Han and the Yang-tsz, he said: "I am a barbarian savage, and do not concern myself with Chinese titles, living or posthumous." In 706, when the reigning king made his first conquest of a petty Chinese principality (North Hu Pêh), he said again: "I am a barbarian savage; all the vassals are in rebellion and attacking each other; I want with my poor armaments to see for myself how Chou governs, and to get a higher title." On being refused, he said: "Do you forget my ancestor's services to the father of the Chou founder?" Later on, as has already been mentioned, he put in a claim for the Nine Tripods because of the services his ancestor, "living in rags in the Jungle, exposed to the weather," had rendered to the founder himself. In 637, when the future Second Protector and ruler of Tsin visited Ts'u as a wanderer, the King of Ts'u received him with all the hospitalities "under the Chou rites," which fact shows at least an effort to adopt Chinese civilization. In 634 Lu asked Ts'u's aid against Ts'i, a proceeding condemned by the historical critics on the ground that Ts'u was a "barbarian savage" state. On the other hand, by the year 560 the dying King of Ts'u was eulogized as a man who had successfully subdued the barbarian savages. But against this, again, in 544 the ruler of Lu expressed his content at having got safely back from his visit to Ts'u, i.e. his visit to such an uncouth and distant court. Thus Ts'u's emancipation from "savagery" was gradual and of uncertain date. In 489 the King of Ts'u declined to sacrifice to the Yellow River, on the ground that his ancestors had never presumed to concern themselves with anything beyond the Han and Yang-tsz valleys. Even Confucius, (then on his wanderings in the petty state of CH'ÊN) declared his admiration at this, and said: "The King of Ts'u is a sage, and understands the Great Way (tao)." On the other hand, only fifty years before this, when in 538 Ts'u, with Tsin's approval, first tried her hand at durbar work, the king was horrified to hear from a fussy chamberlain (evidently orthodox) that there were six different ways of receiving visitors according to their rank; so that Ts'u's ritual decorum could not have been of very long standing. The following year (537) a Tsin princess is given in marriage to Ts'u— a decidedly orthodox feather in Ts'u's cap. Confucius affects a particular style in his history when he speaks of barbarians; thus an orthodox prince "beats" a barbarian, but "battles" with an orthodox equal. However, in 525, Ts'u and Wu "battle" together, the commentator explaining that Ts'u is now "promoted" to battle rank, though the strict rule is that two barbarians, or China and one barbarian, "beat" rather than "battle." In 591 Confucius had already announced the "end" of the King of Ts'u, not as such, but as federal viscount. Under ordinary circumstances "death" would have been good enough: it is only in speaking of his own ruler's death that the honorific word "collapse" is used. All these fine distinctions, and many others like them, hold good for modern Chinese. These (apparently to us) childish gradations in mere wording run throughout Confucius' book; but we must remember that his necessarily timid object was to "talk at" the wicked, and to "hint" at retribution. Even a German recorder of events would shrink from applying the word haben to the royal act of a Hottentot King, for whom hat is more than good enough, without the allergnädigst. And we all remember Bismarck's story of the way mouth-washes and finger-bowls were treated at Frankfurt by those above and below the grade of serene highness. Toutes les vices et toutes les moeurs sont respectables.

In 531 the barbarian King of Ts'u is honoured by being "named" for enticing and murdering a "ruler of the central kingdoms." The pedants are much exercised over this, but as the federal prince in question was a parricide, he had a lupinum caput, and so even a savage could without outraging orthodox feelings wreak the law on him. On the other hand, in 526, when Ts'u enticed and killed a mere barbarian prince, the honour of "naming" was withheld. This delicate question will be further elucidated in the chapter on "Names."

It will be observed that none of the testimony brought forward here to show that Ts'u was, in some undefined way, a non-Chinese state is either clear or conclusive: its cumulative effect, however, certainly leaves a very distinct impression that 'there was a profound difference of some sort both in race and in manners, though we are as yet quite unable to say whether the bulk of the Ts'u population was Annamese, Shan, or Siamese; Lolo or Nosu; Miao-tsz, Tibetan, or what. There is really no use in attempting to advance one step beyond the point to which we are carried by specific evidence, either in this or in other matters. It has been said that no great discovery was ever made without imagination, which may be true; but evidence and imagination must be kept rigidly separate. What we may reasonably hope is that, by gradually ascertaining and sifting definite facts and data touching ancient Chinese history, we shall at least avoid coming to wrong positive conclusions, even if the right negative ones are pretty clearly indicated. It is better to leave unexplained matters in suspense than to base conclusions upon speculative substructures which will not carry the weight set upon them.

CHAPTER XXVIII.BARBARIANS

The country of Wu is in many respects even more interesting ethnologically than that of Ts'u. When, a generation or two before the then vassal Chou family conquered China, two of the sons of the ruler of that vassal principality decided to forego their rights of succession, they settled amongst the Jungle savages, cut their hair, adopted the local raiment, and tattooed their bodies; or, rather, it is said the elder of the two covered his head and his body decently, while the younger cut his hair, went naked, and tattooed his body. The words "Jungle savages" apply to the country later called Ts'u; but as Wu, when we first hear of her, was a subordinate country belonging to Ts'u; and as in any case the word "Wu" was unknown to orthodox China, not to say to extreme western China, in 1200 B.C. when the adventurous brothers migrated; this particular point need not trouble us so much as it seems to have puzzled the Chinese critics. About 575 the first really historical King of Wu paid visits to the Emperor's court, to the court of his suzerain the King of Ts'u, and to the court of Lu: probably the Hwai system of rivers would carry him within measurable distance of all three, for the headwaters almost touch the tributaries of the Han, and the then Ts'u capital (modern King-thou Fu) was in touch with the River Han. He observed when in Lu: "We only know how to knot our hair in Wu; what could we do with such fine clothes as you wear?" It was the policy of Tsin and of the other minor federal princes to make use of Wu as a diversion against the advance of Ts'u: it is evident that by this time Ts'u had begun to count seriously as a Chinese federal state, for one of the powerful private families behind the throne and against the throne in Lu expressed horror that "southern savages (i.e. Wu) should invade China (i.e. Ts'u)," by taking from it part of modern An Hwei province: as, however, barbarian Ts'u had taken it first from orthodox China, perhaps the mesne element of Ts'u was not in the statesman's mind at all, but only the original element,—China. An important remark is made by one of the old historians to the effect that the language and manners of Wu were the same as those of Yiieh. In 483, when Wu's pretensions as Protector were at their greatest, the people of Ts'i made use of ropes eight feet long in order to bind certain Wu prisoners they had taken, "because their heads were cropped so close": this statement hardly agrees with that concerning "knotted hair," unless the toupet or chignon was very short indeed. There are not many native Wu words quoted, beyond the bare name of the country itself, which is something like Keu-gu, or Kou-gu: an executioner's knife is mentioned under the foreign name chuh-lu, presented to persons expected to commit suicide, after the Japanese harakiri fashion. In 584 B.C., when the first steps were taken by orthodox China to utilize Wu politically, it was found necessary, as we have seen, to teach the Wu folk the use of war-chariots and bows and arrows: this important statement points distinctly to the previous utter isolation of Wu from the pale of Chinese civilization. In the year 502 Ts'i sent a princess as hostage to Wu, and ended by giving her in marriage to the Wu heir: (we have seen how Tsin anticipated Ts'i by twenty-five years in conferring a similar honour upon Ts'u). A century or more later, when Mencius was advising the bellicose court of Ts'i, he alluded with indignation to this "barbarous" act. In 544 the Wu prince Ki-chah had visited Lu and other orthodox states.

In recognition of this civilized move on the part of an ancient family, Confucius in his history grants the rank of "viscount" to the King of Wu, but he does not style Ki-chah by the complimentary title Ki Kung-tsz, or "Ki, the son of a reigning prince"; that is, the king's title thus accorded retrospectively is only a "courtesy one," and does not carry with it a posthumous name, and with that name the posthumous title of Kung, or "duke'" applied to all civilized rulers. Yet it is evident that the ruling caste of Wu considered itself superior to the surrounding tribes, for in the year 493 it was remarked: "We here in Wu are entirely surrounded by savages"; and in 481 the Emperor himself sent a message through Tsin to Wu, saying: "I know that you are busy with the savages you have on hand at present." In the year 482, when the orthodox princes of Sung, Wei, and Lu were holding off from an alliance with Wu, the prince of Wei was detained by a Wu general, but escaped, and set to work to learn the language of Wu. The motive is of no importance; but the clear statement about a different language, or at least a dialect so different that it required special study, is interesting. When Ki-chah was on his travels, he explained to his friends that the law of succession is: "By the rites to the eldest, as established by our ancestors and by the customs of the country." In 502 the King of Wu was embarrassed about his successor, whose character did not commend itself to him, His counsellor (a refugee from Ts'u) said: "Order in the state ceases if the succession be interrupted; by ancient law son should succeed father deceased." Thus it seems that the ancient Chou rules had been conveyed to Wu by the first colonists in 1200 B.C., and that the succession laws differed from those of Ts'u. Ki-chah's son died whilst he was on his travels, and Confucius is reported to have said: "He is a man who understands the rites; let us see what he does." Ki-chah bared his left arm and shoulder, marched thrice round the grave, and said: "Flesh and bone back to the earth, as is proper; as to the soul, let it go anywhere it chooses!" This language was approved by Confucius, who himself always declined to dogmatize on death and spirits, maintaining that men knew too little of themselves, when living, to be justified in groping for facts about the dead. At first sight it would appear strange that a barbarous country like Wu should suddenly produce a learned prince who at once captivated by his culture Yen-tsz of Ts'i, Confucius of Lu, Tsz-ch'an of Cheng, K'u-peh-yu of Wei, Shuh Hiang of Tsin, and, in short, all the distinguished statesmen of China; but if we reflect that, within half a century, the greatest naval, military, and scientific geniuses have been produced on Western lines in Japan (as we shall soon see, in some way connected with Wu), at least we find good modern parallels for the phenomenon.

When Wu, after a series of bloody wars with Ts'u and Yiieh, was in 473 finally extinguished by the latter power, a portion of the King of Wu's family escaped in boats in an easterly direction. At this time not only was Japan unknown to China under that name, but also quite unheard of under any name whatever. It was not until 150 years later that the powerful states of Yen and Ts'i, which, roughly speaking, divided with them the eastern part of the modern province of Chih Li, the northern part of Shan Tung, and the whole coasts of the Gulf of "Pechelee," began to talk vaguely of some mysterious and beautiful islands lying in the sea to the east. When the First August Emperor had conquered China, he made several tours to the Shan Tung promontory, to the site of the former Yueh capital (modern Kiao Chou), to the treaty-port of Chefoo (where he left an inscription), to the Shan-hai Kwan Pass, and to the neighbourhood of Ningpo. He also had heard rumours of these mysterious islands, and he therefore sent a physician of his staff with a number of young people to make inquiry, and colonize the place if possible. They brought back absurd stories of some monstrous fish that had interfered with their landing, and they reported that these fish could only be frightened away by tattooing the body as the natives did, The people of Wu, who were great fisherfolk and mariners, were also stated to have indulged in universal tattooing because they wished to frighten dangerous fish away. The first mission from Japan, then a congeries of petty states, totally unacquainted with writing or records, came to China in the first century of our era; it was not sent by the central King, but only by one of the island princes. Later embassies from and to Japan disclose the fact that the Japanese themselves had traditions of their descent both from ancient Chinese Emperors and from the founder of Wu, i.e. from the Chou prince who went there in 1200 B.C.; of the medical mission sent by the First August Emperor; of the flight from Wu in 473 B.C. of part of the royal Wu family to Japan; and of other similar matters—all apparently tending to show that the refugees from Wu really did reach Japan; that a very early shipping intercourse had probably existed between Japan, Ts'i, and Wu; and that, in addition to the statements made by later Chinese historians to the effect that the Japanese considered themselves in some way hereditarily connected with Wu, the early Japanese traditions and histories (genuine or concocted) themselves separately repeated the story. One of the later Chinese histories says of Wu: "Part of the king's family escaped and founded the kingdom of Wo" (the ancient name for the Japanese race): the temptation to connect this word with Wu is obvious; but etymology will not tolerate such an identification, either from a Chinese or a Japanese point of view; the etymological "values" are Ua and Gu respectively.

As in the case of Ts'u, there is no really trustworthy evidence to show of what race or races, and in what proportions, the bulk of the Wu population consisted; still less is there any specific evidence to show to what race the barbarian king who committed suicide in 473 belonged; or if those of his family who escaped were wholly or partly Chinese; or if any pure descent existed at all in royal circles, dating, that is to say, from the ancient colonists of the imperial Chou family in 1200 B.C.

So far as purely Chinese traditions and history go, the cumulative evidence, such as it is, needs careful sifting, and is, perhaps, worth a more thorough examination; but as to the Japanese traditions and early "history," these, as the Japanese themselves admit, were only put together in written form retrospectively in the eighth century A.D., and throughout they show signs of having been deliberately concocted on the Chinese lines; that is, Chinese historical incidents and phraseology are worked into the narrative of supposed Japanese events, and Japanese emperors or empresses are (admittedly) fitted with posthumous names mostly copied from imperial Chinese posthumous names. By themselves they are almost valueless, so far as the fixing of specific dates and the identification of political events are concerned; and even when taken as ancillary to contemporary Chinese evidence, except in so far as a few Chinese misprints or errors may be more clearly indicated by comparison with them, they seem equally valueless either to confirm, to check, to modify, or to contradict the Chinese accounts, which, indeed, are absolutely the sole trustworthy written evidence either we or the Japanese themselves possess about the actual condition of the Japanese 2000 years ago.

Meanwhile, as to Wu, all we can say with certainty is, that there is a persistent rumour or tradition that some of its royal refugees (themselves of unknown race) who escaped in boats eastward, may have escaped to Japan; may have succeeded in "imposing themselves" on the people, or a portion of the people (themselves a mixed race of uncertain provenance); and may have quietly and informally introduced Chinese words, ideas, and methods, several centuries before known and formal intercourse between Japan and China took place.

CHAPTER XXIX.CURIOUS CUSTOMS

In laying stress upon the barbarous, or semi-barbarous, quality of the states (all in our days considered pure Chinese), which surrounded the federal area at even so late a period as 771 B.C., we wish to emphasize a point which has never yet been made quite clear, perhaps not even made patent by their own critics to the Chinese themselves; that is to say, the very small and modest beginnings of the civilized patriarchal federation called the Central Kingdom, or Chu Hia—"All the Hia"—just as we say, "All the Russias."

In allotting precedence to the various states, the historical editors, of course, always put the Emperor first in order of mention; then comes CHÊNG, the first ruler of which state was son of an Emperor of the then ruling imperial house; next, the three Protectors Ts'i, Tsin, and Sung; then follow the petty states of Wei, Ts'ai, Ts'ao, and T'êng, all of the imperial family name, or, as we say in English, "surname," and all lying between the Hwai and the Sz systems (T'êng was a "belonging state" of Lu). Then come half a dozen petty orthodox states of less honourable family names; next, three Eastern barbarian states, which had become "Central Kingdom," or which, once genuine Chinese, had become half barbarian; and finally, Ts'u, Ts'in, Wu, and Yiieh, which were frankly, if vaguely, "outer barbarian-Tartar."

It has already been demonstrated that there is evidence, however imperfect, to show that the mass of the population of Ts'u and Wu were of decidedly foreign origin. Even as to Ts'i, which was always treated as an orthodox principality, it is stated that the founder sent there in or about 1100 B.C. "conformed to the manners of the place, and encouraged manufactures, commerce, salt and fish industries." On the other hand, the son of the Duke of Chou (the first vassal prince appointed by his brother the Emperor) changed the customs of Lu, modified the local rites, and induced the people to keep on their mourning attire for three full years. It was considered that the Ts'i policy was the wiser of the two, and it was foretold that Lu would always "look up to" Ts'i in consequence of this superior judgment on the part of Ts'i. On frequent occasions the petty adjoining "Chinesified" states, of which Lu was practically the mesne lord, are stated to have been "tainted with Eastern barbarian rites." From and including modern Sü-chou (North Kiang Su) and eastward, all were "Eastern barbarians"; in fact, the city just named (mentioned by the name of Sü in 1100 B.C., and again about 950 B.C., as revolting against the Emperor) perpetuates the "Sü barbarians" country, which was for long a bone of contention between Ts'i and Ts'u, and afterwards Wu; and the name "Hwai savages" proves that the Lower Hwai Valley was also independent. The Hwai savages, who appear in the Tribute of Yü, founder of the Hia dynasty, 2205 B.C., revolted 1000 years later against the founders of the Chou dynasty. They were present at Ts'u's first durbar in 538 B.C., and are mentioned as barbarians still resisting Chinese methods so late as A.D. 970. In Confucius' time the Lai barbarians (modern Lai-thou Fu in the German sphere) were employed by Ts'i, who had conquered them in 567 B.C., to try and effect the assassination of Confucius' master. Six hundred years before that, these same barbarians were among the first to give in their submission to the founder of Ts'i; and in 602 B.C. both Ts'i and Lu had endeavoured to crush them.

As to the state of Ts'in, there is not a single instance given of any literary conversation or correspondence held by an orthodox high functionary with a Ts'in statesman. While it is not yet quite clear that orthodox China can shake herself entirely free of the reproach of human sacrifices in all senses, it is quite certain that Ts'in had a barbarous and exclusive notoriety in this regard'; and, as the Hiung-nu Tartars also practised it, and Ts'in was at least half Tartar in blood, it is probable that she derived her sanguinary notions from this blood connection with the Turko-Scythian tribes. On the death of the Ts'in ruler in 678 B.C., the first recorded human sacrifices were made, "sixty-six individuals following the dead." In 621, on the death of the celebrated Duke Muh, 177 persons lost their lives, and the people of Ts'in, in pity, "composed the Yellow Bird Ode" (of these popular Chinese odes more anon). This holocaust was given as one reason why Ts'in could never "rule in the East," i.e. assume the Protectorate over the orthodox powers all lying to its east, on account of this cruel defect in its laws. In 387 B.C., the new Earl of Ts'in (who succeeded a nephew, and therefore could, having no paternal duty to fulfil, introduce the innovation more cheaply) abolished the principle of human sacrifices at the death of a ruler. Ten years later, the Emperor's astrologer paid a visit to Ts'in;—evidence that the imperial civilizing influence was still, at least morally, active, This astrologer and historiographer, whose name was Tan, is interesting, inasmuch as he has been confused with Li Tan (the personal name of the philosopher Lao- tsz, who was also an imperial official employed in the historiographical department). It is added that, previous to this visit, for five hundred years Ts'in and Chou had kept apart from each other. Notwithstanding this prohibition of human sacrifices, when the First August Emperor of Universal China died in 210 B.C., the old Ts'in custom was reintroduced, and all his women who had not given birth to children were buried with him. Besides this, all the workmen who had made the secret door and passage to his grave were cemented in alive, so that they might never disclose the secret of its approaches.

It was only after gradually adopting Chinese civilization that Ts'in began to be a considerable power; thus, when Ki-chah of Wu was entertained at Lu with specimens of the various styles of music, he observed, on being regaled with Ts'in music: "Ah! civilized sounds; it has succeeded in refining itself; it is in occupation of the old Chou appanage." So late as 361 B.C., when Ngwei (one of the three royal subdivisions of old Tsin) built a wall to keep off Ts'in, both Ngwei and Ts'u (which by this time was quite as good orthodox Chinese as any other state) treated Ts'in as though the latter were still barbarian, In 326 Ts'in first introduced into her realm the well-known year-end sacrifices of the orthodox Chinese, which fact alone points to a long isolation of Ts'in before this date.

The rule of succession in Ts'in seems to have been of the Tartar kind at one time. Duke Muh, in 660 B.C., succeeded his brother, though that brother had seven sons of his own living: that brother again, had also succeeded a brother.

As to Yüeh, there is no question as to its barbarism, though the one single king around whose name centres the whole glory of Yiieh (Kou-tsien, 496-475) seems to have been a man of great ability and some fine feeling. The native name for Yiieh was Yü-yüeh, as stated in Chapter VII.; and it seems likely that all the coast of China down to Tonquin, or Northern Annam, was then inhabited by cognate tribes, all having the syllable Yüeh, or Viét, in their names. The great empire or kingdom of Yiieh, founded upon the ruins of Wu, soon split up into the "Hundred Yiieh," i.e. (probably) it relapsed into its native barbarism, and ceased to cohere as a political factor. "Southern Yüeh" (the Canton region) has undoubted historical connections with the Tonquin part of Annam, and several other of the subdivisions of Yiieh, corresponding to Foochow, Wênchow, etc., show distinct traces of having belonged to the same race. But it is unsafe to say how the Chinese-transcribed name Yii-yiieh was pronounced; still more unsafe is it to argue that it must have been U or O-viêt simply because the Annamese so pronounce the word now. We have seen that, according to one historical statement, the Wu and Yiieh people spoke the same language; in which case the members of the ruling Wu caste who fled to Japan in 473 B.C. were probably not of the same race as the "savages around them." As an act of bravado, in 481, the King of Wu made five condemned centurions cut their own throats before the Tsin envoy, in order to show what effectively stern discipline he kept, In 484 the King of Yiieh had already committed a similar act of bravado; but neither of these barbarian states is distinctly recorded to have indulged in human sacrifices at the death of a sovereign. Previous to the crushing of Wu by Yiieh, in 473 B.C., Yiieh was nearly annihilated by Wu, and on this occasion Kou-tsien's envoy advanced crawling on his knees to beg for mercy; this is hardly an orthodox Chinese custom. However barbarous Yiieh may have been, its ruling house possessed traditions of descent, through a concubine, from an emperor of the Hia dynasty; for which reason the founder was enfeoffed, near modern Shao-hing, west of Ningpo, in order to fulfil the sacrifices to the founder of the Hia dynasty, who was, and is, supposed to be buried there: like the first colonists who migrated to Wu, he cut his hair, tattooed himself, opened up the jungle, and built a town. In 330 B.C. Kou- tsien's descendant spoke of "taking the road left to Chu- hia," through modern Ho Nan province; that means taking the high-road to China proper. The term originated in times when Ts'u had not yet become a recognized "Hia." The fact that Yüeh, with its new capital then in Shan Tung, could never govern the Yang-tsz and Hwai inland regions, seems to prove that her power was always purely a water power, and that she was comparatively ignorant of land campaigns.

CHAPTER XXX.LITERARY RELATIONS

It is instructive to inquire what were the literary relations between the distinguished statesmen and active princes who moved about quite freely within the limited area so frequently alluded to in foregoing pages as being sacrosanct to civilization and the rites. There seems good reason to suppose that the literary activity which so disgusted the destroyer of the books in 213 B.C. did not really begin until after Confucius' death in 479; moreover, that the avalanche of philosophical works which drenched the royal courts of the Six Kingdoms was in part the consequence of Confucius' own efforts in the literary line. In the pre- Confucian days there is little evidence of the existence of any literature at all beyond the Odes, the Changes, the Book, and the Rites, which, after a lapse of 2500 years or more, are still the "Bible" of China. The Odes, of which 3000 were popularly known previous to Confucius' recension, seem to have been originally composed here and there, and passed from mouth to mouth, by the people of each orthodox state under impulse of strong passion, feeling, or suffering; or some of them may even have been committed to writing by learned folk in touch with the people. Naturally, those songs which specially treated of local matters would be locally popular; but it would seem that a large number of them must have been generally known by heart by the whole educated body all over orthodox China, It will be remembered that in the year 1900, an enterprising American newspaper correspondent took advantage of President Kruger's penchant for quoting Scripture, and telegraphed to him daily texts, selected as applicable to the event, for which the replies to be sent were always prepaid. For instance, on news of a British victory, the American would telegraph: "Victory stayeth not always with the righteous"; on which President Kruger would promptly rejoin: "Yet shall I smite him, even unto the end." This was the plan followed by Chinese envoys, statesmen, and princes in their intercourse with each other: no matter what event transpired, Ki-chah, or Tsz-ch'an, or Shuh Hiang would illustrate it with an ode, or with a reference to the "Book" (of history), or by an appeal to the Rites of Chou, or to some obscure astrological or cosmogonical development extracted from the mystic diagrams of "The Changes." As often as not, the quotations given from the Odes and Book no longer exist in the editions of those two classics which have come down to us. This fact is interesting as proving that the Tso Chwan—or Commentary of Confucius' pupil Tso K'iu-ming on Confucius' own bare notes of history— must have been written before Confucius' expurgated Book of Odes reduced and fixed the number of selected songs; or, at all events, the records from which Tso K'iu-ming took his quotations must have existed before either he or Confucius composed their respective annals and comments. In the times when a book the size of a three-volume novel of to-day would mean a mule-load of bamboo splinters or wooden tablets, it is absurd to suppose that generals in the field, or envoys on the march, could carry their Odes bodily about with them: it is even probable that the four "scriptural" books in question were exclusively committed to memory by the general public, and that not more than half a dozen varnish-written copies existed in any state; possibly not more than one copy. In fact, the only available literary exhilaration then open to cultured friends was to check the memory on visiting strange lands by comparing the texts of Odes, Changes, or Book. A knowledge of the Rites would perhaps be confined to the ruling classes almost entirely, for with them it lay to pronounce the religious, the ritual, the social, or the administrative sanction applicable to each contested set of circumstances. It is very much as though,—as was indeed the case in Johnsonian times,—the French, English, and German wits of the day, and occasionally distinguished literary specimens of even more "barbarous" countries, should at a literary conference indulge in quotations from Horace or Juvenal by way of passing the time: they would not select the Twelve Tables or the Laws of the Pr'tors as matter for the testing of learning.

To take a few instances. In 559 the ruler of Wei had severely beaten his court music-master for failing to teach a concubine how to play the lute. One day the prince invited to dinner some statesmen, the father of one of whom had taken offence at the prince's rudeness; and he ordered the same musician to strike up the last stanza of a certain ode hinting at treason, which the malicious performer did in such a way as to give further offence to the father through his son, and to bring about the dethronement of the indiscreet prince. It gives us confidence in the truth of these anecdotes when we find that K'ü-pêh-yüh was consulted by the offended father as to what course he ought to pursue. This Wei statesman, who has already been twice mentioned in connection with other matters, met Ki-chah of Wu when the latter visited that state in 544, and he was also an admired senior acquaintance of Confucius himself, whom he twice lodged at his house for many months. Three chapters of the "Book" still remain, after Confucius' manipulations of it, to prove how Wei was first enfeoffed by the Duke of Chou, and one of the Odes actually sings the praises of a Ts'i princess who married the prince of Wei in 753 B.C. Thus we see that the ancient classics are intertwined and mutually corroborative.

When the Second Protector (the last of the four Tartar-born brothers to succeed to the Tsin throne) was on his wanderings in 644 B.C., the Marquess of Ts'i gave him a daughter, of whom he became so enamoured that he seemed to be neglecting his political chances amid the pleasures of a foreign country, instead of endeavouring to regain his rightful throne at home. This princess first of all quoted an ode from the group treating of CHÊNG affairs, and secondly cited an apt saying from what she "had heard" the great Ts'i philosopher Kwan-tsz had said, her object being to promote her lively husband's political interests. This all took place a few years after Kwan-tsz's death, and 200 years after the founding of CHÊNG state, and is therefore indirect confirmation of the fact that Kwan-tsz was already a well-known authority, and that contemporary affairs were usually "sung of" in all the orthodox states.

When the Duke of Sung, after the death in 628 B.C. of the picturesque personality just referred to, was ambitious to become the Third Protector of orthodox China and of the Emperor; Confucius' ancestor, then a Sung statesman, approved of this ambition, and proceeded to compose some complimentary sacrificial odes on the Shang dynasty (from which the Sung ducal family was descended): some learned critics make out that it was the music- master of the Emperor who really composed these odes for the ancestor of Confucius. In any case, there the odes are still, in the Book of Odes as revised by Confucius himself about 150 years later; and here accordingly—we have specific indirect evidence of Confucius' own origin; of the "spiritual" power still possessed by the Emperor's court; and of the "Poet Laureate"-like political uses to which odes were put in the international life of the times. This foolish Duke of Sung, who was so anxious to pose as Protector, was the one already mentioned in Chapters X. and XIV., who would not attack an enemy whilst crossing a stream.

Again, in the year 651, when one of the least popular of the four Tartar-born brethren was, with the assistance of the Ts'in ruler (who had been over-persuaded against his own better judgment), reigning in Tsin, the children of this latter state sang a ballad in the streets, prophesying the ultimate success of the self- sacrificing elder brother, then still away on his wanderings in Tartarland. This song was apparently never included among the 3000 odes generally known in China; but it illustrates how such popular songs and popular heroes were created and perpetuated.—It is, perhaps, time now that we should give the personal name of this popular prince, of whom we have spoken so often, and who is as well known to Chinese tradition as the severe Brutus 'is, or as the ravishing Tarquin was, to old Roman history. His name was Ch'ung-êrh, or "the double-eared," in allusion to some peculiarity in the lobes of his ears; besides which, two of his ribs were believed to be joined in one piece: his great success is perhaps largely owing to his robust and manly appearance, which certainly secured for him the eager attentions of the ladies, whether Turks or Chinese. His Turkish wife had been as disinterestedly solicitous for his success, before he went to Ts'i, as his Ts'i wife was when she induced him to leave that country. On arrival in Ts'in, he was presented with five princesses, including one who had already been given to his nephew and immediate predecessor in Tsin. The "rites" were of course decidedly wrong here, but his ally Ts'in was at this time hesitating between Chinese and Tartar culture, and in any case he was probably persuaded in his mind to let the rites go by the board for urgent political purposes. On this occasion his brother-in-law and faithful henchman during nineteen years of wanderings, sang "the song of the fertilized millet" (still existing), meaning that Ch'ung-êrh was the gay young stalk fertilized by the presents and assistance of the ruler of Ts'in: he was, by the way, not so young, then well over sixty. He had married the younger of two Tartar sisters, and had given her elder sister as wife to the henchman in question. (One account reverses the order.)

Ts'u seems to have possessed a knowledge of ancient history and of literature at a very early date. In 597 B.C., after his victory over Tsin, the King of Ts'u had, as previously narrated, declined to rear a barrow over the corpses slain, and had said: "No! the written or pictograph character for 'soldierly' is made up of two parts, one signifying 'stop,' and the other 'weapons.'" By this he meant to say what the great philosopher Lao-tsz, himself a Ts'u man, over and over again inculcated; namely, that the true soldier does not glory in war, but mournfully aims at victory with the sole view of attaining rightful ends. Not only was this half- barbarian king thus capable of making a pun which from the pictograph point of view still holds good to-day, but he goes on in the same speech to cite the "peace-loving war" of Wu Wang, or the Martial King, founder of the Chou dynasty, and to cite several standard odes in allusion to it.

These examples might be multiplied a hundredfold, For instance, in the year 589 a Ts'u minister cites the Odes; in 575 a Tsin officer quotes the Book; in 569 another makes allusion to the ancient attempt made by the ruler of the then vassal Chou state, the father of the imperial Chou founder, and who was at the same time adviser at the imperial court, to reconcile the vassal princes to the legitimate Shang dynasty Emperor (who had already imprisoned him once out of pique at his remonstrances), before finally deciding to dethrone him. In 546 a Sung envoy cites the Odes to the Ts'u government, and also quotes from that section of the "Book" called the Book of the Hia Dynasty, In connection with the year 582 an ode is cited for the benefit of the King of Ts'u, which is not in Confucius' collection. In 541 a Ts'u envoy, who was being entertained in Tsin at a convivial wine party, indulges in apt quotations from the Odes.

There does not seem to be one single instance where any one in Ts'in either sings an ode, quotes orthodox history, or in any way displays literary knowledge. Even the barbarian Kou-tsien, King of Yüeh, has wise saws and modern instances quoted to him in his distress. For instance, whilst hesitating about utterly annihilating the Wu reigning family, he was advised: "If one will not take gifts from Heaven, Heaven may send one misfortune." This is a very hackneyed saying in ancient Chinese history, and is as much used to-day as it was 2500 years ago: it comes from the Book of Chou (now partly lost). It will be remembered that the distinguished Japanese statesman, Count Okuma, in his now notorious speech before the Kobé Chamber of Commerce on the 20th October, 1907, used these identical words to point the moral of Indian commerce. It is doubtful if any other really pregnant Japanese philosophical saying exists which cannot be similarly traced to China. In any case, Count Okuma was only literally carrying out in Kobé the policy of Tsin, Ts'u, Ts'i, and Wei statesmen of China 2500 years ago.

If, as we have assumed, standard books were usually committed to memory (and it must be remembered that the Odes, and much of the Book, the Changes, and the Rites are still so committed to memory in our own times), and were practically confined to the headquarters or the wealthy families of each state, the cognate question inevitably arises: What about the historical records? It has already been observed that Ts'in, the half-Tartar power in the extreme west, was the only state belonging to the recognized federal system (and that only since 771 B.C.) of which nothing literary is recorded, and which, though powerful enough to assist in making Emperors of Chou and rulers of Tsin, was never in Confucian times thought morally fit to act as Protector of the Imperial Federal Union, i.e. of Chu Hia, or "All the Chinas." By a singular irony of fate, however, it so happens that a few Ts'in inscriptions are the only political ones remaining to us of ancient Chinese documents.

When the outlying semi-Chinese states surrounding the inner conclave of orthodox Chinese states, after four centuries of fighting and intrigue for the Protectorate, or at least for preponderance, at last, during the period 400-375 B.C. became the Six Powers, all equally royal, none of them owing any real, scarcely even any nominal, allegiance to the once solitary King or Emperor, then it was that the idea began to enter the heads of the Ts'in statesmen and the rulers of at least three of the Six Royal Powers opposed to Ts'in that it would be a good thing to get rid of the old feudal vassal system root and branch. So unquestionably is this period 400-375 B.C. taken as one of the great pivot points in Chinese history, that the great historian Sz-ma Kwang begins his renowned history, the Tsz-chi Tung-kien, published in 1084 A.D., with the words: "In 403 B.C. the states of Han, Ngwei, and Chao were recognized as vassal ruling princes by the Emperor." Ts'in took to educating herself seriously for her great destiny, and at last, in 221 B.C., after the wars already described in Chapter XXVI., succeeded in uniting all known China under one centralized sway; rounding off the Tartars so as to make the Great Wall (rather than the Yellow River, as of old) their southern limit; conquering the remains of the "Hundred Yüeh" (the vague unknown South China which had hitherto been the special preserve of Ts'u;) and assimilating the ancient empire of Shuh (i.e. Sz Ch'wan, hitherto only vaguely known to orthodox China at all, and politically connected only with Ts'in).

During this process of universal assimilation and annexation, the almost supernaturally active First August Emperor made tour after tour throughout his new dominions, showing a special predilection for the coasts, for Tartarland, and for the Lower Yang-tsz River; but not venturing far up or far south of that Great River; and even when he did so venture a short distance, never leaving the old and well-known water routes: nor did he risk a land journey to Sz Ch'wan, to which country there were at the time no roads of any kind at all possible for armies. It is well known that both he and the legal, international, political, and diplomatical adventurers who had been for a century or more from time to time at his court had been strongly imbued with the somewhat revolutionary and then fashionable democratic principles of the new Taoism, as defined by the philosopher Lao-tsz; but he showed no particular hostility to orthodox literature until, whilst on his travels, deputations of learned men, especially in the ritual centres of Lu and Ts'i, began to suggest to him the re-establishment of the old feudal system, and to "quote the ancient scriptures" to him by way of protesting mildly against his too drastic political changes. It has been explained in Chapter XIII. that in 626 B.C., when his great ancestor Duke Muh had availed himself of the advisory services of an educated Tartar (of Tsin descent), this Tartar had made use of the expression: "The King of the Tartars governs in a simple, ready way, without the aid of the Odes and the Book as in the case of China." Thus it was that, possibly with this ancient warning in his mind, he conceived a sudden, violent, and passionate hatred for didactic works generally, and two books in particular-the very two, passages from which pedants, philosophers, ambassadors, and ministers had for centuries hurled at each other's heads alike in convivial, argumentative, and solemn moments. In other words, the Odes and the Book, together with Confucius' "Springs and Autumns," with its censorious hints for rulers, and all the other local Annals and Histories, were under anathema, But more detestable even than these were the new philosophical treatises of a polemical kind, which girded at monarchs through their subtle choice of words and anecdotes, or which recalled the good old times of the feudal emperors and their not very obsequious vassals. His self-laudatory inscriptions upon stone, scattered about as he travelled from place to place, tell us plainly, in his own royal words, that this hatred of presumptuous vassal claims was his prime motive in destroying all the pedants and books he could secure. He denounces the vassals of bygone times who ignored the Supreme Emperor, fought with each other, and had the insolence to "carve stone and metal in order to record their own deeds." The Changes are quoted in history often enough by statesmen, as well as the Odes and the Book; but, even if the First August Emperor did not entertain the suspicion that the first were (as, indeed, they are according to our Western lights) all "hocus-pocus," he was himself very credulous and superstitious, and the learned word-juggling of the Changes was in any case harmless to him; so that really his rage was confined to the four or five books, known by heart throughout China, setting forth the ancient ritual system of previous dynasties, as perfected by the Chou government; the subordination of all other kings (Ts'in included) to the Chou family; the wrath of Heaven, the divinity of the people, and so on. Things had been made worse during the Fighting State Period (480-230) by the extraordinary literary activity prevailing at the different royal courts, when the old royal tao had been interpreted in one way by Lao- tsz and his followers, in another by Confucius and his school; in countless others by the schools of Legists, Purists, Scholastics, Cosmogonists, Pessimists, Optimists, and so on. A clean sweep was accordingly made, so far as it was possible and practicable, of all literature, with the exception (amongst old books) of the Changes, and of practical modern or ancient books on astronomy, medicine, and agriculture. At the same time copies of the proscribed Odes and Book were kept on record at court for the use of the learned in the service of the Emperor. All "histories," except that of Ts'in, were utterly destroyed, and á fortiori all argumentative works on history or on administrative policy of any kind. The old Tartar blood and Tartar sympathies of the First August Emperor must surely re-appear in a policy so incompatible with all orthodox teaching? In one sense the blight upon Chinese civilization was akin to the blight cast upon that of Eastern Europe 500 years ago by the "unspeakable Turk." The new ruler boldly said: "The world begins afresh, with me. No posthumous condemnatory titles for me! My successor will be 'August Emperor

Number Two,' and so on for ever." It was like the Vendémiaire in 1793.

Thus, except in so far as Confucius may have borrowed from local histories besides that of Lu in making up his "Springs and Autumns," the Annals of Ts'in are the only annals of the feudal states (except the Bamboo Books, or Annals of Tsin, dug up in A.D. 281) now left to us. That there were such annals in each state is certain, for in 627 B.C. the "great historian" of Tsin is spoken of; and in 607 and 510 the names of the Tsin historians are given, in the first case apparently a Tartar. That there should be a Tsin Tartar versed in Chinese literature is not remarkable, for it was shown at the close of Chapter XIII. how a learned Tsin Tartar had acted as adviser to Duke Muh of Ts'in, and had left behind him a work in two chapters, which was still in existence in 50 B.C. Under the year 628 B.C., one of the expanded versions of Confucius' history explains how the anarchy which had then been for some time prevailing in Tsin led to certain Tsin events of the year 630 being omitted by Confucius; this is a very important statement, for it infers that Confucius made use of the Tsin annals. It is recorded of Confucius that when reading the Shi- ki ("Historical Annals"), he expressed very strong views when he came to the events of 632 and 598 B.C., that is, to the place where the "ordering up" of the Emperor by Tsin is described, and to the noble action of the "sage" King of Ts'u; it is interesting to know that this old name, Shi-ki, was chosen by the author of the first real history of China published under that title about 90 B.C., and that he was not the inventor of the name, which had already for centuries been applied in a general sense to the historical annals either of Lu or of China generally.

In 547 B.C. it is stated that the "great historian" of Ts'i made certain remarks: we have already seen in the present chapter how the Ts'i wife of the Second Protector was in 640 B.C. perfectly well acquainted with the historical and philosophical works of Kwan-tsz, the great administrative innovator of Ts'i under the First Protector. In the second century B.C. Kwan-tsz's work of eighty-six chapters was placed at the head of the Taoist works (of course before Taoism became Lao-tsz's speciality). It is mentioned, quite casually, in the year 538, in a political conversation which took place with the King of Ts'u, that the First Protector of Ts'i in the year 647 B.C. had had to contend with the serious rebellion of a subject (who is named). All circumstances point to the truth of this isolated, but otherwise most specific statement; yet it is not mentioned elsewhere,— evidence, if it were wanted, that many historical works, from which facts were borrowed as though the details were well known to all, must have disappeared entirely.

As to Ts'u, its Annals were known by the curious name of "Stinking Wood," by which it is supposed that the evil recorded of men upon wooden tablets was meant. That Ts'u subsequently developed a high literary capacity is evident, for the anniversary of the suicide of the celebrated Ts'u poet K'üh Yiian (envoy to Ts'i during the fierce diplomatic intrigues of 31 B.C.) has been kept up as the annual "dragon festival" down to our own times, in memory of his suicide by drowning in the Tung-t'ing Lake district; and his poems are amongst the most beautiful in the Chinese language. In 656 B.C. the dictatorial First Protector tried to play the rôle of the wolf, with Ts'u in the character of the lamb: he said: "How is it you have not for so many generations past sent your tribute of sedge to the Emperor? How about the other Emperor who visited (modern) Hankow in 1003 B.C. and was never heard of again?" The King replied: "As to our failure to send tribute, we admit it; as to the supposed murder of the Emperor 350 years ago, you had better ask the people of Hankow themselves what they know of it." (Ts'u had hardly yet permanently advanced so far east.)

In 496 B.C. it is recorded of a scholar at the Emperor's court that, being anxious to see his own name in the "Springs and Autumns," he suggested to the Emperor that for a long time no complimentary mission had been sent to Lu. The result was that he was sent himself, and is thus immortalized: it does not follow from this that the knowledge of Confucius' coming book had penetrated to the Chou court, because "Springs and Autumns" was already the accepted term in Lu for "Annals," long before Confucius adopted the already existing general name for his own particular work. In 496 Confucius had left Lu in disgust, and had gone to Wei—the capital of Wei was then on, or near, the then Yellow River (now the River Wei), between the two towns marked "Hwa" and "K'ai" on modern maps—where he collected materials for his History; but he did not begin it until the year 481; so probably the ambitious scholar simply hoped to appear in the "Springs and Autumns" of Lu, as they had already been called before Confucius borrowed the name, just as Sz-ma Ts'ien borrowed the name Shi-ki.

As to Ts'in, Ts'in's own Annals tell us that "in 753 B.C. historians were first established to keep record of events." Hence even the Ts'in records, the sole annals preserved from the flames, must be retrospective from that date. In any case they contain nothing of historical importance farther back than 753 B.C., except the wars with Tartars; the accompanying of the Emperor Muh, as charioteer, by a Ts'in prince on the occasion of his "going to examine his fiefs in the west"; and the cession of the old Chou appanage to Ts'in in 771. By their baldness, and by the baldness of the Bamboo Books, and of Confucius' own "Springs and Autumns," we may fairly judge of the probable insufficiency and dryness of the Annals of Ts'u, Ts'i, Wei, CHÊNG, Sung, and other states interested in the welter of the Fighting State Period. Early Chinese annals contain little more satisfying than the "generations of Adam" in the fifth chapter of Genesis.

CHAPTER XXXI.ORIGIN OF THE CHINESE

Having now derived some definite notions of how the Chinese advanced from the patriarchal to the feudal, from the submissive and monarchical to the emulous and democratic, finally to collapse under the overpowering grasp of a single Dictator or Despot, whose centralized system in the main, still survives; having also seen how the nucleus of China proper was encompassed on three sides by Tibetans, Tartars, Tunguses, Coreans, and by various ill-defined tribes to the south; let us see if there is any evidence whatever to show, or even to suggest to us, whence the orthodox Chinese originally came, and who they were.

First and foremost, it seems primarily unnecessary to suggest at all that they came from anywhere; for, if the position be once assumed as an axiom that all people must have immigrated from some place to the place in which we first find them, or hear of them, then the double question arises: "Why should the persons we find in A., and who, we think, may have come from B., not have migrated from A. to B. before they migrated back from B. to A.?" Or: "If the people we find at A. must have come from B., whence did the people at B. come, before they went to A.?" To put it in another way: given the existence 4000 or 5000 years ago of Chinese in China, Egyptians in Egypt, and Babylonians in Babylonia—why should one group be assumed to be older than the other? The only ground for suggesting that these groups had not each a separate evolution, is the assumption that man was "created" once for all, and created summarily; in which case it follows with mathematical precision that the ultimate ancestry of every man living extends back to exactly the same date. That is to say, the highest and the lowest, the blackest and the whitest, only differ in this, that some men began to keep records earlier than others; for the man who keeps no records loses track of his ancestors, and that is all. Not to mention other races, some of our own noblest English families trace back their ancestry to a favoured or successful person, who was of no hereditary distinction before he distinguished himself; whilst on the other hand the tramp and the street-walker may have as "royal" blood in their veins as any lineal princely personage. It is records, therefore, that differentiate "civilized" from uncivilized people, blue blood from plebeian; and as we see millions of people living without records to-day in various parts of the world, notwithstanding that for centuries, or even for millenniums, they have been surrounded by or in immediate contact with neighbours possessing records, it seems to follow that a nation's greatness may begin at any time, independently of the blueness of its blood, the robustness of its warriors, the beauty of its women; that is, whenever it chooses to keep records, and thus to cultivate itself: for records are nothing more than the means of keeping experiences in stock, instead of having to repeat them every day; they are thus accumulations of national wealth. It by no means follows that because records can be traced back farther in the case of one nation than in the case of another, that the first nation is older than the other; for instance, although in the West our various alphabets appear to refer themselves back to one same source, or to a few sources which probably all hark back ultimately to one and the same, there seems no reason to believe that the Chinese did not independently invent, develop, and perfect their own scheme of written records: the mere fact that we learnt how to write is some evidence in support of the proposition that they also, being men like ourselves, learnt how to write.

There is no documentary evidence for the barest existence of ancient China, or of any part of it, which is not to be found in the Chinese records, and in them alone; no nation anywhere near China has any record or tradition of either its own or of China's existence at a period earlier than the Chinese records indicate. Those records do not contain the faintest allusion to Egypt, Babylonia, India, or any other foreign country or place whatever outside the extremely limited area of the Central Nucleus, and the larger area occupied by the semi-Chinese colonial powers surrounding it. Nor is there the faintest evidence that the Biblical "land of Sinim" had any reference to China, which seems to have been as absolutely unknown to the West previous to, say, 250 B.C., as America was unknown to Europe, or Europe to America previous to 1400 A.D. If any ideas were derived from China by the West, or from the West by China, the records of both China and the West alike point, however, to one obvious connecting link, and that is, the horse-riding nomads of the north, who are now, it is true, in some parts a little more settled than they used to be, and who have been tamed in various degrees by dogmatic religions unknown to them in ancient times, but who remain in many respects now very much what they were 3000 years ago. Of course pedlars, hawkers, and even long-course caravans travelled, whenever the routes were free, from place to place in ancient times as they do now; but it is exceedingly improbable that there would be any through-travellers from Europe to China, except one or two occasional waifs or adventurers buffeted through by chance. If 600 years ago, Marco Polo's through-route adventures were regarded in Europe as almost incredible, notwithstanding the then recent and well-trodden war-path of the Mongol armies, what chances are there of through-travel 2000 years before that? And, even if a rare case occasionally occurred, what chances are there of any one recording it?

The probability is, so far as sane experience takes us, that the Chinese had been exactly where we first find them for many thousand years, or even for myriads of years, before their own traditions begin. With the exception of the discovery of America, which brought a flood of strangers into a strange land, and speedily exterminated the aborigines, there do not appear to be any authenticated instances in history of extensive and robust populations being entirely displaced like flocks of sheep by others. Any one who travels widely in China can see for himself that, wherever unassimilated tribes live in complete or partial independence, and, á fortiori, where the assimilation has been carried out, all those tribes possess at least this point in common with the original Chinese or the assimilated speakers of Chinese—that their language is monosyllabic, uninflected, not agglutinative, and tonic; i.e. that each word is "sung" in a particular way, besides being pronounced in a particular way. Probably those tribes before they were absorbed, or, despite their not having yet been absorbed by the Chinese, had been there as long as the Chinese had been in the contiguous Chinese parts. It seems reasonable to suppose that the Chinese would absorb their own race-classes more readily than they would absorb Tartars, Japanese, and Coreans, all of whom belong to the same dissyllabic, long-worded, agglutinative family. And so it is: the Chinese followed the lines of least resistance (after themselves becoming cultured) and worked their way down the rivers and other watercourses towards what we call South China. From the very first, their passage northwards across the Yellow River was contested by the Tartars, whom they have since partly driven back, and partly (with great effort) absorbed. They have never been able to assimilate the Coreans, not to say the Japanese, though both peoples took very kindly to Chinese civilization after our Christian era, when first friendly missions began to be interchanged. Indo-China contains many more of the monosyllabic and tonic tribes than of others; if, indeed, there are any at all of the dissyllabic and non-tonal classes; and the Chinese have no difficulty in merging themselves with Annamese, Tonquinese, Cambodgians, Siamese, Shans, Thos, Laos, Mons, and such like peoples: but their own administrative base is too far north; the conditions of food and climate in Indo-China are not quite favourable for the marching of armies, especially when it is remembered that the best troops used have always been Tartars, used to warm clothes and heating food. There have, besides, always been rival Indian religion, rival Indian colonization, rival Indian language, and rival Indian trade influence to contend with. No absorption of Indian races has ever been anywhere effected by China. Tibetans never came into question in ancient times; if they were known, it could only have been to Shuh (Sz Ch'wan) and Ts'in or early Chou (Shen Si).

If it had not been the Chinese of Ho Nan who first used records, it is just as probable that the tonic and monosyllabic absorption which, as things were and are, moved from north to south, might have moved from south to north. During the Chou dynasty (1122 B.C.-222 B.C.), when the extension of the Chinese race took place (which had probably already for long gone on) in the clear light of history, it will be noticed that the rulers of all the great colony nations of the south—Ts'u, Wu, and Yüeh—had, in turn, to remind the Emperor of China of their perfect equality with him in spiritual claim and ancient descent; of their connection with dynasties precedent to his; of times when his ancestor was a mere vassal like themselves. No Tartars of those times ever put forth claims like these, though, it is true, in much later times some of the (non-Turkish) Tartar rulers of North China traced their ancestors back to the mythical Chinese emperors who reigned in Shan Tung. Again, the founder of the Hia dynasty (2205 B.C.) is repeatedly said to have been buried at modern Shao-hing (between Hangchow and Ningpo), and the King of Yüeh even sacrificed to him there. So the Emperor Shun, the predecessor and patron of the same founder, was traditionally buried near Ch'ang-sha in modern Hu Nan province. The First August Emperor included both these "lions" in his pleasure tours among the great sights of China. No sound historical deduction, of course, can be drawn from these traditions, however persistent: if false, they were, at any rate, open to the criticism of a revolutionary and all-powerful Emperor over 2000 years ago, and to a second, almost equally powerful, who visited both places a century later; the suggestion inevitably follows from the existence of these traditions in the south that either the cultured Chinese whom we first find in Ho Nan had moved northwards from Hu Nan, Kiang Si, and the lake districts generally, before they spread themselves backwards; or that the uncultured Chinese had moved north before the cultured Chinese moved south; or that both north and south Chinese were at first equally cultured, until within historical times the north Chinese (i.e. in Ho Nan, along the Yellow River) so perfected their system of records that they carried all before them. After all there is no strain on the imagination in suggesting this, for early Western civilization grew up in the same way.

There is not the smallest hint of any immigration of Chinese from the Tarim Valley, from any part of Tartary, from India, Tibet, Burma, the Sea, or the South Sea Islands: in fact, there is no hint of immigration from anywhere even in China itself, except as above hypothetically described. There the Chinese are, and there they were; and there is an end to the question, so far as documentary evidence goes. Of course, the persistent Tarim Valley scheme proposed is only a means to get in the thin end of the wedge, in order to drive home the thick end in the shape of a definite start from the Tower of Babel, and an ultimate reference to the Garden of Eden. If there are still people who believe it their duty on Scriptural principle to accept this naïve Western origin of the Chinese, there is no reason why religious belief or imagination should not be perfectly respected, and even find a working compromise with the principle of strict adherence to human evidence. If supernatural agencies be once admitted (as the limited human intellect understands Nature), there seems to be no more reason for accepting the creation of a complete whale (already a hundred years old, according to the growth period of later whales), than for accepting the creation of complete men with 1000 years' history behind them instead of 100; or that of the earth with 20,000, or even 20,000,000 years' history behind it, and even before it; for as the first whale, or pair of whales, must set the standard of natural history for all future whales, so the man created with history behind him may equally well have history created in front of him. "Nature," according to the imperfect human understanding, is no more outraged in one case than in the other, nor can mere time or size count as anything towards increasing our wonder when we tell ourselves what supernatural things unseen powers superior to ourselves may have done. This amounts to the same thing as saying that dogmatic belief, personal religious conviction, agnosticism, superstition, and imagination are all on equal terms, and are equally respectable factors when confronted with human historical evidence, so long as they are kept rigidly apart from the latter, As an eminent Catholic has recently said: "The Church has no more reason to be afraid of modern science than it was of ancient science." In other words, however pious and religious a man may be (as we understand the words in Europe), there is no reason why, as a recreation apart from his faith, he should not rigidly adhere to the human evidence of history so far as it goes. On the other hand, however sceptical and discriminating a man may be, from the point of view of imperfect human knowledge, in the admittance of humanly proved fact, there is no reason why, from the emotional and imaginative side of his existence, he should not rigidly subscribe to dogma or personal conviction, whether the abstract idea of virtue, the concrete idea of love for some cherished human being, or the yearning for some supernatural state of sinlessness be concerned. A distinguished financier, for instance, may regale his imagination with socialistic dreams of a perfect Utopia; but, when the weekly household bills are presented to him, he deals with overcharges in pence like any other practical individual.

From one point of view, the Chinese, already provided with their tonic language at the Confusion of Tongues, marched to the Yellow River, where we find them. From the other, there is no evidence whatever to connect the Chinese with any people other than those we find near them now, and which have from the earliest times been near them; no evidence that their language, their civilization, their manners, ever received anything from, or gave anything to, India, Babylonia, Persia, Egypt, or Greece, except so far as has been suggested above, or will be suggested below.

CHAPTER XXXII.THE CALENDAR

Allusion has already been made to the eclipses mentioned in Confucius' history as a means by which the probability of his general truth as a historian may in a certain measure be gauged. A few words upon the Chinese calendar, as it is and was, may therefore not be amiss. The Chinese month has from first to last been uncompromisingly lunar; that is to say, the first day of each month, or "moon" as it may strictly and properly be called, always falls within the day (beginning at midnight) during which the new moon occurs. Of course, Peking is the administrative centre now, and therefore the observations are taken there with reference to the Peking meridian. As Confucius took his facts and records mainly from the Lu archives, and (we must suppose) noted celestial movements from what was seen by the Lu astronomers, it has always been presumed that the eclipses mentioned by him were observed from Lu too; that is, from a station over four degrees of longitude and one of latitude removed from the imperial capital as it then was (modern Ho-nan Fu). It was the duty of all sovereign princes to proclaim the first day of the moon at their ancestral temple; and even if the Chinese of those days had discovered the difference in "time" between east and west, these princes must each of them have proclaimed the day during which the new moon occurred as it occurred to themselves, in their own State, and not as it occurred to the Emperor's astronomers. On the other hand, when eclipses were observed from the comparatively small territory of Lu, it must have occurred, at least occasionally, that visitors from other states had either the same eclipse or other eclipses to report. If the Emperor's astronomer reported eclipses in Ho-nan- Fu on a given day, it is difficult to see how Lu, which was a centre almost of equal standing with the imperial capital for orthodoxy in rites and records, could have entirely ignored such reports.

But the Chinese year has always been luni-solar. From the earliest times they had observed the twelve ecliptical "mansions" and zodiacal signs, and also that the time occupied by the sun in travelling through a mansion was rather longer than one lunation, or the time intervening between two new moons. Their object has accordingly always been to bring the lunar and solar years into manageable combination, so that the equinoxes, solstices, and "seasons" might occur with as much regularity as possible in the same months, and so that the husbandman might know when to sow his grain. Formerly they regulated this discrepancy according to the mean movements of the sun and moon; but, ever since the Jesuits first instructed them more accurately, they have regulated the two years, that is, the solar year and the twelve lunations, according to the true movements, and with reference to the meridian of Peking. If the moons were each exactly 29 1/2 days in length, instead of being 44 minutes 2.87 seconds longer, it would have been a simple matter to halve the ordinary lunar year, and make six months "large" (30 days) and six "small" (29 days); but the extra 44 minutes and a fraction accumulate, and the result is that there must always be a larger number of "great" months than "small" in the year. The way the Chinese arranged this was to call a month "great" (30 days) if the interval between mid-night (beginning of the new-moon day) and the hour of the next new moon was full 30 days or over in duration; if less than 30 days, then the month was a "small" one (29 days). Not more than two long months ever followed in succession, and two short months never did so.

But, in any case, even twelve regular moons of 291/2 days only make 354 days, whereas a solar year is about 3651/4 days, whilst the sun's time in passing through a "mansion" (one-twelfth of the solar year) is about 301/2 days. Thus there was a "superfluity" of about ten days in every lunar year, or about one lunation in every third year; not to mention that a "mansion" was about a day longer than a lunation, and that therefore the husbandman was liable to be thrown out of his reckoning. In order to remedy this, the Chinese intercalated a month once in about thirty-three moons, and called the intercalary month by the same name as the one preceding it, both with regard to the common numbers 1-12, and with regard to the two endless cycles of twelve signs and sixty signs, by which moons are calculated for ever, in the past and in the future. Regarding the difficulty of seasons, the solar year was divided into twenty-four "joints," and each "joint" was about half a "mansion" (the difference rarely exceeding one hour). However, the spring equinox is always the sixth "joint," and is the middle of spring season: this and the other "joints" being all about 15 1/4 days in length, the Chinese seasons can be symmetrically divided with relation to both equinoxes and both solstices; for the intercalary moon (judiciously made unobtrusive, and kept out of vulgar sight as far as possible) settles the lunar year difficulty; and the seasons conform, as of course they should do, to the heat of the sun, which is a much more natural and practical arrangement than our own arbitrarily assorted and unequal months.

The endless sixty-year cycle of years is usually referred back to for a beginning to either 2697 or 2637 B.C.; but, apart from the fact that there is little or no accurate knowledge anterior to 842 B.C., it is of no importance when it began, so long as sixty pairs of equinoxes and solstices are calculated backwards indefinitely. It goes back, in any case, to a date beyond which the memory of Chinese man runneth not to the contrary; it is unbroken and continuous; we are free to take up any date we like at sixty-year intervals, and say "here I agree to begin": we cannot deny that 1908 is the cycle year it purports to be; and even if we did, batches of sixty years backwards from any other cyclic year called 1908, would always have a fixed relation to the other 4604 years recorded; nor, having accepted 1908, can we deny 1808, 1708, and so on, as far back as we like, in order to test how any given event, eclipse or other, coincides relatively with our own date: it is not a question of beginning, but of counting back, and stopping. We find Confucius of Lu (Chou clan state) using the calendar of the Chou dynasty (1122 B.C.-249 B.C.); whose founder had said: "In future we make the eleventh month the beginning of the year instead of the twelfth month." The previous dynasty of Shang (1766-1123) had similarly said: "In future we make the twelfth month begin the year instead of the first." The previous dynasty of Hia (2205-1767) and the individual emperors before had all said (or taken for granted): "The year begins in the first month," from which we may naturally conclude that there could not have been an earlier calendar, as no "sage" could reasonably begin anywhere but at the beginning. At the same time, it must be explained that the astronomical order of the months, counting the first as being that when the sun enters Capricorn, is different from the civil order. Thus the Hia, Shang, and Chou first civil months were the third, second, and first astronomical months, representing the sun's entry into Pisces, Aquarius, and Capricorn, respectively. When the First August Emperor conquered the whole of China, and proceeded to unify cart-axles, weights and measures, written characters, and many other discrepant popular arrangements, he said: "Let the tenth month be in future the first in the year instead of the eleventh." That is to say, he took as civil first month the twelfth astronomical month, or that in which the sun enters Sagittarius. Thus we see that in 2000 years the calendar had got about 90 days out of gear; or, roughly, about an hour a year.

All the above may, perhaps, be understood more clearly by considering the following unmistakably genuine statement made by the Emperor in 104 B.C., a hundred years after the Ts'in dynasty had been destroyed; after he had contemplated the tombs of the ancient monarchs as explained in the last chapter; after the West of Asia had been discovered; and when it is possible (though there is no record of it) that Persians, Indians, Greeks, etc., may have intervened in discussion upon the calendar. He says: "After the Emperors Yu and Li (the two who fled from their metropolis in 771 B.C. and 842 B.C. respectively, as related), the Chou dynasty went wrong, and those who were doubly subjects began to wield power; astrologers ceased to keep reckoning of seasons; the princes no longer proclaimed the first day of each moon. Hereditary astronomers got scattered; some remained in All the Hia (orthodox China); others betook themselves to the various barbarians. In the twenty-sixth year of the Emperor Siang (626 B.C.) there was an intercalary third month, which arrangement the 'Springs and Autumns' condemns (it should have been at the end of the year)... The First August Emperor took the tenth month as the beginning of the year... The present Emperor (of the Han dynasty) appointed two astronomers, the second of whom (a native of East Sz Ch'wan) advanced the calculations and improved the calendar. Then it was found that the measures of the Sun and the Mansions agreed with the principles adopted by the Hia dynasty... The first cyclic day and also the first lunar day of the eleventh moon has now been proved to be the winter solstice. I change the seventh year (of my present reign-period), and I make of it the first year of the new reign-period, to be called 'Great Beginning.'"—Accordingly what had up to that date been the seventh year (of a reign-period bearing another name) now became a year of 442 days; that is to say, the three months postponed in turn by the Hia, Shang, and Chou dynasties were taken up again, and accordingly that one correcting year consisted of fifteen months. With slight changes, always adopted only to be again rejected after a few years of trial, this has been the basis of all later calendars; and for this reason Confucius' birthday is kept on the twenty-seventh day of the eighth moon instead of during the tenth moon, as it would have been according to Chou dates.

The above examination into the calendar question tends to show still more clearly the good faith of the historians and the administration; it also illustrates the continuity and painstaking accuracy of the Chinese records, whatever other defects they may otherwise disclose.

CHAPTER XXXIII.NAMES

One of the difficulties of Chinese ancient history is the unravelling of proper names; but, as with other difficulties, this one is owing rather to the novelty and strangeness of the subject, to the unfamiliarity of scene and of atmosphere, than to any inherent want of clearness in the matter itself. In reading Scottish history, no one is much disconcerted to find a man called upon the same page (as an imaginary instance), Old John, John McQuhirt, the Master of Weel, the McQuhirt, the Laird o' Airton, the Laird of the Isle, and the Earl of Airton and Weel; there are many such instances to be found in Boswell's account of the Johnsonian trip to the Hebrides; but the puzzled Englishman has at least his own language and a fairly familiar ground to deal with. When, however, we come to unpronounceable Chinese names of strange individuals, moving about amid hitherto unheard-of surroundings 2500 years ago, with a suspicion of uncertainty added about the genuineness and good faith of the whole story, things are apt to seem hopelessly involved, even where the best of good-will to understand is present. Thus Confucius may be called K'ung-tsz, K'ung Fu-tsz, or Chung-ni, besides other personal applications under the influence of tabu rules, Tsz-ch'an may be spoken of as Kung-sun K'iao, or (if he himself speaks) simply as K'iao. And so on with nearly all prominent individuals. In those times the family names, or "surnames" as we say in English, were not used with the regularity that prevails in China now, when every one of standing has a fixed family name, such as Li or Yiian, followed by an official personal name, like Hung-chang or Shï- k'ai. In old times the clan or tribe counted first; for instance the imperial clan of Ki included princes of several vassal states. But, after five generations, it was expected that any given family unit should detach itself. Thus, in 710 B.C., Confucius' ancestor, son of the composer of odes mentioned on page 175, took, or was given by the ruler of his native state, Sung, the detached family name of K'ung-fu (Father K'ung), "Father" being the social application, and K'ung the surname, which thence became the family name of a new branch. The old original clan- names were little used by any one in a current sense, just as the English family name of Guelph is kept in the dim background so far as current use goes. Nor were the personal names, even of Chinese emperors and kings, so grave and decorous in style as they have always been in later times. For instance, "Black Buttocks," "Black Arm," "Double Ears";—such names (decidedly Turkish in style) are not only used of Tsin princes with an admixture of Tartar blood nearly always coursing more or less in their veins, but also in such states as the orthodox Lu. The name "Black Arm," for instance, is used both by Lu and by Ts'u princes; also by a Ts'u private individual; whilst an orthodox Duke of Sung bears the purely Turkish name of T'ouman, which (and exactly the same pictograph characters, too) was also the name of the first historical Hiung-nu (later Turkish) Khan several centuries later. The name Luh-fu or "Emoluments Father," belonging to the son of the last Emperor of the Shang dynasty in 1123 B.C., was also the personal name of one of the rulers of Ts'i many centuries later. In the same way we find identical personal names in CH'ÊN and Lu, and also in Ts'u and Lu princes. Eunuchs were not considered to possess family names, or even official personal names. If there had been then, as now, a celibate priestly caste, no doubt then, as now, priests would also have been relieved of their family name rights.

It seems quite clear that many if not most family names began in China with the name of places, somewhat after the Scotch style: even in Lancashire the title of the old lord of the manor is often the family surname of many of the village folk around. Take the Chinese imperial domain for instance; in the year 558 one Liu Hia goes to meet his master the new Emperor. His name (Hia) and surname (Liu) would serve just as well for current use to-day, as for example with the late viceroy Liu K'un-yih; but we are told Liu Hia was so "named" by the historian in full because his rank was not that of first-class statesman, and it is explained that Liu was the name of his tenancy in the imperial appanage. At a Lu funeral in 626 B.C. the Emperor's representative to the vassal state is spoken of complimentarily by his social appellation in view of his possessing first-class ministerial rank: he cannot be spoken of by his detached clan-name, or family name, "because he has not yet received a town in fee." A few years later, another imperial messenger is spoken of as King-shuh (Glory Uncle), "Glory" being the name of his manor or fee, and "Uncle" his social appellation. In 436 B.C. the Emperor sent a present of sacrificial meat to Lu by X. As X is thus "named," he must be of "scholar" rank, as an imperial "minister" (it is explained) could not be thus named. The ruler alone has the right to "affront a man" at all times with his personal name, but even a son in speaking of his own father to the Emperor may "affront" his father, because both his father and himself are on equal subject footing before the Emperor. To "name" a man in history is not always like "naming" a member in the House of Commons. For instance, the King of Ts'u, as mentioned in Chapter XXVII., was named for killing a Chinese in 531, but not for killing a barbarian prince in 526 B.C. It was partly by these delicate shades of naming or not naming, titling or not titling, that Confucius hinted at his opinions in his history: in the Ts'u case, it seems to have been an honour to "name" a barbarian. Wei Yang, Kung-sun Yang, or Shang Kiin, or Shang Yang, the important personage who carried a new civilization to Ts'in, and practically "created" that power about 350 B.C., was, personally, simply named Yang, or "Bellyband." As he came originally from the orthodox state or principality of Wei, he might be called Wei Yang, just as we might say Alexander of Fife. As he received from Ts'in, as a reward for his services, the petty principality of Shang (taken in war by Ts'in from Ts'u), he might be called the prince or laird (kün) of Shang (of. Lochiel), or Shang Kün. As he was the grandson (sun) of a deceased earl (called kung, or "duke," as a posthumous compliment), he was entitled to take the family name of Kung-sun, just as we say "Fitzgeorge" or "Fitzwilliam." Finally, he was Yang (= John) of Shang (= Lochiel). In speaking of this man to an educated Chinese, it does not in the least matter which of the four names be used. In the same way, Tsz-ch'an (being a duke's grandson) was Kung-sun K'iao. The word tsz, or "son," after a family name, as for instance in K'ung-tsz (Confucius), is defined as having the effect of "gracefully alluding to a male." It seems really to be the same in effect as the Latin us, as in Celsius, Brutus, Thompsonius, etc. When it precedes, not the family name or the tabu'd personal name, but the current or acquaintance name, then it seems to have the effect of Don or Dom, used with the most attenuated honorificity; or the effect of "Mr." Fu-tsz means "The Master."

As to tabus, the following are curious specific instances. King, or "Jungle," was the earliest name for Ts'u, or "Brushwood," the uncleared region south of the River Han, along the banks of the Yang-tsz; and it afterwards became a powerful state. But one of the most powerful kings of Ts'in (249-244) was called Tsz-ts'u, or "Don Brushwood," so his successor the First August Emperor (who was really a bastard, and not of genuine Ts'in blood at all) tabu'd the word Ts'u, and ordered historians to use the old name King instead. In the same way the philosopher Chwang Chou, or Chwang-tsz, was spoken of by the Han historians as Yen Chou, because chwang was an imperial personal name. Both words mean "severe": it is as though private Romans and public scribes had been commanded to call themselves and to write Austerus, instead of Severus, out of respect for the Emperor Septimius Severus. The business-like First August Emperor, himself, evidently had no hand in the pedantic King and Ts'u tabu business, for one of his first general orders when he became Supreme Emperor in 221 B.C., was to proclaim that "in ancient times there were no posthumous names, and they are hereby suppressed. I am Emperor the First. My successor will simply be Emperor the Second, and so on for ever." There is no clear record of posthumous names and titles anterior to the Chou dynasty; the first certain instance is the father of the founder, whose personal name was Ch'ang, and who had been generally known as the "Earl of the West." His son, the founder, made him W&n Wang, or the "Civilian King," posthumously. In the same way the Duke of Chou, a son of the Civilian King, made his brother the founder, personally called Fah, Wu Wang, or the "Warrior King." The same Duke of Chou (the first ruler of Lu, and Confucius' model in all things) was the virtual founder of the Chou administrative system in general, and also of the posthumous name rules which were "intended to punish the bad and encourage the good"; but counsellors have naturally always been very gingerly and roundabout in wounding royal family feeling by selecting too harsh a "punishing" name.

Not only royal and princely personages had posthumous names. In 817 and 796 B.C., each, we find a counsellor of the Emperor spoken of both by the real and the posthumous name. In 542 B.C. a concubine of one of the Lu rulers is spoken of by her clan-name and her posthumous name. In 560 B.C. the dying King of Ts'u modestly alludes to the choice of an inferior posthumous name befitting him and his poor talents, for use at the times of biennial sacrifice to his manes, and adds: "I am now going to take my place á la suite, in company with my ancestors in the temple."

Persons of the same clan-name could not properly intermarry. Thus the Emperor Muh, who is supposed to have travelled to Turkestan in the tenth century B.C., had a mysterious liaison during his expedition with a beauteous Miss Ki (i.e. a girl of his own clan), who died on the way. The only way tolerant posterity can make a shift to defend this "incest," is by supposing that in those times the names of relatives were "arranged differently." However, the mere fact that the funeral ceremonies were carried out with full imperial Chou ritual, and that incest is mentioned at all, seems to militate against the view (noticed in Chapter XIII.) that it was Duke Muh of Ts'in who (400 years later) undertook this journey, for he did not belong to the Ki family at all.

Curiously enough, it fell to the lot of the son and successor of the Emperor Muh to have to punish and destroy a petty vassal state whose ruler had committed the incestuous act of marrying three sisters of his own clan-name. In 483 B.C. the ruler of Lu also committed an indiscretion by marrying a Ki girl. As her clan-name must, according to rule, be mentioned at her burial, she was not formally buried at all, but the whole affair was hushed up, and she was called by the fancy name of Mêng-tsz (exactly the same characters as "Mencius"),

Another instance serves to illustrate the above-mentioned imperial journey west, and the fief questions jointly. When the Emperor Muh went west, he was served as charioteer by one of the ancestors of the future Ts'in principality, who for his services was enfeoffed at Chao (north of Shan Si province). Chao was one of the three states into which Tsin broke up in 403 B.C., and was very Tartar in its sympathies. Thus, as both Ts'in and Chao bore the same original clan-name of Ying, granted to the Ts'in family as possessions of the Ts'in fief (Eastern Kan Suh province) by the early Chou emperors in 870 B.C., Ts'in is often spoken of as having the sub-clan-name of Chao. These facts, again, all militate against the theory that it was Duke Muh of Ts'in who made the voyage of discovery usually attributed to the Chou Emperor Muh; for Duke Muh's lineal ancestor, ancestor also of the original Ts'in Ying, himself acted as guide in Tartary to the Emperor Muh. The First August Emperor, who was, as already stated, really a bastard, was borne by the concubine of a Chao merchant, who made over the concubine whilst enceinte to his (the Emperor's) father, when that father was a royal Ts'in hostage dwelling in the state of Chao; hence the Emperor is often called Chao CHÊNG (CHÊNG being his personal name). He had thus a double claim to the family name of Chao, first because—granting his legitimacy—his Ts'in ancestor (also the ancestor of all the Chao family) was, during the ninth century B.C., enfeoffed in Chao; and secondly because, when Chao became an independent kingdom, he was, during the third century B.C., himself born in Chao to a Chao man of a Chao woman.

A great deal more might of course be said upon the subject of names, and of their effect in sometimes obscuring, sometimes elucidating, historical facts; but these few remarks will perhaps suffice, at least, to suggest the importance of scrutinizing closely the possible bearing of each name upon the political events connected with it.

CHAPTER XXXIV.EUNUCHS, HUMAN SACRIFICES, FOOD

Mention has been made of eunuchs, a class which seems to have originated with the law's severity rather than from a callous desire of the rich to secure a craven and helpless medium and means for pandering to and enjoying the pleasures of the harem without fear of sexual intrigue. Criminals whose feet were cut off were usually employed as park-keepers simply because there could be no inclination on their part to gad about and chase the game. Those who lost their noses were employed as isolated frontier pickets, where no boys could jeer at them, and where they could better survive their misfortune in quiet resignation. Those branded in the face were made gate-keepers, so that their livelihood was perpetually marked out for them. It is sufficiently obvious why the castrated were specially charged with the duty of serving females in a menial capacity. One name for eunuch is "cleanse man," and it is explained by a very old commentator that the duty of these functionaries was to sweep and cleanse the court; but it is perhaps as likely that the original idea was really "purified man," or man deprived of incentive to certain evils. It is often said disparagingly of the Chou dynasty that they introduced the effeminate Persian custom of keeping eunuchs; but the Chou family, which was in full career before Zoroaster existed, is perhaps entitled to a much greater antiquity in civilization than Persia—Cyrus himself was a contemporary of Lao- tsz and Confucius—and probably the castrated were only utilized as menials because they already were eunuchs by law, and were not made eunuchs against the spirit of natural law simply in order that their services as menials should be conveniently rendered. In 655 B.C. the Tsin ruler despatched a eunuch to try and assassinate his half-brother (the future Second Protector of China) when in Tartar exile. When the Second Protector in 636 at last came to his rights as ruler of Tsin, the same eunuch offered to commit an assassination in his interest; arguing, by way of justifying his previous attempt, that a servant's duty was to serve his de facto master for the time being, and not to question de jure claims, which were a matter beyond the competence of a menial. In 548 the ruler of Ts'i was assassinated by a eunuch who would not even grant his master permission to commit suicide decently in the ancestral hall; (see p. 62). A year later, the succeeding ruler under urgent circumstances secured the services of a eunuch as coachman. In contrast to these traitors, in 481 a faithful eunuch tries to save the ruler of Ts'i from assassination by one of the supplanting great families: this was the case that so horrified Confucius that he died soon after, in despair of ever seeing "divine right" regain the upper hand in China. In 544 B.C. the ruler of Wei was assassinated by a eunuch door-keeper. In 537 the King of Ts'u conceived the idea of castrating and cutting the feet off the two Tsin envoys for use as a palace gate-keeper and for service in his harem; but he was prudently dissuaded by his chief counsellor from incurring the risks consequent upon such an international outrage; (see p. 46). Three centuries later, in the year 239, the First August Emperor's (real) father, for his own spying purposes, got a sham eunuch appointed to a post in the service of the ex-concubine made over, as explained in the last chapter, to the First Emperor's father; by the dowager-queen, as she then was, the supposed eunuch had two sons. When subsequently this dangerous person revolted, the First August Emperor's own real eunuchs took part in opposing his murderous designs.—It must be mentioned that this objectionable father of the Emperor was himself a very distinguished man notwithstanding, and has left a valuable historical and philosophical work of twenty-six chapters behind him, put together under his direction by a number of clever writers. It is usually considered a Taoist work, because it savours in parts of Lao-tsz's doctrine; but, like the works of Hwai-nan-tsz (an imperial prince of the Han dynasty 150 years later) it was classified in 50 B. C. as a "miscellany."—Finally, a eunuch played an important part as witness when the Second August Emperor was assassinated. Thus all the states—those around the original nucleus of Old China at least—employed eunuchs in the royal harems, even if the vassal princes of orthodox China as a general rule did not.

It is much the same thing with another disagreeable feature in the manners of those times— human sacrifices. Many instances have already been given of such practices in the state of Ts'in. The tomb of the King of Ts'u who died in 591—of that king whose death Confucius condescended to record, decently and in ritual terms, because of his many good qualities—which tomb appears to be still in existence near King-chou Fu, is surrounded by ten other smaller tombs, supposed so be those of the persons who "followed him to the grave." At all events, when in the year 529 a later king of Ts'u hanged himself, a faithful follower buried two of his own daughters with the royal body. In A. D. 312 the tomb of the first Protector, who died in 643 B.C., was opened under circumstances so graphically described that there can scarcely be a doubt of the substantial truth: the stench was so great that dogs had to be sent in first to test the effects of the poisoned atmosphere; so many bones were found lying about that there can be little doubt many women and concubines were buried with him. It is often said by modern writers that it was a general custom to do so all over ancient China, and possibly the fact that in the second century B.C. a humane Chinese emperor (of Taoist principles) ordered the discontinuance of the practice may be thought to give colour to this supposition. But it must be remembered that the great house of Han had only then recently overthrown the dynasty of Ts'in, and had incorporated nearly the whole of China as we now view it: the Emperor would naturally therefore be referring to Ts'i, Ts'in, Ts'u, and possibly also to Wu and Yüeh, three of which states had, as we see, once practised this cruel custom.

Wine, or rather spirit, was known everywhere; in Confucian times the Far West had not yet been discovered, and there were neither grapes nor any names for grapes; no grape wine, nor any other fruit wine. Even now, though the Peking grapes are as good as English grapes, no one nearer than Shan Shi makes wine from them. Spirits seem to have been served from remote times at the imperial and princely feasts. Here, once more, as with the two vicious practices described, the drunkards appear to be found more among those peoples surrounding orthodox China than in the ancient nucleus. In 694 B.C., when the ruler of Lu was on a visit to his brother-in-law, the ruler of Ts'i, whose sister he had married, brother and sister had incestuous intercourse; which being detected, the ruler of Ts'i made his Lu brother-in-law drunk, and suborned a powerful ruffian to squeeze his ribs as he was assisted into his chariot. Thus the Duke Hwan of Lu perished. In 640 B.C., as we have seen, when the future Second Protector was dallying with his Ts'i wife, it was found by his henchman necessary to make him drunk in order to get him away. In 574 a Ts'u general was found drunk when sent for by his king to explain a defeat by Tsin troops. In 560 the Ts'u envoy—the philosopher Yen-tsz—was entertained by the Ts'u court at a wine. In 531 the ruler of Ts'u first made drunk, and then killed, one of the petty rulers of orthodox China. In 537 it had already been explained to the King of Ts'u that on the occasions of the triennial visits of vassals to the Emperor (probably only theoretical visits at that date) wine was served at long tables in full cups, but was only drunk at the proper ritualistic moment. Two years after that the King of Ts'u was described as being at his wine, and therefore in the proper frame of mind to listen to representations.

In 541 the Ts'u envoy was entertained at a punch d'honneur by the Tsin statesmen, one of whom seized the occasion to chant one of the Odes warning people against drunkenness. It is well known that Confucius enjoyed his dram; indeed, it is said of him: "As to wine, he had no measure, but he did not fuddle himself." In the year 506 the ruler of Ts'in is described as being a heavy drinker. In 489 a Ts'i councillor is described as being drunk. A few years later the ruler of Ts'i and his wife are seen drinking together on the verandah, and some prisoners escape owing to the gaoler having been judiciously plied with drink.

Meat seems to have been much more generally consumed in old China (by those who could afford it) than in modern times; and, as we might expect, among the Tartar infected people, horse-flesh in particular. In the second century B.C. the question of eating horse-liver is compared by a witty Emperor with the danger of revolutionary talk. He said: "We may like it, but it is dangerous." (Last year, when in Neu Brandenburg, I came across a man whose brother was a horse-butcher in Pomerania, and, remembering this imperial remark, I asked about horse-liver. The man said he always had a feast of horse-liver when he visited his brother, and that he much preferred it to cows' liver, or to any other part of the horse; but, he added, "you must be careful about eating it in summer.") In 645 Duke Muh of Ts'in was rescued from the Tsin troops by what was described to him as a body-guard of horse-flesh eaters. It appeared, when he sought for explanation, that the same Ts'in ruler had, some time before, been robbed of a horse by some "wild men," who proceeded to cut it up and eat it. They were arrested; but the magnanimous duke said: "I am told horse-flesh needs spirits to make it digest well," and, instead of punishing them, he gave them a keg of liquor, adding: "no sage would ever injure men on account of a mere beast.", He had forgotten the circumstance, but it now transpired that these men had, out of gratitude, since then enlisted as soldiers. This story is the more interesting as it proves how incompletely civilized the neighbourhood of Ts'in then was.—Bears' paws are often spoken of as a favourite dish. In 626 the King of Ts'u, about to be murdered by his son and successor, said: "At least, let me have a bear's paw supper before I die." But it takes many hours to cook this dish to a turn, and the son easily saw through the paternal manoeuvre, pleaded only to gain time. It may be here mentioned, too, that Ts'u made regular use of elephants in battle, which circumstance is another piece of testimony in favour of the Annamese connection of Ts'u. In the Rites of Chou, supposed to be the work of the Duke of Chou, mention is made of ivory as one of the products of the "Jungle province," as then called. In modern times Annam has regularly supplied the Peking Government with elephants, the skin of which is eaten as a tonic. After the annihilation of Wu by Yiieh, the cunning Chinese adviser of Yiieh decided to retire with his fortune to Ts'i, on the ground that the "good sleuth-hound, when there is no more work for him, is apt to find his way to the cooking-pot." Dogs (fed up for the purpose) are still eaten in some parts of China, and (as we shall soon see) they were eaten in ancient Yiieh.

CHAPTER XXXV. KNOWLEDGE OF THE WEST

The question of the expedition of the Emperor Muh to the West in the year 984 B.C., or during that year and the two following, is worthy of further consideration for many reasons; and after all that has been said about the rise of the Chou dynasty, the decay of the patriarchal system, the emulous ambitions of the vassals, the destruction of the feudal Empire, and the substitution of a centralized administration under a new dynasty of numbered August Emperors, it will now be comparatively easier to understand.

We have seen that, if any local annals besides those of Lu have been in part preserved, those of Ts'in at least were deliberately intended by the First August Emperor to be wholly preserved, and must therefore hold first rank among all the restored vassal annals published by Sz-ma Ts'ien in or about 90 B.C.; and it must be remembered that the original Lu annals have perished equally with those of Ts'i, Sung, and other important states; it is only Confucius' "Springs and Autumns,"—evidently composed from the Lu archives,—that have survived. Well, the Ts'in Annals, as given by Sz-ma Ts'ien, record that one of the early Ts'in ancestors "was in favour with the Emperor Muh on account of his admirable skill in manipulating horses" [names of four particularly fine horses given]. The Emperor "went west to examine his fiefs"; he was so "charmed with his experiences that he forgot the administrative duties which should have called him back." Meanwhile, a revolt broke out in East (uncivilized) China, and the manipulator of horses was sent by the Emperor back to China at express speed, in order to stave off trouble till the Emperor could get back himself. It is also stated of him that, in spite of remonstrances, he made extensive war upon the Tartars, and that, in consequence, his uncivilized vassals ceased to present themselves at court. No other mention is made of this expedition by Sz-ma Ts'ien in the imperial annals, and, so (apart from the fictitious importance afterwards given to the expedition, and especially by European investigators in quite recent times), there is really no reason to attach any more political weight to it than to the other innumerable exploring expeditions of emperors into the almost unknown regions surrounding the nucleus of orthodox China so often defined in these chapters. We have already (page 184) cited the case in which the father and predecessor of King Muh had ventured on a tour of inspection as far as modern Hankow on the Yang-tsz River, or, as some say, as far as some place on the River Han, where he was murdered; in 656 the First Protector raked up this affair against Ts'u, whose capital was very near King-thou Fu, above Hankow. Finally, scant though Sz-ma Ts'ien's two references to this affair may be, they at least agree with each other, i.e. the Emperor did actually go to Tartar regions, and a revolt of non-Chinese tribes did actually break out in the immediate sequel.

But in A.D. 281 a certain tomb at a place once belonging to Wei, but later attached to the kingdom of Ngwei formerly part of Tsin, was desecrated by thieves, and, amongst other books written in ancient characters found therein (unfortunately all more or less injured by the rummaging thieves), were two of paramount interest. One was an account of, and was entirely devoted to, the Emperor Muh's voyage to the West; the other was the Annals of Ngwei (i.e. of that third part of old Tsin which in 403 B.C. was formally recognized by the Emperor as the separate state of Ngwei), including those of old Tsin, and also what may be termed the general history of China, narrated incidentally. These Annals of Tsin or Ngwei are usually styled the Bamboo Books, because they were written in ink on bamboo tablets strung together at one end like a fan or a narrow Venetian blind. They also speak shortly of the Emperor Muh's expedition, and thus they also are useful for comparing hiatuses, names, faults, and dates; both in general history, and in the account of King Muh's expedition. Since the discovery of these old documents (which had been buried for well- nigh 600 years, and of which no other record whatever had been preserved either in writing or by tradition), Chinese literary wonder-mongers have exercised their wits upon the task of identifying the unheard-of places mentioned; the more so in that one place, and one king bearing the same foreign name as the place—Siwangmu—was so written phonetically that it might mean "Western-King-Mother." They endeavoured to show how this and other places might have lain in relation to the genuine places discovered by Chinese generals after these ancient documents were buried, seven centuries after the events recorded therein. Then came the foreigner with his Jewish Creation, Confusion of Tongues, Accadian and Babylonian origin of all science, etc., etc. Of course Marco Polo's adventures at once suggested to the European, thus biased, that 3000 years ago the Emperor Muh might have found his way to Persia, and might have been this or that Babylonian, Egyptian, or Persian hero; in fact, Professor Forke of Berlin even takes his Chinese majesty as far as Africa, and introduces him to the Queen of Sheba (= Western-King-Mother).

The distinguished Professor Edouard Chavannes of Paris has recently attempted to show, not only that the Emperor Muh never got beyond the Tarim (which, indeed, is absolutely certain from the text itself), but that it was not the Emperor Muh at all who went, but the semi-Turkish Duke Muh of Ts'in, in the seventh century B.C., who made the expedition.

To begin with, let us see what the expedition purports to be. In the first place, the thieves used as torches, or otherwise destroyed, the first few pages of the bamboo sheaf book, and we do not know, consequently, whence the Emperor started: there is much indirect evidence, however, to show that he started from some place on the headwaters of the Han River, in what must then have been his own territory (South Shen Si); especially as his three expeditions all ended there. It is certain, however, that he had not travelled many days on his first journey before he reached a tribe of Tartars very frequently mentioned in all histories, and bearing the same name as the Tartars whom Sz-ma Ts'ien says the Emperor Muh did conquer. He crossed the Yellow River on the 169th day, came to two rivers, the Redwater (222nd day), and the Blackwater (248th day), which rivers in after ages have been frequently mentioned in connection with Tibetan, Turkish, and Ouigour wars, and are apparently in the Si-ning and Kan-chou Fu, or possibly Kwa Chou regions (cf. p. 68); but first he passed, after the 170th day, a place called "Piled Stones," a name which has never been lost to history, and which corresponds to Nien-po, between Lan-thou Fu and Si-ning, as marked on modern maps. In other words, he went by the only high-road there was in existence, and ever since then has continued in existence (just traversed by Bruce), leading to the Lob Nor region; whence again he branched off, presumably to Turfan, or to Harashar; thence to Urumtsi, and possibly Kuché, as they are respectively now called; but on the whole it is not likely that he got beyond Harashar and Urumtsi. Even 800 years later, when the Chinese had thoroughly explored all the west up to the Hindu Kush, their expeditions had all to proceed from Lob Nor to Khoten, or from Lob Nor (or near it) viâ Harashar and Kuché along the Tarim Valley: it was not for long after the discovery of these routes that the later Chinese discovered the northerly Hami route, and the possibility of avoiding Lob Nor altogether. His charioteer is said in this account to have been a man (named) whose name is exactly the name, written in exactly the same way, as the name of the ancestor of Ts'in, who, Sz-ma Ts'ien tells us, actually was the charioteer of the Emperor when he marched forth against the Tartars, and who hurried back to China when the revolts broke out owing to the Emperor's absence. As the Emperor received, from various princes, presents of wine, silk, and rice, it is almost certain that he must have avoided bleak, out-of-the-way places, and have made for the productive regions of Harashar, Turfan, and possibly Kuché, any or all three of these. With a little more care and patience we may yet succeed in identifying, and by the same names, several more of the places mentioned by the old chronicler. In about ten months (286 days from the first day already mentioned, and 17 days out from "Piled Stones") he reached Siwangmu. This is not at all unlikely to be Urumtsi, or a place near it, possibly Ku- CH'ÊNg or Gutchen, because Siwangmu (also the name of the king of that place), gave him a feast on a certain lake, which lake, written in exactly the same way, became the name of a quite new district in 653 A.D., when it was abolished; and that district was at or near Urumtsi; the presumption being that, in the seventh century A.D., it was so named on account of old traditions, then well known. Roughly speaking, it took the Emperor 300 days to go, and a second 300 to get back; stoppages, feasts, functions, all included. The total distance travelled, as specified from chief station to chief station, is 13,300 li (say 4000 miles) to Siwangmu and to the hunting grounds near but beyond it. When 200 days out he came to the place where his feet were washed with kumiss; this place is frequently mentioned in history; even Confucius names it, as one of the northernmost conquests of the Chou dynasty. The only doubt is whether it is near Lan-thou Fu in Kan Suh province, or near the northern bend of the Yellow River. The journey back was hurried and shorter (as we might well suppose from Sz-ma Ts'ien's accounts above given), that is to say, only 10,000 li. But the total for the whole double journey of 660 days in all, including all by-trips, excursions, and hunts, was 38,000 li, or about 12,000 miles—say 20 miles a day. I have myself travelled several thousand miles in China and Tartary, always at the maximum rate of 30 miles a day; more usually 20, allowing for delays, bad roads, and accidents. In Dr. Legge's translation of the "Book of Odes," p. 281, there is a song about a great expedition against the Tartars in 827 B.C., one line of which is precisely, as translated by Dr. Legge: "and we marched thirty li every day,"-which means only ten miles. This is the chief journey; and whether the Chou Emperor in 984 B.C., or the Ts'in Duke in 650 B.C., made it, there are really no difficulties, no contradictions. Four important places at least are named which are known by exactly the same names, and are frequently mentioned, in very much later history. The Emperor had hundreds of carts or chariots with him, and we have seen that these were a special feature of orthodox China. He came across a huge moulting-ground of birds in the desert regions, and the later Chinese very frequently speak of it in Tartar-land. Being caught in the waterless desert, he had to cut the throats of some of his best horses and drink their warm blood: two friends of my own, travelling through Siberia and Mongolia, were only too glad, when nearly starving from cold, to cut a sheep's throat and drink its warm blood from the newly-gashed throat itself. Fattening up horses for food is mentioned, and washing the feet with kumiss— both incidents purely Tartar. "Cattle," distinct from horses and oxen, are alluded to— probably camels, for which no Chinese word existed until about the time of our era.

The second and third journeys, which occupied another 600 days between them, both ended at, and therefore it is assumed began at, the same place as the first journey's terminus; that is, at a place marked on modern maps as Pao-CH'ÊNg, on the Upper Han River. In later times it belonged to the semi-Chinese kingdoms of Shuh and Ts'u in turn. One of these narratives is taken up with a description of the Emperor's infatuation for a clever wizard from a far country, and of his liaison with a girl bearing his own clan-name, who died about two months before he reached home, and was buried on the road with great pomp. These two later journeys have no geographical value at all; but as the Emperor in each case again crossed the Yellow River, it is plain that he was amusing himself somewhere along the main Tartar roads, as in the first case. It may be added that the Taoist author Lieh-tsz, in his third chapter, repeats the story of the magician, who, he says, came from the "Extreme West Country." He also explains that it was through listening to this man's wonderful tales that the Emperor "neglected state affairs, and abandoned himself to the delights of travel,"—thus anticipating by three centuries the language of Sz- ma Ts'ien in 90 B.C. The story of the particular tribe of Tartars (named with the same sounds, but not with the same characters) who washed the Emperor's feet with kumiss is also told by Lieh-tsz. The position of the Redwater River is defined, to which textual remarks the commentators add more about the River Blackwater. Curiously enough, in himself commenting upon the Emperor Muh's conversations with the chieftain of Siwangmu, Lieh-tsz mentions the traditional departure, west, of the philosopher Lao-tsz, his own master.

Now, although there is considerable doubt as to the authorship, date, and genuineness of Lieh-tsz's book, which at any rate was well known to Chinese bibliophiles long before our era, the fact that it mentions and repeats even part of the Emperor Muh's travels 600 years before the ancient book describing those travels was found, proves that the manipulators of the ancient book thus found did not invent the whole story after our era. It also seems to prove that in Lieh-tsz's time (i.e. immediately after Confucius) the story was already known (and probably the book of travels too), Confucius himself having mentioned one of the tribes visited by the Emperor. The Bamboo Books bring history down to 299 B.C., and were found, together with the travels of the Emperor Muh, in A.D. 281. The Bamboo Books not only support part of the story of the Emperor Muh's travels, but their accuracy in dates has been shown by Professor Chavannes to strengthen the credibility of Confucius' own history: a reference to Chapter XXXII. on the Calendar will explain what is meant by "accuracy in dates." Finally, we have Sz-ma Ts'ien's history of go B.C., citing the Chou Annals and the Ts'in Annals, or what survived of them after incessant wars between 400 and 200 B.C., and after the destruction of literature in 213 B.C.

This point settled, the next thing is to consider Professor Chavannes' reasons for supposing that Duke Muh of Ts'in (650 B.C.) and not the Emperor Muh of Chou (984 B.C.) was the real traveller:—

1. He shows that the ruling princes of Ts'in and Chao hailed from the same ancestors, were contiguous states, and, besides being largely Tartar themselves, ruled all the Tartars along the (present) Great Wall line: also that the naming of individual horses and other features of the Emperor's travels recalls features equally prominent in later Turkish history. This is all undoubtedly true: compare page 206.

2. He shows that the Duke Muh's chief claim to glory was his successes against the Tartars of the West. This is also quite certain. 3. He thinks that in 984 B.C. the literary capacity of China was not equal to the composition of such a sustained work as the Travels.

4. He also thinks that the real Chinese found in Ts'in the traditions relating to Duke Muh, and then, for the glory of China, appropriated them to the Emperor Muh, and foisted them upon orthodox history.

There is a great deal to be said for this view, which has, besides, many other minor points of detail in its favour. But it may be answered:—

1. Chou itself was in the eyes of China proper, once a "barbarian" tribe of the west, as the founder of the Chou dynasty in 1122 B.C. himself showed when he addressed his neighbours and allies, the eight other states of the west, and exhorted them, as equals, to assist him in the conquest of China. It was only in 771 B.C. that the original Chou appanage (since 1122 the western half of the imperial appanage) had been ceded to Ts'in, which in 984 was a petty state, still of the "adjunct-function" (cf. page 144) type, and not "sovereign." In 984 there was no intermediate sovereign "power" between the Emperor and the Tartars, with whom, in fact, he had been directly engaged in war independently of Ts'in. He was as much under Tartar social influences as was Ts'in: in fact, the Chou principality, under the Shang dynasty, was a sort of first edition of Ts'in principality under the Chou dynasty. Just as in 1122 B.C. Chou ousted Shang as the imperial house, so in 221 B.C. Ts'in definitely replaced Chou.

2. If Duke Muh distinguished himself by Tartar conquests, so did the Emperor Muh before him, and the authorities are all agreed on this point.

3. If in 984 B.C. the long-standing orthodox Chinese literary capacity was unequal to this effort, how is it that semi-barbarous Ts'in, the least literary of all the states (not only Chinese, but also half-Chinese), into which state records had only been introduced at all in 753 B.C., was able to compose such a book; or, if not to write the book, then to dictate so sustained and connected a story? Besides, the Emperor Muh left several inscriptions carved on stone during the progress of his travels.

4. The instances M. Chavannes cites of the tombs of Yü and Shun in South China, as being parallel instances of appropriation by orthodox Chinese of semi-Chinese traditions have already been put to quite another use above, as tending to show, on the contrary, that those two Emperors either came from the south, or had ancestral traditions in the south; (see pp. 138,191).

5. Finally, about a third of the Travels is taken up with a description of the incestuous intrigue with Lady Ki, and of her sumptuous ritual funeral. Why should Duke Muh trouble himself about the rites due to members of the Ki family, to which the Emperor belonged, but he himself did not? Why should the warlike Duke Muh (who had just then been recommended by an adviser (an ex- Chinese, since become a Tartar) to adopt simple Tartar ways instead of worrying himself with the Odes and the Book "as the Chinese did") waste his time in pomp and ritual? (see p. 180). Again, when, as the Travels tell us, various vassal rulers from orthodox China (even so far as Shan Tung in the extreme east) arrived to pay their respects to the Emperor as their liege-lord, how is it possible to suppose that these orthodox counts and barons would come to pay court to a semi-barbarian count (for that was all he was) like Duke Muh (as he is posthumously called), one of their equals, a man who took no part in the durbar affairs, and who, on account of his human sacrifices, was not even thought fit to become an emergency Protector of China? What could the semi- Tartar ruler of Ts'in have known of all these wearisome refinements in pomp, mourning, and music? Once more, the place the Emperor started from and came back to, though part of his appanage in 984 B.C. and possessing an ancestral Chou temple, was not part of the Ts'in dominions in 650 B.C., and never possessed a Ts'in temple: if not independent, it was at that time a bone of contention between Ts'in and Ts'u, and by no means a safe place for equipping pleasure expeditions. Finally, if it is marvellous that the Chou Annals of Sz-ma Ts'ien do not

give full details of the voyage, is it not at least equally marvellous that the Ts'in Annals should not mention it in 650 B.C., when M. Chavannes supposes it took place, whilst they do so mention it under 984 B.C., when he thinks it did not take place? All accounts agree that the ancestor of Ts'in (named) was there with the Emperor as charioteer; he was, as we have seen, equally ancestor of Chao, and the Chao Annals of Sz-ma Ts'ien say exactly what the Ts'in Annals say.

Hence we may gratefully accept Professor Chavannes' most illuminating proofs, so far as they tend to show that the Travels of the Emperor Muh are genuine history for a tour no farther than the middle Tarim Valley; but, so far as Duke Muh of Ts'in is concerned, he must be eliminated from all consideration of the matter, and we must ascribe the tour, as the Chinese do, to the Emperor Muh. Lastly, are there any proved instances of such radical tamperings with history by the Chinese annalists as M. Chavannes suggests? I do not know of any; and such superficial tamperings as there are the Chinese critics always expose, coûte que coûte, even though Confucius himself be the tamperer.

CHAPTER XXXVI.ANCIENT JAPAN

The development of China is not only elucidated by documents and events probably antecedent to the strictly historical period, such as the supposed voyage of an Emperor to the Far West, but it is also made easier to understand when we consider its possible indirect effects upon Japan. The barbarian kingdom of Wu does not really appear in Chinese history at all, even by name, until the year 585 B.C. It was found then that it had traditions of its own, and a line of kings extending back to the beginning of the Chou dynasty (1122 B.C.), and even farther beyond. In 585 B.C. the new King, Shou-mêng, hitherto an unknown and obscure vassal of Ts'u, altogether beyond the ken of orthodox China, felt quite strong enough, as we have seen in Chapter VII., to strike out an independent line of his own. It is a singular thing that, when the Japanese set about constructing a nomenclature (on Chinese posthumous lines) for their newly discovered back history in the eighth century A.D., they should have fixed upon exactly this year 585 B.C. for the death of their supposed first Mikado Jimmu (i.e. Shên-wu, the "divinely martial"). The next three Kings of Wu, all of whom, like himself, bore dissyllabic and meaningless barbarian names, were sons of Shou-mêng, and a fourth son was the cultured Ki-chah, who visited orthodox China several times, both as a spy and in order to improve himself. Then follow two sons of the last and first, respectively, of the said three brothers. The second of these royal cousins was killed in battle, and his son Fu-ch'ai vowed a terrible, vengeance against Ts'u, whose capital he subsequently took and sacked in 506 B.C. Now appears upon the scene his own vassal, Yiieh, and at first Wu gets the best of it in battle. Bloodthirsty wars follow between the two, full of picturesque and convincing detail, until at last the King of Yiieh, in turn, has the King of Wu at his mercy; but he was, though a barbarian, magnanimously disposed, and accordingly he offered Fu-ch'ai the island of Chusan (so well known to us on account of our troops having occupied it in 1840) and three hundred married families to keep him company. But Fu-ch'ai was too proud to accept this Elba, the more especially so because he had it on his conscience that he had been acting throughout against the earnest advice of his faithful minister (a Ts'u renegade), whom he had put to death for his frankness. This adviser as he perished had cried out: "Don't forget to pluck my eyes out and stick them on the east gate, so that I may witness the entry of the Yiieh troops!" He therefore committed suicide, first veiling his face because, as he said: "I have no face to offer my adviser when I meet him in the next world; if, on the other hand, the dead have no knowledge, then it does not matter what I do." After the beginning of our Christian era, when the direct communication between Japan (overland viâ Corea) and China (also by sea to Wu) was first officially noticed by the historians, it was recorded by the Chinese annalists that part of Fu-ch'ai's personal following had escaped in ships towards the east, and had founded a state in Japan. But it must not be forgotten that then (473 B.C.) orthodox China had never yet heard of Japan in any form, though of course it is possible that the maritime states of Wu and Yiieh may have had junk intercourse with many islands in the Pacific.

We have already ventured upon a few remarks upon this subject in Chapter XXIII., but so much is apt to be made out of slight historical materials-such, for instance, as the pleasure expedition of a Chinese emperor in 984 B.C. to the Tarim Valley— that it may be useful to suggest the true proportions, and the modest possible bearing of this "Japanese" migration—assuming the slender record of it to be true; and the basis of truth is by no means a broad one; still less is it capable of sustaining a heavy superstructure.

Any one visiting Japan will notice that there are several distinct types of men in that country, the squat and vulgar, the oval-faced and refined, and many variations of these two; just as, in England, we have the Norman, Saxon, Irish, and Scotch types of face, with many other nuances. It is also clear from the kitchen-midden and other prehistoric remains; from the presence, even now, in Japan of the bearded Ainus (a word meaning in their own language "men"); and from the numerous accounts of Ainu- Japanese wars in both Chinese and Japanese history, that there were (as there still are) manners, and possibly yet other men, in ancient Japan, both very different from the manners and appearance of the cultured and gifted race, viewed as a homogeneous whole, we are now so proud to have as our political allies. But that brings us no nearer a historical solution, It is a persistent way with all ethnologists to search out whence this or that race came. Of course all races move and mingle, and must always have moved and mingled, when by so doing they could better their circumstances of life; but even if movement has taken place in Japan as it has elsewhere, there is no reason why, if comparatively uncivilized Japanese displaced Ainus, Ainus should not have, before that, displaced quite uncivilized Japanese; or, if other races came over the seas to displace the people already there, the natives already there should not have, later on, ejected these new-comers by sea routes.

In other words, it is quite futile (unless we can lay hands on definite objects, or definite facts recorded—even definite traditions) to try and account for hypothetical movements in prehistoric times. We are totally ignorant of early Teutonic, Hungarian, and Celtic movements-though, thanks solely to Chinese records, we are pretty certain, within defined limits, about early Turkish movements. How much more, then, must we be ignorant about the Japanese movements? If "people" must have come from somewhere, whence did these arrivals start, and why should they not go back; or why not meet other movers going to the place whence they themselves started? If we are to accept the only historical records or quasi-records we possess at all, that is, the Chinese records, then we must accept them for what they are worth on the face of them, and neither add to nor mutilate them; imperfect things that do exist are necessarily better than imaginary things that might have existed in their place. A few hundred families at most, we are told, escaped; and if it be true that they went intentionally to Japan, it is probable that the expert Wu sailors (none existed elsewhere in China) had already for long known the way thither, or to Quelpaert and Tsushima, which practically means to both Corea and Japan; in fact, if they sailed east from Ningpo, there is no other place to knock up against, even if the special intention were not there. Everything tends to show that Fu-ch'ai, though perhaps a barbarian in 473 B.C., was of orthodox if remote pedigree dating from 1200 B.C., and that the ruling class of Wu was very different from the "barbarians" by whom (as we are specifically told) Wu was surrounded; the situation was like that of the Egyptians and Phoenicians, like Cecrops and Cadmus, amongst the earliest barbarous Greeks. It amounts, then, to this, that, just as Chinese colonies and adventurers emerged under the stress of increased population, or under the impulses of curiosity, tyranny, and ambition, to found states in Ts'u, Ts'in, Tsin, Ts'i, Lu, Wu, Yüeh, and other places round the central nucleus, so (they being the sole possessors of that magic POWER, "records") other parties would from time to time sally forth either from the same orthodox centre, or from the semi-orthodox places surrounding that centre, to still remoter spots, such as, for instance, Corea, Japan, Formosa, Annam, Burma, Tibet, and Yiin Nan. Fu-ch'ai's surviving friends had indeed a very lively stimulus indeed-the fear of instant death-to drive them tumultuously over the seas; and doubtless, as they must have been perfectly harmless after tossing about hungry in open boats for weeks together, they would be as welcome to the Japanese king, or to the petty chief or chiefs who received the waifs, as in our own times was the honest sailor Will Adams when he drifted friendless to Japan, and whose statue now adorns a great Japanese city as that of a man who was, in a humble way, also a "civilizer" of Japan (600 A.D.). Doubtless, many Wu words, or Chinese words as then pronounced in Wu, had already been brought over by fishermen; but here at last was a great haul of (possibly) books and the way to interpret them; at least there was a great haul of the best class of the Wu ruling folk. It is true that the first Japanese envoys who came to China made as much of their Wu "origin" as they could; firstly, because it probably paid them as traders to do so; secondly, because it necessarily gave them a respectable status in China; and, thirdly, because they were, in the first century of our era, gradually beginning to understand the mystic power of the Chinese written character, and they would therefore naturally take an intense interest in all records, rumours, traditions, and fables about themselves, which they would embellish and "confirm" whenever it suited their interests to do so. Which of us does not begin to furbish up his pedigree when he is made a peer of the realm?

As to the bulk of the Japanese race, be it mixed or unmixed, it is surely in the main to be found now where it always was, or close by? It is no more depreciating to early Japan to give her a dynasty of Chinese adventurers, or perhaps to give her only hereditary Chinese advisers and scribes, than it is derogatory to the states of Europe to possess dynasties which belong by their origin, as a general rule, to almost any place but the countries they now govern as sovereigns. As to the ancient chiefs or kings of Japan, some of their genuine native names may have been preserved in the memories of men; whether they were or not, they were, even without records, as "ancient" chiefs as the best recorded chiefs of Egypt, Babylonia, or China; and it must be remembered that Egyptian and Babylonian records were non-existent to us for all practical purposes during many thousands of years, until we recently discovered how to read them: that is to say, what was once no history at all—the present condition of the prehistoric races of High Asia—suddenly becomes history when we find the records and know how to read them.

When, a few centuries later on, the Japanese had begun thoroughly to understand Chinese books, they decided to have an historical outfit of their own; they took what vague traditions they had, and, in the absence of any long-forgotten genuine records, or visible remains having part of the effect of records, simply fitted on to their heroes, real or imaginary, the Chinese posthumous system, and a selection of the historical facts recorded about the Chinese. Even the Emperor Muh in China was not so named until he died. If a man can be given a complimentary title three years after death (that was the Chinese rule at first), why not give it him 300 years after his death? The king or chief hitherto known, whether accurately or not, whether honestly or not, as X, had most certainly existed; that is, the tenth great-grandfather of the reigning prince; the ninth, eighth, and so on; must positively have been there at some remote period of the past. By calling him Jimmu (a Chinese emperor had already been posthumously so called) he is none the less there than he was before he was called Jimmu, and his new title therefore does not make him less of an entity than he was before. And so on with all the other Japanese emperors who, in the eighth century A.D., were similarly provided with imaginary names. Possibly this is how the Japanese argued with themselves when they set about the task. The situation is a curious one, and perhaps unique in the world; but it does not matter much (as suggested in Chapter XXXI.) so long as we keep imagination separate from real evidence.

CHAPTER XXXVII.ETHICS

We propose to say a few words now about peculiar customs which had vogue all over or in certain parts of China; of course some of them may be traced back to the "Rites of Chou," and to what is prescribed therein; but general administrative schemes representing in general terms things as they ought to be, or as the Chou federal and feudal oligarchy would have liked them to be, do not give us such a life-like picture of ancient China as specific accounts of definite events which really did happen. Take, for instance, the peculiar formalities connected with abject surrender.

After a great defeat in 699 B.C., just when Ts'u was beginning to emerge from its narrow confines between the Han and Yang-tsz Rivers, the defeated Ts'u generals had themselves bound in fetters, or with ropes, in order to await their king's pleasure. In 654, when Ts'u had one of the small orthodox states (in the Ho Nan nucleus) at its mercy, the baron presented himself with his hands tied behind, a piece of jade in his mouth, followed by his suite in mourning, carrying his coffin. It is evident that at this date Ts'u was still "barbarous," for the king had to ask what it all meant. It was explained to him that, when the Chou founder conquered China, and mutilated the last Shang dynasty emperor, that emperor's elder brother by an inferior mother had presented himself before the founder half naked, with his hands tied behind his back, his left hand leading a ram (or goat), and his right carrying sedge for wrapping round the sacrificial victim; he was enfeoffed as Duke of Sung. In 537 the same thing happened to a later King of Ts'u in connection with another petty principality, and the king had to be reminded of the 654 precedent. Thus there must have been records of some kind in Ts'u at an early date. In 645 B.C., when the ruler of Ts'in took prisoner his brother-in- law, the ruler of Tsin, and was seriously contemplating the annexation of Tsin, together with the duty of discharging Tsin sacrifices, his own sister, with bare feet, wearing mourning, and bound with a mourning belt, intercedes successfully for her husband. In 597 B.C. the ruler of the important orthodox state of Cheng went through the form of dragging along, with the upper part of his own body uncovered, a ram or goat into the presence of the King of Ts'u. In 511, when the ruler of Lu had to fly the country and throw himself upon the generosity of Tsin, in order to escape from the dangerous machinations of the intriguing great families of Lu, the six Tsin statesmen (who were themselves at that moment, as heads of great private clans, gradually undermining their own prince's rights) sent for the arch-intriguer, and called upon him to explain his conduct. At that time Lu was coquetting between its two powerful neighbours, Tsin and Ts'i. The conspirator duly presented himself before the Areopagus of Tsin grandees, barefoot and attired in common cloth (i.e. not of silk, but of hemp), in order to explain to them the circumstances of the duke's exile: it is characteristic of the times, and also of the frankness of history, to find it added that he succeeded in bribing the grandees to give an unjust decision. When the Kings of Yüeh and Wu were in turn at each other's mercy, in 494 and 473 respectively, their envoys, in offering submission, in each case advanced to the conqueror "walking on the knees," with bust bared: this knee-walking suggests Annamese, Siamese, and possibly Japanese forms rather than Chinese. The Wu servants at dinner are said to have "waited" on their knees. The third and last August Emperor in 207 submitted to the conquering Han dynasty seated in an unadorned chariot, drawn by a white horse (with signs of mourning), carrying his seal-sash round his neck (figurative of hanging or strangling himself), and offered the seals of the Son of Heaven to the Prince of Han.

Something has already been said about the rules of succession in Ts'u and Ts'in. When the Duke of Sung just mentioned died, in 1078 B.C., he was succeeded by his younger brother because his own son was dead; this was in accordance with the Shang dynasty's ritual laws. Even the Warrior King himself, founder of the Chou dynasty, was not the eldest son of his father, the (posthumously) Civilian King; the latter had set aside the elder of the two sons; and it will be remembered that, several generations before that, two of the royal Chou brothers had voluntarily retired to colonize the Wu Jungle country, in order that their younger brother, father of the future Civilian King, might succeed to the then extremely limited vassal state of Chou. Later on, in 729, a Duke of Sung on his death-bed bequeathed the succession to his younger brother instead of to his own son, on the ground that the rule is, "son to father, younger to elder brother"—a "universal rule" approved by Mencius in later times. The younger brother in this case thrice refused the kingly crown, but at last accepted, and Confucius in his history censures the act, which, it is considered, contributed to Sung's ultimate downfall. (It must be remembered that Confucius' ancestors were themselves of royal Sung extraction.) In 652 the younger brother by the superior spouse wished, at his father's death-bed, to cede his right to the succession of Sung to his elder brother by an inferior wife; the dying father commended the spirit, but forbade the proposed sacrifice of prior right, and the elder therefore served the younger as counsellor. In 493 a Duke of Sung, irritated on account of his eldest son having left the country, nominated a younger son as successor, and after his death his wife confirmed by decree her late husband's nomination; but the younger brother firmly declined, on the ground that the rule of succession was a fixed one, and that he was unworthy to perform the sacrifices to the gods of the land and grain. It is a curious coincidence that the question of status in wives affects the present rulers of both China and Japan. Though the dowager was Empress-Mother, she always ceded the pas to the senior dowager, who had no children. And as to the Mikado's mother, who died last October, she was, it seems, never officially considered as an Empress.

In 817 B.C. the Emperor himself is censured by history for having, "contrary to rule," wished to set up as ruler of Lu a second son in preference to the elder son; he repeated the act in 796, as has already been explained in Chapter XX., when a few other instances were cited to illustrate the general rule in China. At this time the waning power of the emperors still evidently flickered. In 608, through the meddlesome political interference of Ts'i, a concubine's son succeeded to the Lu throne in preference to the legitimate wife's son; curiously enough, the legitimate wife was a Ts'i princess. The result of this irregularity was that the "three powerful families" of Lu (themselves descendants of the ruling family) grew restless, and the state began to decline. On the death of a King of Ts'u in 516, it was proposed to put on the throne, instead of the king's young son, the king's younger brother by an inferior mother, on the ground that the mother of the young son in question was the wife obtained from Ts'in by the king for marriage to his eldest son (who had since joined the king's enemies), which young lady the king had subsequently decided to marry himself. Even under this irregular and complicated family tangle, the proposed succession was disapproved by the counsellors, on the ground that irregular successions invariably produced trouble in the state. In the year 450 B.C. the ruler of Ts'i insisted, against advice, on the succession of a younger son by a favourite concubine in preference to his elder sons by superior mothers, including the first and most dignified spouse. But here, again, the powerful families intervened; one of the elder sons, who had fled to Lu, was brought back secretly in a sack; the wrongful successor was murdered, and the "powerful family" which took the lead in state affairs soon afterwards, to the horror of Confucius, by intrigue and by further assassination, secured the Ts'i throne for itself. It will thus be noticed that all the great states except Ts'in had their full share of succession troubles.

There were several customs practised in warfare which are worthy of short notice. In 633 B.C. a Ts'u general, in the interests of discipline, flogged several military men, and "had the ears of others pierced by arrows, according to military regulation." In 639 this same king had sent as a present to some princesses of other states, who had congratulated him on his victory over Sung, "a pile of the enemy's left ears." As the historians express their disgust at this indelicate act, it was presumably not an orthodox practice, at all events in this particular form. In 607 there were captured from Sung 450 war-chariots and 250 soldiers; the latter had their left ears cut off; in this case the victors were CHÊNG troops, acting under Ts'u's orders, and it is presumed that CHÊNG officers cut off the ears under Ts'u's commands. A few years later two or three Ts'u generals were discussing what the ancients did when they challenged for a battle; it was decided that the best "form" was to rush up to the entrenchments, cut off an enemy's left ear, carry him away in your chariot, and rush back to your own camp. As there is a special Chinese character or pictograph for "ears cut off in battle," it thus appears that to a certain extent even the orthodox Chinese practised the "scalping" art, which was doubtless intended to furnish easy proof of claims for reward based upon prowess; in fact, even in modern official Chinese, a decapitated head is called a "head-step," an expression evidently dating from the time when a step in rank was given for each head or group of heads taken.

Rulers, whether the Emperor or vassals, faced south in the exercise of their sovereign powers. Thus, when the Duke of Chou, after the death of his brother the Martial King, acted as Regent pending the minority of the Martial King's son, his own nephew, he faced south; but he faced north once more when he resumed his status of subject. It has already been mentioned, in Chapter XX., that in 640 B.C. the state of Lu made the south gate of the Lu capital the Law Gate, because it was by the south gates that all rulers' commands emanated. In 546 a counsellor of Ts'u explained to the king how, since Tsin influence had predominated in the orthodox state of CHÊNG, this last had ceased to "face south towards its former protector." Thus, though the Emperor faces south towards the sun, and his subjects in turn face north in his honour, those subjects face their other protector in whatever direction he may lie, supposing the Emperor's protection to be inadequate. It is evidently the same principle as "bowing towards the east," and "turning towards Mecca," both of which formalities must be modified according to place. In 315 B.C., when Yen (the Peking plain) had become one of the six independent kingdoms, a usurper (to whom the King of Yen had foolishly committed full powers) "turned south" to perform acts of sovereignty in the king's name. In 700 B.C., in the orthodox state of Wei, we hear of "princes of the left and right," which is explained to mean "sons of mothers whose official place is left or right of the principal spouse." Right used to be more honourable than left in China, but left now takes precedence of right. Thus the provinces of Shan Tung and Shan Si are also called "Left of the Mountains" and "Right of the Mountains," because the Emperor faces south.

Notwithstanding, the ancient phraseology sometimes survives; for instance, "stands right of him" means "is better than he is," and "to left him" means "to prove him wrong or worse." All yamêns in China face south; there are rare exceptions, usually owing to building difficulties. Once, in the province of Kwei Chou, I was officially invited by the mandarin to take my seat on his right instead of on his left, because, as he explained, his yamên door did not face south, but west; and, he added, it was more honourable for me, as an official guest, to sit north, facing west, than to sit south, facing west. In Canton, the Viceroy used out of courtesy to sit south, facing north, and make his own interpreter sit north, facing south; the consul sat east, facing west, and the consul's interpreter sat west, facing east. But the consul could not have presumed to occupy the north seat thus given to an inferior on the principle of de minimis non curat lex; nor was the Viceroy willing to assert his "command" to a guest. In 436 the armies of Yiieh marching north through Ho Nan called the Chinese places lying to their west the "left" towns; but that was perhaps because Yiieh came marching from the south. In 221 B.C., when for the first time South China to the sea became part of the imperial dominions, the Emperor's territory was described as extending southward to the "north-facing houses." Hong Kong and Canton are just on the tropical line; but the island of Hainan, and also Tonquin, are actually in the tropics. Whether the houses there do really face north—which I have never noticed—or whether the expression is merely symbolical, I cannot say; but the idea is "to the regions where, when the sun is on the tropic, you have to turn north to see him."

A point of honour in China was not to make war on an enemy who was in mourning, but this rule seems to have been honoured in the breach as much as in the observance thereof. Two centuries before the Chou dynasty came into power, an emperor of the Shang dynasty distinguished himself by not speaking at all during the three years he occupied the mourning hut near the grave. As we have seen, the first rulers of Lu (as a Chou fief) modified existing customs, and introduced the three years' mourning rule there. In connection with a Sung funeral in 651 B.C., it is explained that the bier lay between the two front pillars, and not, as with the Chou dynasty, on the top of the west side steps; it will be remembered that Sung represented the sacrifices of the extinct Shang dynasty. That same year the future Second Protector (then a refugee among the Tartars) declined to put in a claim to the Tsin succession against his brothers "because he had not been in mourning whilst a fugitive." In 642 Sung and her allies made war on Ts'i, which was then mourning for the First Protector; by a just Nemesis the Tartars came to the rescue and saved Ts'i. In 627, after the Second Protector's death, Ts'in declared war, whilst Tsin was mourning, upon a petty orthodox principality belonging to the same clan as Tsin and the Emperor, and belonging also to the Tsin vassal system. This so enraged the new ruler of Tsin that he dyed his white mourning clothes black, so as to avenge the insult, and yet not to outrage the rites: moreover, white was unlucky in warfare: victorious over Ts'in, he then proceeded to mourn for his father, and ever after that black was adopted, by way of memento, as the national colour of Tsin. In 626 and 622 the Emperor sent high officers to represent him at Lu funerals, and to carry gems to place in deceased's mouth, "to show that he (the Emperor) had not the heart to leave the deceased unsupplied with food." In 581 the ruler of Lu, being on a visit to Tsin, was forcibly detained by Tsin, in order to swell the importance of a Tsin ruler's funeral. Lu (like the petty orthodox states of Wei, Sung, CHÊNG, etc., further south) was nearly always under the rival political constraint of either Ts'i, Tsin, or Ts'u; and this factor must accordingly also be taken into account in explaining Confucius' longing for the good old days of imperial predominance. In 572 Tsin attacked Cheng, though of the same clan as itself, whilst in mourning; but in 567 semi-barbarian Ts'u set a good example to orthodox Tsin by withdrawing its troops out of deference to a later official mourning then in force in Cheng: in 564 the King of Ts'u withdrew his armies home altogether on account of the mourning due to his own deceased mother. In 560 barbarian Wu attacked Ts'u whilst in mourning for the above king (the one who first conquered the Canton region for Ts'u); but, here again, by a just Nemesis, Wu's army was cut to pieces, and Wu's own ally, Tsin, censured her for having done such an improper thing. In 544 the prime minister of Tsin mourned for his Ts'u co-signatory of the celebrated Peace Conference Treaty of 546; and this graceful act is explained to be in accordance with the rites. In 544 Ts'u herself was in mourning, and in accordance with the terms of the Peace Conference Treaty, under which the Tsin vassals and the Ts'u vassals were to pay their respects to Ts'u and Tsin respectively—Ts'in and Ts'i, as great powers, being excused, or, rather, discreetly left alone—Ts'u put great pressure on Lu to secure the personal presence of the Lu ruler at the Ts'u funeral. The orthodox duke did not at all like this "truckling to a barbarian"; but one of his counsellors suggested behaving before the corpse as he would behave to a vassal of his own: this was done, and the unsophisticated Ts'u was none the wiser at the time, though, later on, the king discovered the pious fraud. In 514 B.C. Wu wished to attack Ts'u while, mourning, and the virtuous Ki-chah was promptly sent by Wu to sound Tsin about the facheuse situation. At a Lu funeral in 509, it was explained that the new duke could only mount the throne after the burial was over; it was added "even the Son of Heaven's commands do not run in Lu during this critical period; á fortiori is the duke not capable of transacting his own subjects' business." But long before this, when the First Protector died, in 643, his body lay for sixty-seven days in the coffin unattended, whilst his five sons were wrangling about the succession; in fact, the worms were observed crawling out of the coffin. These painful details have a powerful historical interest, for when (as mentioned on p. 209) his tomb was opened nearly 1000 years later, dogs had to be sent in ahead to test the air, as the stench was so great. In 492 an unpopular prince of Wei was in Tsin, which state had an interest in placing him on the throne. There happened to be in Tsin at that moment a scoundrel who had fled to Tsin from Lu, because he had found Confucius too strong for him in Lu; and this man suggested to Tsin that it would be a good plan to send seventy Wei men back to Wei in mourning clothes and sash, so as to make the Wei people think that the prince was dead, and thus gain an opportunity to "run him in" by surprise, and set him up as ruler. In 489, when the King of Ts'u died in the field of battle, his three brothers, all of whom had declined his offer of the throne, but one of whom had at last accepted in order to give the dying man peace, decided to conceal the king's death from the army whilst they sent for his son by a Yiieh mother, pleading that the king had been non compos mentis when he proposed an irregular succession, and that the promise made to him was, therefore, of no avail. In 485 Lu and Wu joined in an attack upon Ts'i during the latter's mourning—a particularly disgraceful political combination: no wonder Confucius was hastily sent for from the state of CH'ÊN, whither he had previously retired in disgust at the corruption of his native land. In 481 a conspiracy which was going on in Ts'i was delayed because one of the chief actors, being in mourning, could not attend to public business of any kind. In 332 B.C. Ts'i took ten towns from Yen by successfully attacking her whilst in mourning; one of the travelling diplomats and intriguers so common in China at that period insisted upon the towns being restored. This was at the exact moment when the philosopher Mencius, who seems to have also been a great political dilettante, was circulating to and fro between such monarchs as the Kings of Ts'i and Ngwei, alias Liang, as is fully explained in the still extant book of Mencius.

All the above quaint instances, novel though they may be in detail, strongly recall to us in principle our own "rules" of international law, which are always liable to unexpected "construction" according to the exigencies of war and the power wielded by the "constructor." Inter arma leges silent. As usual in these ritual matters, Ts'in is distinguished by total absence of mention.

CHAPTER XXXVIII. WOMEN AND MORALS

So far as it is possible to judge from the concrete instances in which women are mentioned, it appears that in ancient Chinese times their confinement and seclusion was neither nominally nor actively so strict as it has been in later days, and they seem to have been much more companionable to men than they have been ever since the ridiculous foot-squeezing fashion came into vogue over a thousand years ago. When the Martial King addressed his semi-barbarous western allies, as he prepared his march upon the last Shang Emperor in 1122 B.C., he observed: "The ancient proverb says the hen crows not in the morn; when she does, the house will fall"—in allusion to the interference of the debauched Emperor's favourite concubine in public affairs; and we have seen, under the heading of Law in Chapter XX., how one of the imperial statutes, proclaimed or read regularly in the vassal kingdoms, prohibited the meddling of women in public business. But, in spite of this, so far as promoting the succession rights and political interests of their own children goes, wives and concubines certainly exerted considerable influence, whether legitimate or not, in all the states. The murder of an Emperor and flight of his successor in 771 B.C. was in its inception owing to the intrigues of women about Court. A few years only after that event, we find the orthodox ruler of Wei marrying a beautiful Ts'i princess (her beauty is a matter of history, and is celebrated in the Odes, which are themselves a popular form of history); and then, because she had no children, further marrying a princess of Ch'en. This princess unfortunately lost her offspring; but her sister also enjoyed the prince's favour, and her son was, after her death, given in adoption to the first childless Ts'i wife. This son succeeded to the Wei throne, but was ultimately murdered by a younger brother born of a concubine, who was next succeeded by still another younger brother, whose queen had also been one of his father's concubines. Thus in the most orthodox states (Wei was of the imperial clan), the rites often seem not to have counted for much in practice.—This book, it must here be repeated, deals with specific recorded facts, and not with civilization as it ought to have been under the Rites of Chou.—So, even in comparatively modern China, 1500 years later, the third emperor of the T'ang dynasty married his father's concubine, and she ultimately reigned as empress in her own right, which is in itself an outrage upon the "rites."

In 694 B.C. the ruler of Lu (also of the imperial clan) married a Ts'i princess, who, as has been stated in Chapter XXXIV., not only had incestuous relations with her brother of Ts'i, but led that brother to procure the murder of her husband. In connection with this woman's further visit to Ts'i two years later, the rule is cited: "Women, when once married, should not recross the frontier." The same rule is quoted in 655 when a Lu princess, who had married a petty mesne-vassal of Lu in 670, recrossed the Lu frontier in order to visit her son in Lu.

The Second Protector, during his wanderings, we know, married first a Tartar wife and then a Ts'i wife, both of whom showed disinterested affection for him, and genuine regard for his rights to the Tsin succession, Yet the ruler of Ts'in supplied him with five more royal girls, of whom one had already been married to the Second Protector's predecessor and nephew, the Marquess of Tsin. It is but fair to the memory of this uxorious Tsin ruler to say that he only took her over under protest, and under the immediate stress of political urgencies; he ultimately made her his principal spouse at the expressed desire of his ally the Ts'in ruler. He must have later married a daughter of the Emperor too, for, after the succession of a son and grandson, another of his sons named "Black Buttocks," being the youngest, and also "son of a Chou mother," came to the throne. Thus in those troublous times the honour of imperial princesses evidently did not count for very much at the great vassal courts. The readiness of Ts'in to induce the Tsin ruler to take over his nephew's wife (being a Ts'in princess) accentuates the semi-Tartar civilization of Ts'in at least, if not of Tsin too; for both Hiung-nu (200 B.C.) and Turks (A.D. 500) had a fixed rule that a Khan successor should take over all his predecessor's women, with the single exception of his own natural mother. In the year 630 the King of Ts'u married or carried off two CHÊNG sisters (of the imperial clan). The ruler of CHÊNG had been insolent to the future Second Protector during his wanderings in the year 637, and, in order to avoid that Protector's vengeance, had been subsequently obliged to throw himself under Ts'u protection. "This ignoring of the rites by the King of Ts'u will result in his failing to secure the Protectorship," it was said. However, these princesses, though of the imperial Ki clan by marriage into it, were really daughters of a CHÊNG ruler by two separate Ts'i and Ts'u wives: moreover, previous to the accession of the Hia dynasty (in 2205 B.C.), a Chinese elective Emperor had married the two daughters of his predecessor, whose own son was unworthy to succeed: and, generally, apart from this precedent, the rule against marrying two sisters, even if it existed, seems to have been loosely applied (cf. Chapter XXXIII.).

In connection with the Cheng succession in 629, it is mentioned that "the wife's sons being all dead, X, being wisest of the secondary wives' or concubines' sons, is most eligible" (cf. Chapter XXXVII.).

Great political complications arose in connection with a clever and beautiful princess of Cheng who had had various liaisons with high personages in the state of Ch'en and elsewhere; in the end she was carried off in 589 by a treacherous Ts'u statesman to Tsin; and indirectly this adventure led to his being charged by Tsin with a mission to Wu; to the subsequent entry of Wu into the conclave of federal princes; and to the ultimate sacking of the Ts'u capital by the King of Wu in 506: it is easy to read between the lines that the Kings of Ts'u were considered unusually arbitrary and tyrannical rulers; over and over again we find that their most capable statesmen took service with powers inimical to Ts'u. In 581 the ruler of Cheng, being forcibly detained in Tsin whilst on a political visit there, was temporarily replaced in Cheng by his elder brother, born of an inferior wife.

A marriage between the two states of Sung and Lu having been arranged, the imperial clan states of Lu and Wei had certain duties to perform at the wedding, which took place in 583; and it is recorded that the latter sent "handmaids" The explanation given is a little involved, but it seems to throw some light on the marriage of sisters question. It seems that the legitimate spouse and her "left and right handmaids" were each entitled to three "cousins or younger sisters" of the same clan-name as themselves, "thus making a total of nine girls, the idea being to broaden the base of succession." Not content with this, Lu sent a special envoy to Sung the next year to "lecture" the princess. It is explained that "women at home are under the power of their father; married, under that of their husbands." Tsin also sent handmaids this year. It is further explained that "handmaids are a trifling matter, and they are only mentioned in this Lu princess case because her marriage turned out so badly." The following year Ts'i despatched handmaids, but, "being of a different clan-name, Ts'i was not ritual in doing so."

The precise functions of these paranymphs, or under-studies of wives, together with the rules governing their selection, are doubtless clearly enough described in the Rites of Chou; but we are only dealing here with concrete facts as recorded.

In 526 B.C., when Ts'in gave a princess in marriage to the Ts'u heir, the Ts'u king decided to keep her for himself (see p. 234). Only a few years before that, Ts'u had given a princess of her own in marriage to the heir-apparent of one of the petty orthodox states (imperial clan), and the reigning father had had improper relations with her, which in the end led to his murder by his son; thus Ts'u, however delinquent, had already been given a bad example by the imperial clan.

After his humiliating defeat by the King of Wu in 494 B.C., the King of Yiieh introduced a veritable Lex Julia into his dominions, in order to increase the population more quickly, and to prepare for his great revenge. Robust men were forbidden to marry old women, and old men to marry robust women. Parents were punished if girls were not married by the time they were seventeen, and if boys were not married by twenty. Enceinte women had to be placed under the care of public midwives. For every boy born, a royal bounty of two pots of wine and a dog were given: for every girl born, two pots of wine and a sucking-pig;— the dog, it is explained, being figurative of outdoor, the pig of internal economy. Triplets were to be suckled at the public expense; twins to be fed, when big enough, at the public expense. The chief wife's son must be mourned, with absence from official duty, for three years; other sons for two; and both kinds of son were to be equally buried with weeping and wailing. Orphans, and the sons of sick or poor widows, were to receive official employment. Distinguished sons were to have their apartments cleansed for them, and had to be well fed and handsomely clothed. Learned men from other states were to be officially welcomed in the ancestral temple. With reference to this curious law, which is totally un-Chinese in its startling originality, it may be mentioned that it seems to have gradually led to that laxity of morals in ancient Yiieh which is still proverbial in those parts; for, when the First August Emperor was touring over his new empire in 212 B.C., he left an inscription (still on record) at the old Yiieh capital, denouncing the "pig-like adultery" of the region, and, more especially, the remarrying of widows already in possession of children. Only a few years ago, proclamations appeared in this region denouncing the pernicious custom of forcing widows to remarry. Although Kwan-tsz is supposed to have "invented" the Babylonian woman for Ts'i, nothing is said in any ancient Chinese history about common prostitution; nor is female infanticide ever mentioned. In 502 B.C. the Lu revolutionary, already mentioned in Chapter XXXVII., who was driven to Tsin by Confucius' astute measures, had, before leaving Lu, formed a plot to murder all the sons, by wives, of the three "powerful families" who were intriguing against the ducal rights, and to put concubine sons-being creatures of his own-in their place; thus the succession principles applied not only to ruling families, but also to private houses; though, as a matter of fact, these three were all, in their origin, descended from previous ruling dukes. As explained in Chapters XII. and XXXIII., after five generations a fresh "family" is supposed to spring out of the common clan.

In spite of Wu's barbarism, the fact of its belonging, by remote origin, to the imperial clan (through its first: ruler having magnanimously migrated from Chou before Chou conquered China in 1122), made it technically incest for Lu to intermarry with Wu; thus, when in 482 B.C., a Wu princess (evidently forced for political purposes upon Lu) died, her husband, the ruler of Lu, was obliged to refrain from a public burial, as has been explained in Chapter XXXIII. on Names.

CHAPTER XXXIX.GEOGRAPHICAL KNOWLEDGE

It will have been noticed that, even in strictly historical times subsequent to 842 B.C., orthodox China was, mutatis mutandis, like orthodox Greece, a petty territory surrounded by a fringe of little-known regions, such as Macedonia, Asia Minor, Phoenicia, Egypt, and Italy; not to say distant Marseilles, and the Pillars of Hercules-all places at best very little visited except by navigators, and even then only by a few specially enterprising navigators or desperate adventurers; though later on Greek influence and Greek colonies soon began to replace the Phoenician, and to exhibit surrounding countries in a more correct and definite light.

As touches the surrounding regions of ancient China, and the knowledge of it possessed by the orthodox nucleus, such traditions as there are all point to acquaintance with the south and east rather than with the north and west. Persons who are persistently bent on bringing the earliest Chinese from the Tower of Babel by way of the Tarim Valley, are eager to seize upon the faintest tradition, or what seems to them an apparent tradition, in support of these preconceived views; ignoring the obviously just argument that, if we are to pay any attention to mere traditions at all, we must in common fairness give priority in value to such traditions as there are, rather than such traditions as are not, but only as might be. For instance, there was a Chinese tradition that the founder of the Hia dynasty (2205 B.C.) was, in a sense, somehow connected with the barbarous kingdom of Yiieh, inasmuch as the great-great-grandson of the founder of the Hia empire a century later enfeoffed a son by a concubine in that remote region. The earliest Chinese mention of Japan is that it lay to the east of Yiieh, and that the Japanese used to come and trade with Yiieh. If the Japanese traditions, on the other hand, as first put into independent writing in the eighth century A.D., are worth anything, then the Japanese pretend that their ancestors were present at a durbar held by the above-mentioned great-great- grandson of the Hia founder; and they also firmly derive their ruling houses (both king and princes) from the kingdom of Wu. We have seen in former chapters that both Wu and Yiieh, the most ancient capitals of which were within 200 miles of each other, spoke one language, and that both were derived (i.e., the administrative caste was derived) from two separate Chinese imperial dynasties. Now, the founder of the Hia dynasty is celebrated above all things for his travels in, and his geography of China, usually called the "Tribute of Yii" (his name),—a still existing work, the real origin of which may be obscure, but which has come down to us in the Book (of History). This geography is not only accurate, but it even now throws great light upon the original direction of river-courses which have since changed; in this work there is not the faintest tradition or indirect mention of any Chinese having ever migrated into China from the west.

There is no foundation, however, for the supposition, favoured by some European writers, that the Nine Tripods (frequently mentioned above) contained upon their surface "maps" of the empire; they merely contained a summary, or a collection of pictures, symbolizing the various tribute nations. On the other hand, there is no trace in the "Tribute of Yii" of any knowledge of China south of the Yarig-tsz River, south of its mouths, and south of its connection with the lakes of Hu Nan. The "province" of Yang Chou is vaguely said to extend from the Hwai River "south to the sea." The "Blackwater" is the only river mentioned which exhibits any knowledge of the west (i.e. of the west half of modern Kan Suh province), and this "Blackwater" was crossed in 984 B.C. by the Emperor Muh.

Then there is the tradition of Yii's predecessor, the Emperor Shun, who, as mentioned in the last chapter, married the two daughters of the Emperor Yao, and is buried at a point just south of the Lake Tung-t'ing, in the modern province of Hu Nan: it is certain that in 219 B.C., when the First August Emperor was on tour, the mountain where the grave lay was pointed out to him at a distance, if he did not actually go up to it. Again, the grandfather of the Warrior King who founded the Chou dynasty in 1122 B.C. was, as already repeatedly pointed out, only a younger brother, his two elder brothers having migrated to the Jungle, and, proceeding thence eastward, founded a colony in Wu (half-way between Nanking and Shanghai). Both Wu and Yiieh, for very many centuries after that, were extremely petty states of only 50 or 60 miles in extent, and for all practical purposes of history may be considered to have been one and the same region, to wit, the flat, canal-cut territory through which the much-disputed Shanghai- Hangchow railway is to run. After the death of the Martial King, when his brother the Duke of Chou was Regent for his son, the duke incurred the suspicion of other brethren and relatives as to his motives, and had to retire for some time to Ts'u, or, as it was then called, the Jungle country, for two years. There is a tradition that a mission from one of the southern Yiieh states found its way to the Duke of Chou, who is supposed to have fitted up for the envoys a cart with a compass attached to it, in order to keep the cart's head steadily south. This tradition, which only appears as a tradition in one of the dynastic histories of the fifth century A. D., is not given at all in the earlier standard history, and it is by no means proved that the undoubtedly early Chinese knowledge of the loadstone extended to the making of compasses. Yet, as Rénan has justly pointed out in effect, in his masterly evidences of Gospel truth, a weak tradition is better worth considering than no tradition at all. Besides, there is some slight indirect confirmation of this, for in 880 B.C. or thereabout, a King of Ts'u gave one of his younger sons a Yiieh kingdom bearing almost the same double name as that Yüeh kingdom from which the envoys in 1080 B.C. came to the Duke of Chou; in each case the first part of the double name was Yiieh, and the second part only differed slightly. Again, in or about 820, some of the sons of the king exiled themselves to a place vaguely defined as "somewhere south of the Han River," which can scarcely mean anything other than "the country of the Shan or Siamese races," who lived then in and around Yiin Nan, and some of whom are still known by the vague name used as here in 820 B.C. The vagueness of habitat simply means that all south of the Han and Yang-tsz was terra incognita to China proper. There is another tradition, unsupported by standard history, to the effect that the Martial King enfeoffed a faithful minister of the emperor and dynasty he had just supplanted as a vassal in Corea. Here, again, if the emperor's own grandfather, or grand-uncles and trusted friends, could find their way to Wu, and, later, to Japan, not to mention Shan Tung and the Peking plain, it is reasonable to permit a respected adherent of the dethroned monarch to find his way to Corea, the more in that the centre of administrative gravity of Corea was then Liao Tung and South Manchuria—at the utmost the north part of modern Corea—rather than the Corean peninsula.

In the year 649 the First Protector began to boast of having done as much as any of the' three dynasties, Hia, Shang, and Chou, during the 1500 years before him; he then defines the area of his glory, which is circumscribed by (at the very utmost) the west part of Shan Si, the south part of Ho Nan, the north part of the Peking plain, and the Gulf of "Pechelee." The Second Protector, when he safely reached his ancestral throne after nineteen years of wanderings as Pretender, said to his faithful Tartar henchman and father-in-law: "I have made the tour of the whole world (or whole empire) with you." As a matter of fact, he had been with the Tartars, certainly in central, and possibly also in northern Shan Si; in Ts'i, which means the northern part of Shan Tung and southern part of Chih Li; thence across the four small orthodox states of Sung, Wei, Ts'ao, and CHÊNG (which simply means up the Yellow River valley into Ho Nan), to Ts'u; and thence Ts'in fetched him to put him on the Tsin throne. The Emperor was already an obscure figure-head beneath all political notice, and no other parts of what we now call China were known to the Protector, even by name. As we shall see in a later chapter, Confucius covered the same ground, except that he never went to Tsin or to Tartarland. The first bare mention of Yiieh is in 670 B.C., when the new King of Ts'u, who had assassinated his elder brother, and who therefore wished to make amends for this crime and for his father's rude conquests, and to consolidate his position by putting himself on good behaviour to federal China, made dutiful advances to Lu and to the Emperor (these two minor powers then best representing the old ritual civilization). The Emperor replied: "Go on conquering the barbarians and Yiieh, but let the Hia (i.e. orthodox Chinese) states alone." In 601 Ts'u and Wu came to a friendly understanding about their mutual frontiers, and Yiieh was also admitted to the conclave or entente; but this was a local act, and had nothing whatever to do with China proper, which first hears of Yiieh as an independent or semi-independent power in 536, when the King of Ts'u, with a string of conquered orthodox Chinese princes in train as his allies, and also a Yiieh contingent, makes war on Wu. In later days there is evidence showing that there was not much general knowledge of China as a whole, and that interstate intercourse was chiefly confined to next-door neighbours. For instance, when Tsin boldly marched an army upon Ts'i in 589 B.C., it was considered a remarkable thing that Tsin chariots should actually gaze upon the sea. In 560, when the Ts'i minister and philosopher, Yen-tsz, was in Ts'u as envoy, and the Ts'u courtiers were playing tricks upon him (as previously narrated in Chapter IX.) he said: "I have heard it stated that when once you get south of the Hwai River the oranges are good. In the same way, we northerners produce but sorry rogues; the genuine article reaches its perfection in Ts'u." Thus, even at this date, the Yang-tsz was regarded much as the Romans of the Empire regarded the Danube—as a sort of vague barrier between civis and barbarus. In no sense was the Ts'u capital—at no time were the bulk of the Ts'u dominions—south of that Great River; nor, in fact, were the capitals of Wu and Yiieh south of it either, for one of the three mouths (the northernmost was as now), corresponded to the Soochow Creek and the Wusung River, as they pass through the Shanghai settlement of to-day; whilst the other ancient mouth entered the sea at modern Hangchow. We have given various other evidence above to show that, even earlier than this, the Yang-tsz was an unexplored region, known, and that only imperfectly and locally, to the Ts'u government alone. In the year 656 B.C. the First Protector called Ts'u to book because, in 1003 B.C., the Emperor had made a tour to the Great River and had never returned (see Chapter XX-XV.). Again, when the imperial power collapsed in 771 B.C., the first Earl of CHÊNG (a relative of the Emperor) consulted the imperial astrologer as to where he had better establish his new fief: his own idea was to settle southwards on the borders of the Yang-tsz; but he was dissuaded from this step on the ground that the Ts'u power would grow accordingly as the Chou power declined, and thus CHÊNG would all the easier fall a prey to Ts'u in the future if she migrated now so far south. The astrologer makes another observation which supports the view that Ts'u and orthodox China were originally of the same prehistoric stock. He says: "When the remote ancestor of Ts'u did good service to the Emperor (2400 B.C.), his renown was great, yet his descendants never became so flourishing as those of the Chou family." In 597 B.C., when the Earl of CHÊNG really was at the mercy of Ts'u, he said: "If you choose to send me south of the Yang-tsz towards the South Sea, I shall not have the right to object"; meaning, "no exile, however remote, is too severe for my deserts." In 549, when the Tsin generals were marching against Ts'u, they were particularly anxious to find good CHÊNG guides who knew the routes well. Finally, in 541, a Tsin statesman made the following observations to a prince (afterwards king) of Ts'u, who was then on a mission to Tsin, by way of illustrating for his visitor the conquests and distant expeditions of ancient times:—"The Emperor Shun (who married Yao's two daughters, and employed the founder of the Hia dynasty as his minister) was obliged to imprison the prince of the Three Miao (in Hu Nan; the savages of Hu Nan and Kwei Chou provinces are still called Miao); the Hia dynasty had to deal with quarrels in (modern) Shan Tung and Shen Si; the Shang dynasty had to do the same in (modern) Kiang Su; the early Chou monarchs the same in (modern) North Kiang Su and South Shan Tung: but, now that there are no able emperors, all the vassals are at loggerheads. Wu and P'uh (the supposed Shan or Siamese region above referred to) are giving you trouble; but it is no one's concern but yours."

From all this it is quite plain, though the Chinese historians and philosophers never seem to have discerned it clearly themselves, that the cultivated or orthodox Chinese, that is, the group of closely related monosyllabic and tonic tribes which alone possessed the art of writing, and thus inevitably took the lead and gradually civilized the rest, covered but a very small area of ground even at the time of Confucius' death in 479 B.C., and were completely ignorant of everything but the bare names of all the regions surrounding this orthodox nucleus, which nucleus was therefore rightly called the "Central State," as China is, by extension, now still called.

CHAPTER XL. TOMBS AND REMAINS

The Chinese, with the single exception of their Great Wall, have always been flimsy builders, and there is accordingly very little left in the way of monuments to prove the antiquity of their civilization. Mention has already been made of the tombs of the Emperors Shun and Yii (2200 B.C.). The tomb of another Hia dynasty emperor (1837 B.C.) lay twenty miles north of Yung-ning in Ho Nan,' where Ts'in, in 627 B.C., was annihilated by Tsin (see p. 30). The tomb (long. 115ø, lat. 33ø) of the King of Ts'u who died in 689 B.C. was pillaged about 500 years later, but landslips defeated the thieves' objects. The First Protector's tomb, seven miles south of his capital in Shan Tung—the town still marked on the maps as Lin-tsz—was desecrated in A.D. 312. A small pond of mercury was found inside, besides arms, valuables, and the bones of those buried with him. The palace of the Ts'u king of 617 B.C.,—son of the one whose death that year was respectfully chronicled by Confucius—is still the yam&. or protorium of the district magistrate at King-thou Fu, and can perhaps even yet be seen from any passing steamers that circulate above the treaty- port of Sha-shf. There is a doubt about the date of this king's tomb (d. 593); some place it near the palace, others over 100 miles north, near the modern city of Siang-yang. It is possible that, after the sacking of the capital by Wu, in 506, the bodies of former kings were at once removed to the new temporary capital (far to the north) to which the old name was given. For instance, it is certain that the king who died in 545 was buried quite close to the capital (King-thou Fu). Ki-chah's tomb, with Confucius' inscription upon it in ancient character, is still shown at a place ten miles west of Kiang-yin (where the modern forts are, below Nanking) and twenty miles east of Ch'ang-chou; probably the new "British" railway passes quite close to the place, as do the steamers: for the past 400 years sacrifices have been annually offered to Ki-chah's memory: as Confucius never visited Wu, the inscription, if genuine, must have been sent thither. The tomb of Ki-chah's nephew, King of Wu, is still to be seen outside one of the gates of Soochow; or, rather, the temple built on the site is there, for the tomb itself was desecrated and pillaged by the armies of Yueh, when they sacked the capital in 482. There was, originally, a triple copper coffin, a small pond, and some water birds made of gold (probably symbolic of sport), arms, valuables, etc.; but nothing is said of human beings having been sacrificed. It was said (2000 years ago) that elephants had been employed in carrying the earth and building materials for this tomb. In 506 the vengeful Ts'u officer who had fled to Wu, and had incited the King of Wu to do all he could to ruin Ts'u, actually opened the royal grave, in or near the capital, and flogged the corpse of the dead king who had so grievously offended him and his family.

In the year 501 the original bow and sceptre given by the warrior king to his brother, the Duke of Chou, founder of the State of Lu, was stolen from its resting-place, but was luckily recovered the following year. Incidentally this statement is of value; for when the King of Ts'u, as narrated above, was making his demands upon the Emperor, one of his grievances was that he possessed no relics of the founder such as the presents which had been made by him to Ts'i, Lu, Yen, Tsin, and other favoured states of no greater status than his own. The above are only a few instances out of many which show how, from age to age, the Chinese have seen with their own eyes things which in the vista of the distance now seem to us uncertain and incredible. As usual, Ts'in gives us nothing in the way of antiquity; another proof that, until she conceived the idea of conquering China, she was totally unknown (internally) to orthodox China. Confucius' own house, temple, grave, and park form an absolutely unbroken link with the past. There are remains and the relics of the Duke of Chou in the immediate neighbourhood, and it must not be forgotten that the Duke of Chou and his ritual system were Confucius' models: as Confucius insisted, "I am only a transmitter of antiquity." Moderns, and especially foreigners, have forgotten or reck nothing about the Duke of Chou; yet his remains and temples were just as much a matter of visible history to Confucius as Confucius' grounds are to us. Each successive generation in China alludes to existing antiquities, or to contemporaneous objects which have since become antiquities, with the quiet confidence of those who actually possess, and who doubt not of their possessions. The very lacunae are pointed out by themselves—no scepticism of ours is required; for whenever any historian, or any less formal writer, has outstepped the bounds of truth or probability, the critics are immediately there, and they always frankly say what they believe. In a word, the Chinese documents, be they iron, stone, wood, silk, paper, buildings, or graves; and their traditions, are the sole evidence we possess: Chinese critics were the sole critics of that evidence; and they are the sole light by which we foreigners can become critics. The great Chinese defect in criticism is the failure to work out general principles, and to criticize constructively as well as analytically. Their history is a rule of thumb, hand to mouth, diary sort of arrangement, like a vast museum of genuine but unclassified and unticketed objects. But there is no good reason whatever for our doubting the genuineness of either traditions or documents beyond the point of scepticism to which native Chinese doubts go, for it must be remembered that no foreigner possesses one tenth of the mass of Chinese learning that the professional literatus easily assimilates. All we can do is to re-group, and extract principles.

CHAPTER XLI. THE TARTARS

It is important to insist on the very close relations that existed between the Chinese and the Tartars from the very earliest times. All that we are told for certain is that they were north and west of the older dynasties, and especially in occupation of the Upper Wei River, on the lower part of which the old metropolis of Si- ngan Fu lies; which means that they were exactly where we find them in Confucian times, and where we find them now, except that they have been pushed a little further back, and that Chinese colonists have appropriated most of the oases. The Chou ancestor who died in 1231, i.e. the father of the founders of Wu, and the great-grandfather of the founder of the Chou dynasty (1122), had to abandon to the encroaching Tartars his appanage on the Upper King River (a northern tributary of the Wei, which runs almost parallel with it, and joins it at Si-ngan Fu), and was obliged to move southwards to the Upper Wei River. For nearly 1000 years previous to this, his ancestors, who had originally been forced to fly to the Tartars in order to avoid the misgovernment of the third Hia emperor, had lived among and had, whilst continuing the Chinese art of cultivating, partly become Tartars; for in 1231 B.C. the migrating host is said to have renounced Tartar manners, and to have devoted themselves seriously to building and cultivating; from which it necessarily follows that Tartar manners must for some time have been definitely adopted by the Chou family. The grandson of the migrator, the father of the Chou founder, had various little wars with a tribe called the Dog Tartars. Over 1000 years after that first flight to Tartardom, we have seen that the Emperor Muh, great-grandson of the Chou founder, not only had brushes with the Tartars, but extended his tours amongst them to the Lower Tarim Valley, Turfan, Harashar, and possibly even as far as Urumtsi and Kuché; but certainly no farther. Two hundred years later, again, the then ruling Emperor was defeated by the Tartars in (modern) Central Shan Si province, and the descendant in the sixth generation of the Ts'in Jehu who had conducted the Emperor Muh's chariot into Tartarland, only just succeeded in saving the Emperor's life; but this family of Chao, which was thus (cf. p. 206) of one and the same descent with the Ts'in family, subsequently found its account in abandoning the imperial interest altogether, and in serving the rising principality of Tsin (Shan Si), where it became one of the "six families," three of which six in 403 B.C. were ultimately recognized by the Emperor as independent rulers. As we have said over and over again, in 772 B.C. the Chou Emperor, through female intrigues, got into trouble with the Tartars, and was killed: his successor had to move the metropolis east to (modern) Ho-nan Fu, thus abandoning the western part of his patrimony—the semi-Tartar half—to Ts'in. Thus Ts'in in 771 B.C. was to the Chou Emperors what Chou, previous to 1200 B.C., had been to the Shang Emperors.

We now come to strictly historical times, and we shall have no difficulty in showing that even then—h fortiori in times not strictly historical—the various Tartar tribes were still in practical possession of the whole north bank of the Yellow River, all the way from the Desert to the sea. In fact, in 494 B.C., when the King of Wu sent a giant's bone to Lu for further explanation, Confucius said that the "Long Tartars" (who had frequent fights with Lu in the seventh century B.C.) used to extend south-east into (modern) Kiang Su, almost as far as the mouth of the Yang-tsz River: he also says that, had it not been for the energy of the First Protector and his statesman adviser, the philosopher Kwan- tsz of Ts'i, orthodox China would certainly have become Tartarized. It was Confucius also whose learning enabled him to recognize a (Manchu) arrow found in the body of a migrating goose. In the eighth and seventh centuries B.C. the Tartars made repeated and obstinate attacks upon Yen (Peking plain), Ts'i (coast Chih Li and north Shan Tung), Wei (south Chih Li and north Ho Nan), Sung (extreme east Ho Nan), Ts'ao (central Ho Nan), and the Emperor's territory (west Ho Nan). This situation explains to us why the Protector system arose in China, in competition with the waning imperial power. Ts'in and Tsin, being already half Tartar themselves, were always well able to cope with and even to annex the Tartar tribes in their immediate vicinity; but orthodox China was ever a prey to the more easterly Tartar attacks; and thus the Emperors, threatened by Ts'u to their south, and in a measure also by Ts'in and Tsin to their north and west, not only could not any longer protect their orthodox vassals lying towards the east from Tartar attacks, but could not even protect themselves.

It was Ts'i that drove back the Mongol-Manchu tribes and rescued Yen in 662; it was the Ts'i ruler who led a coalition of princes against other groups of Tartars and placed back on his ancestral throne the ruler of Wei, who had been driven from his country by Tartars in 658; it was the First Protector, ruler of Ts'i, who managed to pacify the more westerly Tartars we find persistently menacing the Emperor in 648; to whose rescue the Tartars came in 642, when a coalition of orthodox Chinese princes shamelessly took advantage of the First Protector's death to attack Ts'i during the mourning period. Now it was that the Second Protector, still a refugee among his Tartar relatives, started for Ts'i, his original idea being to replace the philosopher Kwan-tsz as adviser to the First Protector; but, shortly after he reached Ts'i, the First Protector died, and it was only by stratagem that his friends succeeded in rescuing the future Second Protector from the arms of his Ts'i Delilah and his d'elices de Capue. His chief adviser, and at the same time his brother-in-law from a Tartar point of view, was the lineal descendant of the Chao man who had saved the Emperor in 800 B.C. He set out, via the orthodox states, for his own country. These petty orthodox states, such as Wei, Cheng, and Ts'ao, which did not then see their way to profit politically by the Pretender's visit, paid the penalty of their meanness and their rudeness to him later on. Sung was polite, as at that time Sung and Ts'u were both aiming at the Protectorship. Ts'u's hospitality was bluff and good-natured, the King being too strong to fear, and too unsophisticated to intrigue after Chinese fashion. Just then news coming from Ts'in that the Pretender's brothers had all resigned or died, and that his chance had now come, the Pretender hurried to Tsin, regained his throne, and was acclaimed Protector of China exactly at the critical moment when a strong hand was urgently required to check the particular ambitions of Ts'in, Ts'i, and Ts'u. Ts'u was too barbarous; Sung was too pedantic; Tsin alone had unrivalled experience both of Tartars and Eastern barbarians, and also of Southern barbarians (Ts'u). Probably it was only the fact of the Tsin ruling family bearing the same clan-name as the Emperor that had decided Tsin throughout to be orthodox Chinese instead of Tartar. The Tartar family into which the Second Protector had married as a comparatively young man was, however, also of the imperial clan- name, i.e. it was of orthodox Chinese origin, but (even like the Chou imperial family at one time) it had adopted Tartar customs. A large number of the one thousand or more petty Chinese principalities, attached not directly to the Emperor, but to the greater vassals as mesne lords, were in the same predicament; that is to say, they were of Chinese origin, but they had found that it paid them best to adopt barbarian ways. It was exactly as though Scipio should settle in Carthage, and become a Carthaginian: C'sar in Gaul, and adopt Gallic customs; and so on with other Roman adventurers who should find a comfortable gîte in Persia, Asia Minor, Syria, Egypt, or even in Britain and Germany.

The main point upon which to fix the attention is this. The Chinese nucleus was very small, and only by rudely thrusting aside incompetent emperors and fussy ritual did it succeed in emancipating itself from Tartar bondage. That this is not an exaggerated view is additionally plain from the fact that Tartars have, even since Confucian times, ruled more and longer than have Chinese over North China; the Mongols (1260-1368) were the first Tartars to rule over all China, and nominally over all West Asia; the Manchus (1643-1908) are the first Tartars to rule all China, all Manchuria, and all Mongolia, at all effectively; and they have even added parts of Turkestan, with Tibet, Nepaul, and other countries over which the Peking imperial Mongol influence was always very shadowy.

CHAPTER XLII.MUSIC

In these pictures of ancient Chinese life which we are endeavouring to present, the idea is to repeat from every point of view the main characteristics of that life, so that a strange and unfamiliar subject, very loosely depicted in the straggling annals of antiquity, may receive fresh rays of light from every possible quarter, and thus stand out clearer as a connected whole.

Take, for instance, the subject of music, which always played in Chinese ceremonial a prominent part not easy for us now to understand. One of the chief sights of the modern Confucian residence is the music-room, containing specimens of all the ancient musical instruments, which, on occasion, are still played upon in chorus; a picture of them has been published by Father Tschepe. (See page 128.) According to the description given by this European visitor, the music is of a most discordant and ear- splitting description: but that does not necessarily dispose of the question; for even parts of Wagner's Ring are a meaningless clang to those who hear the music for the first time, and who are unable to read the score or to follow out the "classical" style. As we have said before, the ancient emperors, at their banquets given to vassals and others, always had musical accompaniment.

In 626 B.C., when the ruler of Ts'in received a mission from "the Tartar king" (probably a local king or chief), he was much struck with the sagacity of the envoy sent to him. This envoy still spoke the Tsin language or dialect; but his parents, who were of Tsin origin, had adopted Tartar manners. The envoy was also an author, and his work, in two sections, had survived at least up to the second century B.C.: he is classed amongst the "Miscellaneous Writers." The subject of the conversation was the superiority of simple Tartar administration as compared with the intricate ritual of the Odes, the Book, the Rites, and the "Music" of orthodox China. The beginnings of Lao-tsz's Taoism seem to peep out from this Tartar's words, just as they do with other "Miscellaneous" authors. The wily Ts'in ruler, in order to secure this clever envoy for his own service, sent two bands of female musicians as a present to the Tartar king, so as to make him less virile; 140 years later the cunning ruler of Ts'i did much the same thing in order to prevent the Duke of Lu from growing too strong; and the immediate consequence was that Confucius left his fickle master in disgust. Ki-chah, Prince of Wu, was entertained whilst at Lu with specimens of music from the different states. When he came to the Ts'in music, he said: "Ha! ha! the words are Chinese! When Ts'in becomes quite Chinese, it will have a great future." This remark suggests a Ts'in language or dialect different from that of Tsin, and also from that of more orthodox China. In 546 B.C., when a mission from Ts'u to Tsin was accompanied by a high officer from the disputed orthodox state of Ts'ai lying between those two great powers, the theory of music as an adjunct to government was discussed. Confucius' view a century later was that music best reflected a nation's manners, and that in good old times authority was manifested quite as much in rites and ceremonies as in laws and pronouncements. Previous to that, in 582, it had been discovered that Ts'u had a musical style of her own; and in 579, when the Tsin envoy was received there in state, among other instruments of music observed there were suspended bells.

Thus both Ts'in and Ts'u at this date were still in the learning stage. Before ridiculing the idea that music could in any way serve as a substitute for preaching or commanding, we must reflect upon the awe-inspiring contribution of music to our own religious services, not to mention the "speaking" effect of our Western nocturnes, symphonies, and operatic music generally.

In 562 B.C., when a statesman of Tsin (whose fame in this connection endures to our own days) succeeded in establishing a permanent understanding with the Tartars, based upon joint trading rights and reasonable mutual concessions, the principle of interesting the Tartars in cultivation, industry, and so on; as a reward for his distinguished services, he was presented with certain music, which meant that he had the political right to have certain musical airs performed in his presence. This concession ceases to seem ridiculous or even strange to us if we reflect what an honour it would have been to, say, the Duke of Wellington, or to Nelson, had the right to play "God Save the King" at dinner been granted to his family band of musicians. Four centuries before this, when the Emperor Muh made his tour amongst the Tartars, he always commanded that one particular musical air (named) should be struck up by his musicians on certain occasions (always stated in the narrative). In Tsin, and probably elsewhere, music-masters seem to have combined soothsaying and philosophy with their functions; thus, in 558 the music-master of that state was questioned on the arts of good government, to which he replied: "Goodness and justice"—two special antipathies, by the way, of Lao-tsz the Taoist, who lived about this time as an archive-keeper at the metropolis. In the year 555, either this same man or another musical prophet in Tsin reassured his fellow- countrymen who were dreading a Ts'u invasion with the following words: "I have just been conducting a song consisting of north and south airs, and the latter sound as though the south would be defeated." But music also had its lighter uses, for we have seen in Chapter VI. how in 549 two Tsin generals took their ease in a comfortable cart, playing the banjo, whilst passing through Cheng to attack Ts'u. Music was used at worship as well as at court; in 527 the ruler of Lu, as a mark of respect for one of his deceased ministers, abandoned the playing of music, which otherwise would have been a constituent part of the sacrifice or worship he had in hand at the moment. Even in modern China, music is prohibited during solemn periods of mourning, and officials are often degraded for attending theatrical performances on solemn fasts. In 212 B.C., when the First August Emperor was, like Saul or Belshazzar, beginning to grow sad at the contemplation of his lonely and unloved greatness, he was suddenly startled at the fall of a meteoric stone, bearing upon it what looked like a warning inscription. He at once ordered his learned men to compose some music treating of "true men" and immortals, in order to exorcise the evil omen; it may be mentioned that this emperor's Taoist proclivities have apparently had the indirect result that the word "true man" has come century by century down to us, with the meaning of "Taoist priest," or "Taoist inspired person."

CHAPTER XLIII.WEALTH, SPORTS, ETC.

A traveller in modern China may still wonder at the utter absence of any sign of wealth or luxury except in the very largest towns. Fine clothes, jewels, concubines, rich food, aphrodisiacs, opium, land, cattle—these represent "wealth" as conceived by the Chinese rich man's mind. In 655 Ts'in is said to have paid five ram-skins to Ts'u in order to secure the services of a coveted adviser. Not many years after that, when the future Second Protector was making his terms with the King of Ts'u, he remarked: "What can I do for you in return? You already possess all the slaves, musicians, treasures, silks, feathers, ivory, and leather you can want." In 606 a magnificent turtle was sent as a new year's dinner present from Ts'u to Cheng; in modern China this form of politeness would never do at all, as the turtle has acquired an evil reputation as a term of abuse, akin to the Spanish use or abuse of the word "garlic": however, I myself once experienced, when inland, far away from the sea, a curious compliment in the shape of a live crab two inches long (sent to me as a great honour) in a small jar. Of course chairs were unknown, and even the highest sat or squatted on mats; not necessarily on the ground, but spread on couches. Hence the word survives the object, just as with us ("covers" at dinner are "provided" but never seen; thus in China a host is "east mat" and a guest "west mat.") In 626, when the ruler of Ts'in was talking politics with the Tartar envoy just mentioned above, he allowed him, as a special favour, to sit alongside of his own mat (on the couch). These couches probably resembled the modern settee, sofa, k'ang, or divan, such as all visitors to China have seen and sat on. Tea was quite unknown in those days, and is not mentioned before the seventh century A.D.; but possibly wine may have been served, as tea is now, on a low table between the two seats. "Tartar couches" (possibly Turkish divans) are frequently mentioned, even in the field of battle, and in comparatively modern times. In 300 B.C. Ts'u made a present to a distinguished renegade prince of the Ts'i house of an "elephant couch," by which is probably meant a couch inlaid with ivory, in the present well-known Annamese style.

In 589 B.C., when Tsin troops reached the Ts'i capital and the sea (as already related in Chapters VI. and XXXIX. under the heads of Armies and Geographical Knowledge), T'si endeavoured to purchase peace by offering to the victor the state treasure in the shape of precious utensils. In 551 a rich man of Ts'u was considered insolently showy because he possessed forty horses. In 545 the envoy from Cheng, acting under the Peace Conference agreement so often previously described and alluded to, brings presents of furs and silks to Ts'u; and in 537 Tsin speaks of such articles as often being presented to Ts'u. In 494, when the King of Yiieh received his great defeat at the hands of the King of Wu, his first desperate idea was to kill his wives and children, burn his valuables, and seek death at the head of his troops; but the inevitable wily Chinese adviser was at hand, and the King ended by taking his mentor's advice and successfully bribing the Wu general (a Ts'u renegade) with presents of women and valuables. When this shrewd Chinese adviser of the Yueh king had, by his sagacious counsels, at last secured the final defeat of Wu, he packed up his portable valuables, pearls, and jades, collected his family and clients, and went away by sea, never to come back. As a matter of fact, he settled in Ts'i, where he made an enormous fortune in the fish trade, and ultimately became the traditional Croesus of China, his name being quite as well known to modern Chinese through the Confucian historians, as the name of Croesus is to modern Europeans through Herodotus. He had, between the two defeats of Yiieh by Wu and Wu by Yiieh, served for several years as a spy in Wu, and the fact of his reaching Shan Tung by sea confirms in principle the story of the family of his contemporary, the King of Wu, having similarly escaped to Japan. The place where he landed was probably the same as where the celebrated pilgrim Fah Hien landed, after his Indian pilgrimage, in 415 A.D., i.e., at the German port of Ts'ing-tao.

We do not hear much of gold in the earlier times, but in 237 B.C., when Ts'in was straining every nerve to conquer China, the (future) First August Emperor was advised that "it would not cost more than 300,000 pounds weight in gold to bribe the ministers of all the states in league against Ts'in." Yet in 643 B.C., on the death of the First Protector, the orthodox state of Cheng (lying between Ts'i and Tsin to the north and Ts'u to the south), was bribed with "metal" of some sort—probably gold or silver—to abandon Ts'i. In 538 the celebrated Cheng statesman Tsz-ch'an informs his Ts'u colleagues that the Tsin officers "think of nothing but money." What kind of money this was is doubtful, but it will be remembered that about this time the "powerful family" of Lu had succeeded in bribing the Tsin ministers, or the "six great families" then managing Tsin, to deny justice to the fugitive Lu duke. In 513 B.C. the powerful Wu king who made (modern) Soochow his capital is said to have possessed both iron and gold mines, and it is stated that not even China proper could turn out better weapons. Large "cash" are said to have been coined by the Emperor who reigned from 540 to 520 B.C.; and in 450 B.C. the King of Ts'u is reported to have "closed his depot of the three moneys." As only copper was coined, it is not easy to say now what the other two "moneys" were. In 318 B.C. a bribe of "one hundred golds" was given by Yen to one of the well-known political diplomats or intriguers then forming leagues with or against Ts'in; it is not known for certain how much this was at that particular time and place; but a century or two later it meant, under the Ts'in dynasty, twenty-four ounces; during the Han dynasty, conquerors of the Ts'in dynasty, it was only about half that. Cooks seem to have held official positions of considerable dignity. "Meat-eaters" in Confucian times was a term for "officials" or "the rich." Thus when the haughty King of Wu was suddenly recalled home, from his high-handed durbar with Tsin, Lu, and other orthodox states, to go and deal with his formidable enemy of Yueh, he turned quite pale. By dint of bold "bluff" he managed after all to gain most of his political points, and to retire from an awkward corner with honour; but Chinese spies had their eyes on him none the less, and reported to the watchful enemy that "meat-eaters are not usually blackfaced"—meaning that the King of Wu evidently had some very recent bad news on his mind, for "the well-fed do not usually look care-worn."

Silk was universally known. When the Second Protector (to be) was dallying with his lady-love in Ts'i, the maid of his mistress happened to overhear important conversations from her post in a mulberry tree; the presumption is that she was collecting leaves for the silkworms. Again in 519, a century later, there was a dispute on the Ts'u-Wu frontier (North An Hwei province), about the possession of certain mulberry trees. Cotton (Gossypium) was unknown in China, and the poorer classes wore garments of hempen materials; the cotton tree (Bombyx) was known in the south, but then (as now) the catkins could not be woven into cloth. It was never the custom of officers in China to wear swords, until in 409 B.C. Ts'in introduced the practice; but it probably never extended to orthodox China, so far, at least, as civilians' were concerned. The three dynasties of Hia, Shang, and Chou had all made use of jade or malachite rings, tablets, sceptres, and so on, as marks of official rank.

As to sports, hunting, and especially fowling, seem to have been the most popular pastimes. In 660 a prince of Wei (orthodox) is said to have had a passion for egret fights. In 539 four-horsed chariots are mentioned as being used in a great Ts'u hunt south of the modern Teh-an in northern Hu Peh province, then mostly jungle: these hunts were used as a sort of training for war as well as for sport. The celebrated "stone drums" discovered in the seventh century A.D. near the old Chou capital describe the war-hunts of the active emperor mentioned in Chapter XLI. As might be expected, Yen (Peking plain) would be well off for horses-to this day brought by the Mongols in droves to Peking: in 539 it is said of Yen: "She was never a strong power, in spite of her numerous horses." In 534 a great hunt in Lu is described with much detail; here also chariots were used, and their shafts were reared in opposite rows with their tips meeting above, so as to form a "shaft gate," on which, besides, a flag was kept flying. The entrance to Chinese official yamens is still called "the shaft gate";-in fact, the ya was orginally a flag, and "yamen" simply means "flag gate." In the Middle Ages the Turkish Khans' encampments were always spoken of as their ya—thus: "from hence 1500 miles north-west to the Khan's ya." Cockfighting was a common sport in Ts'i and Lu. In 517 B.C. two prominent Lu functionaries had a quarrel because one had put metal spurs on his bird, whilst the other had scattered mustard in the feathers of his fighting cock: owing to the ambiguity or double meaning of one of the pictographs employed, it is not quite certain that "mustard in the wings" may not mean "a metal helmet on the head." Lifting weights was (as now) a favourite exercise; in 307 a Ts'in prince died from the effects of a strain produced in trying to lift a heavy metal tripod. In Ts'i games at ball, including a kind of football, were played. As a rule, however, it is to be feared that the wealthy Chinese classes in ancient (as in modern) times found their chief recreation in feasting, literary bouts, and female society. Curiously enough, nothing is said of gambling. Women are depicted at their looms, or engaged upon the silk industry; but it is singular how very little is said of home life, of how the houses were constructed, of how the hours of leisure were passed. In modern China the bulk of the male rural population rises with or before the dawn, and is engaged upon field or garden work until the shades of evening fall in; there is no artificial light adequate for purposes of needlework or private study; even the consolations of tobacco and tea—not to say opium, and now newspapers—were unknown in Confucian days. It is presumed, therefore, that life was even more humdrum than it is now, except that women at least had feet to walk upon. We gain some glimpses of excessive taxation and popular misery, forced labour and the press-gang; of callous luxury on the part of the rich, from the pages of Lao-tsz and Mencius; the Book of Odes also tells us much about the pathetic sadness of the people under their taskmasters' hands. In all countries popular habits change slowly; in none more so than in China. We are driven, therefore, by comparison with the life of to-day to conclude that life in those times was sufficiently wretched, and it is therefore not to be wondered at that the miserable people readily sold their services to the first ambitious adventurer who could protect them, and feed them from day to day.

CHAPTER XLIV.CONFUCIUS

Confucius has hitherto appeared to many of us Westerners as a stiff, incomprehensible individual, resting his claim to immortality upon sententious nothingnesses directed to no obvious practical purpose; but, from the slight sketches of the manners of the times in which he lived given above, it will be apparent that he was a practical man with a definite object in view, and that both his barebones history and his jerky moral teachings were the best he could do with sorry material, and in the face of inveterate corruption and tyranny. It has been explained how the Warrior King who conquered China for the Chou family in 1122, about a dozen years later enfeoffed the elder brother of the last Shang dynasty emperor in the country of Sung, where he ruled the greater part of what was left of the late dynasty's immediate entourage, and kept up the sacrifices. This is what Confucius meant when he said: "There remain not in K'i sufficient indications of what the institutions of the Hia dynasty were; but I have studied in Sung what survives of the Shang dynasty institutions. In practice I follow the Chou dynasty institutions, as I have studied them at home in Lu." K'i was a very petty state of marquess rank situated near Lu, to which, indeed, it was subordinate; but just as Sung had, as representatives of the Shang dynasty, the privilege of carrying out certain imperial sacrifices, so had K'i, as representatives of the Hia dynasty (enfeoffed by Chou in 1122), an equal right to distinction. Confucius' ancestors were natives of Sung and scions of the ducal family reigning there; in fact, in 893 his ancestor ought to have succeeded to the Sung throne: in 710 B.C. the last of these ancestors to hold high official rank in Sung was killed, together with his princely master; and several generations after that the great-grandfather of Confucius, in order to avoid the secular spite of the powerful family who had so killed his ancestor, decided to migrate to Lu. In other words, he just crossed the modern Grand Canal (then the river Sz, which rose in Lu), and moved a few days' journey north-east to the nearest civilized state of any standing. Confucius' father is no mythical personage, but a stout, common soldier, whose doughty deeds under three successive dukes are mentioned in the Lu history quite in a casual and regular way. When still quite a child, Confucius disclosed a curious fancy for playing with sacrificial objects and practising ceremonies, just as English children in the nursery sometimes play at "being parson and sexton," and at "having feasts." When he grew up to manhood, a high officer of Lu foretold his future greatness, not only on account of his precociously grave demeanour, but also because he was in direct descent from the Shang dynasty, and because the intrigues that had taken place in Sung had deprived him of his succession rights there also. This high officer's two sons, both frequently mentioned by various contemporary authors, and one of whom subsequently went with Confucius to visit Lao-tsz at the imperial court, thereupon studied the rites under the man of whom their father had spoken so well. The only official appointment in Lu that Confucius was able to obtain at this period was that of steward to one of the "powerful families" then engaged in the task, so congenial in those times all over China, of undermining the ducal authority; this appointment was a kind of stewardship, in which his duties consisted in tallying the measures of grain and checking the heads of cattle. One of the two sons of the above-mentioned statesman who had foreseen Confucius' distinction, some time after this submitted a request to the ruler of Lu that he might proceed in company with Confucius to visit the imperial capital; and it is supposed by Sz-ma Ts'ien, the historian of 100 B.C., that this was the occasion on which took place the philosopher's famous interview with Lao-tsz. In this connection there are two or three remarks to make. In the first place, it is recorded of nearly all the vassal states that they either did pay visits to, or wished to visit, the metropolis; and that royal dukes and royal historians, either at vassal request or under imperial instruction, took part in advising vassal states. In the second place, as Confucius then held no high office, his visit, being a private affair, would not be considered worth mentioning in the Lu annals, and it would therefore almost follow as a matter of course that the young man who accompanied him, being of official status by birth, would count as the chief personage. In the third place, there is no instance in the Confucian histories of a mere archive-keeper or a mere philosopher being mentioned on account of his importance in that capacity. Such men as Tsz-ch'an, Shuh Hiang, Ki-chah, and the other distinguished "ritualists" of the time, are not mentioned so much on account of their abstract teachings as they are on account of their being able statesmen, competent to stave off the rising tide of revolutionary opinions. Even Confucius himself only appears in contemporary annals as an able administrator and diplomat; there is no particular mention of his "school," and, a fortiori, he himself does not mention Lao-tsz's "school," even if Lao-tsz had one; for he disapproved of Lao-tsz's republican and democratic way of construing the ancient tao. Finally, neither Confucius nor Lao-tsz, however great their local reputations, were yet universally "great"; they were consequently as little the objects of hero-worship as was Shakespeare when he was at the height of his activity; and of the living Shakespeare we know next to nothing. At this time Lu was in a quandary, surrounded by the rival great powers of Tsin, Ts'i, and Ts'u, all three of which absolutely ignored the Emperor, except so far as they might succeed in using him and his ritualistic prestige as a cat's-paw in their own selfish interests. When Confucius was thirty years of age (522 B.C.) the ruler of Ts'i, accompanied by his minister the philosopher Yen-tsz, paid a visit to Lu, and had a discussion with Confucius upon the question: "How did Ts'in, from beginnings so small and obscure, reach her present commanding position?" Besides this, the Ts'i ruler and his henchman Yen-tsz both took the opportunity to study the rites at Lu. This fact seems to support the (later) statement that Confucius had himself been to study the rites at the metropolis, and also to explain Confucius' own confession that he did not understand much about the Hia dynasty institutions that used to exist in K'i,—a state lying eastward of Ts'i. In 520 the last envoy ever sent from Lu to the Chou metropolis reported on his return that the imperial family was in a state of feud and anarchy: if, as it is stated, this was really the last envoy from Lu, then Confucius and his friend must have visited Lao-tsz before the former reached the age of thirty. Tsin and Lu were both now in a revolutionary condition, and a struggle with the "powerful families" was going on in each case; it was also beginning in Ts'i, and in principle seems to have been exactly akin to our English struggle between King John and his barons (as champions of popular rights) against the greed of the tax-collector. To avoid home troubles, Confucius at the age of thirty-five went to Ts'i, in order, if possible, to serve his friend the Marquess, who had a few years before consulted him about the rise of Ts'in. There perhaps it was that he found an opportunity to study the music of the Hia dynasty at the petty state of K'i, only one day's journey east of the Ts'i capital, on the north-east frontier of Lu; and then it must have been that he formed his opinion about the surviving Hia rites. His advice to the reigning prince of Ts'i was so highly appreciated that it was proposed to confer an estate upon him. It is interesting to note that the jealous Yen-tsz (who was much admired as a companionable man by Confucius) protested against this grant, on the ground that "men of his views are sophistical rhetoricians, intoxicated with the exuberance of their own verbosity; incompetent to administer the people; wasting time and money upon expensive funerals. Life is too short to waste in trying to get to the bottom of these inane studies." From this it will be seen that Lao-tsz was by no means alone in despising Confucius' conservative and ritualistic views, though it is quite possible that Yen-tsz may still have respected him as a man and a politician. Finally, Confucius, finding that the Ts'i ministers were all arrayed against him, and that the Marquess fain confessed himself too old to fight his battles for him, quitted the country and returned home. His own duke died in exile in 510 B.C., power remaining in the intriguing hands of an influential private family; and for at least ten years Confucius held no office in his native land, but spent his time in editing the Odes, the Book, the Chou Rites, and the

Music; by some it is even thought that he not only edited but composed the Book (of History), or put together afresh such parts of the old Book as suited his didactic purposes. Meanwhile the private family intrigues went on more actively than ever; until at last, in 501, when Confucius was fifty years of age, the most formidable agitator of them all, finding his position untenable, escaped to Ts'i; it even seems that Confucius placed, or thought of placing, his services at the disposal of one of these rebel subjects. Possibly it was in view of such contingencies that the reigning duke at last gave Confucius a post as governor of a town, where his administration was so admirable that he soon passed through higher posts to that of Chief Justice, or Minister of Justice. Confucius' views on law are well known. He totally disapproved of Tsz-ch'an's publication of the law in the orthodox state of Cheng, as explained in Chapter XX., holding that the judge should always "declare" the law, and make the punishment fit the crime, instead of giving the people opportunities to test how far they could strain the literal terms of the law. He also said: "I am like others in administering the law; I apply it to each case; it is necessary to slay one in order not to have to slay more. The ancients understood prevention better than we do now; at present all we can hope to do is to avoid punishing unjustly. The ancients strove to save a prisoner's life; now we can only do our best to prove his guilt. However, better let a guilty man go free than slay an innocent one."

Confucius' old friend the ruler of Ts'i was still alive (he reigned fifty-eight years, one of the longest reigns on record in Chinese history), and he had just suffered serious humiliation at the hands of the barbarous King of Wu, to whose heir-apparent he had been obliged to send one of his daughters in marriage. The Protectorate of China was going a-begging for want of a worthy sovereign, and it looked at one time as though Confucius' stern and efficient administration would secure the coveted prize for Lu. The Marquess of Ts'i therefore formed a treacherous plot to assassinate both master and man, and with this end in view sent an envoy to propose a friendly conference. It was on this occasion that Confucius uttered his famous saying (quoted, however, from what "he had heard") that "they who discuss by diplomacy should always have the support of a military backing." A couple of generals accordingly accompanied the party to the trysting-place; and it is presumed that the generals had a force of soldiers with them, even though the indispensable common people be not worth mention in Chinese history. In conformity with practice, an altar or dai's was constructed; wine was offered, and the usual rites were being fulfilled to the utmost, when suddenly a Ts'i officer advanced rapidly and said: "I now propose to introduce some foreign musicians," a band of whom at once entered the arena, with brandished weapons, waving feathers, and noisy yells. Confucius saw through this sinister manoeuvre at once, and, hastily mounting the dais (except, out of respect, the last step), expostulated in the plainest terms. The ruler of Ts'i was so ashamed of his position that he at once sent the dancers away. But a second group of mountebanks were promptly introduced in spite of this check. Confucius was so angry, that he demanded their instant execution under the law (presumably a general imperial law) "providing the punishment of death for those who should excite animosity between princes." Heads and legs soon covered the ground; and Confucius played his other cards so well that he secured, in the sequel, a formal treaty, actually surrendering to Lu certain territories that had unlawfully been held for some years by Ts'i. On the other hand, Lu had to promise to aid Ts'i with 22,500 men in case Ts'i should engage in any "foreign" war—probably alluding to Wu. Two or three years after that stirring event there was civil war in Lu, owing to Confucius having insisted on the "barons" dismantling their private fortresses.

At the age of fifty-six Confucius left his post as Minister of Justice to take up that of First Counsellor: his first act was to put to death a grandee who was sowing disorder in the state. It was during these years of supreme administration that complete order was restored throughout the country; thieves disappeared; "sucking-pigs and lambs were sold for honest prices"; and there was general content and rejoicing throughout the land. All this made the neighbouring people of Ts'i more and more uneasy, even to the point of fearing annexation by Lu. The wily old Marquess therefore, again at the instigation of the man who had planned the attempted assassination of 500 B.C., made a selection of eighty of the most beautiful women Ts'i could produce, besides thirty four- horsed chariots of the most magnificent description. The reigning Marquess of Lu, as well as his "powerful family" friend against whom Confucius had once thought of taking arms (who, indeed, acted as intermediary) both fell into the trap: public duty and sacrifices were neglected; and the result was that Confucius at once threw up his offices and left the country in disgust. His first visit was to Wei (imperial clan), the capital city of which state then stood on the Yellow River, in the extreme north-east part of modern Ho Nan province; and through this capital the river then ran: the metropolis of one of the very ancient emperors previous to the Hia dynasty had nearly 2000 years before been in the immediate neighbourhood, as also had been the last capital of the Shang dynasty, of which, as we have seen, Confucius was a distant scion. After a few months' stay there, he was suspected and calumniated; so he decided to move on, although the ruler of Wei had generously appropriated to him a salary (in grain) suitable to his high rank. He accordingly proceeded eastwards to a town belonging to Sung (in the extreme south of modern Chih Li province): here he had the misfortune to be mistaken for the dangerous individual who had fled from Lu to Ts'i in 501, in consequence of which he returned to stay in Wei with his friend K'u-peh-yuh, who, as mentioned in Chapter XXVIII., had been visited by Ki-chah of Wu in 544 B.C. Here, as a distinguished traveller, he was asked (practically commanded) by one of the ruler's wives to pay her a visit; and, though the reluctant visit was paid with all propriety and reserve, the fact that this woman was at the time suspected of having committed incest with her own brother is considered by uncompromising native critics to leave a slight stain on Confucius' character. Worse still, the reigning prince took his wife out for a drive with a eunuch sitting in the same carriage, ordering the sage to follow the party in an inferior carriage. This was too much for Confucius, who then resumed his original journey through Sung, from which he had turned back, and proceeded to the small state of Ts'ao (imperial clan; still called Ts'ao-thou, extreme south-west of modern Shan Tung province). To-day he would have had to cross the Yellow River, but of course none is here mentioned, as Confucius had already left it behind at the Wei capital: in fact, he had been on the right bank ever since he left his own country. This was 495 B.C. After a short stay in Ts'ao, the philosopher proceeded south towards the capital of Sung (modern Kwei-teh Fu in the extreme east of Ho Nan). For some reason the Minister of War there wished to assassinate him—probably because the arch-intriguer whom Confucius had driven out of Lu in 501, and who had taken refuge first in Ts'i and then in Sung, had calumniated him there. Confucius thereupon made his way westwards, over the various headwaters of the River Hwai, to Cheng (imperial clan), the state which had been for a generation so admirably administered by Tsz- ch'an: in fact, a man outside the city gate observed "how like Tsz-ch'an" the stranger looked. Some accounts make out that Tsz- ch'an was then only just dead, but the better opinion is that he had already then been dead for twenty-seven years: in any case it is curious that Confucius, who was a very tall man, should twice be mistaken for other persons. Thence Confucius turned back south- east to the orthodox state of Ch'en (modern Ch'en-chou Fu in Eastern Ho Nan). This was one of the very oldest principalities in China, dating from even before the Hia dynasty (2205 B.C.); and the Warrior King of Chou, after conquering the empire in 1122 B.C., had industriously sought out the most suitable lineal descendant to take over the ancient fee of his remote ancestor, and continue the sacrifices.

Confucius remained in Ch'en over three years, and during that time the barbarian King of Wu annexed several neighbouring towns, whilst Tsin and Ts'u ravaged the surrounding country in turn, in their rival efforts to secure a predominant influence there. Here it was, too, that a bird of prey, pierced with a strange arrow, fell near the prince's palace: from the wood used in making the arrow and the peculiar stone barb employed to tip it, Confucius was able to explain that the bird must have flown from (modern) Manchuria. (This annual flight of bustards and geese, to and from the Steppes, may be observed any winter to-day.) He next turned north, and arrived once more at the spot in Sung he had visited in 496: here he was arrested, but set free on his solemn promise that he would not go to Wei, which state at the moment was considering the advisability of attacking that very Sung town. Confucius deliberately broke his plighted word, on the ground that "promises extorted by violence are void, and are not recognized by the gods." (These words, which, after all, are good English law, were quoted by the irate Chang Chf-tung when Russia "extorted" the Livadia Treaty from Ch'unghou.) On his arrival in Wei, he advised his old friend, the Wei duke, to attack the Sung town he had just left. But the duke thought it best to have the Yellow River between himself and the rival states of Ts'u and Tsin (this specific mention of the Yellow River as being west of a city in long. 114ø 30' E. is interesting). The latter state, Tsin, then held most of the left bank. Confucius even thought of accepting the invitation of a Tsin rebel to go and assist him: this was just at the moment when the "six families" were gradually breaking up the once powerful northern orthodox state. He also hesitated whether he would not do better, as the prince of Wei would not employ him, to proceed west to Tsin in order there to serve one of the contending six families: in fact he actually got as far as the Yellow River (another proof that it must then have run on the west side of Wei-hwei Fu in Ho Nan); but turned back to Wei on hearing unfavourable news from the Tsin capital (in south Shan Si). As the Wei prince treated him somewhat cavalierly during an interview, he decided to go back once more due south to the ancient state of Ch'en. Here (492) he heard news of the destruction by fire of some of the Lu ancestral temples, and of the death of the "powerful family" minister whose disgraceful conduct with the singing girls had led to his departure from Lu in disgust. This minister was a sort of hereditary maire du palais, an arrangement which seems to have been customary in many states, and his last words to his son were: "When you succeed me, send for Confucius: my administration has failed: I did wrong in dismissing him." The son had not the courage to ask Confucius himself, but he sent instead for one of the philosopher's disciples, and it was arranged with Confucius' friends that this disciple on taking office should send for Confucius himself, who really wished to be employed in Lu again. Meanwhile Confucius decided to visit the orthodox state of Ts'ai (imperial clan), lying to the south of Che'n: the capital of this state had been originally a town on the upper waters of the Hwai River, right in the heart of modern Ho Nan province; but, under stress of the Tsin and T'su wars, it had twice moved its chief city eastwards, and owing to a Ts'u invasion, it was now (491) on the main Hwai River in modern An Hwei province, and was at the moment under the political influence of Wu; it is not clear, however, whether Confucius visited the old or the new capital. After a year's stay here, Confucius went further westwards to a certain Ts'u town (near Nan-yang Fu in Ho Nan), passing, on his way, near the place in which Lao-tsz was born. He soon returned to Ts'ai, where he stayed three years. It will be observed that ever since 700 B.C. it had been the deliberate policy of Ts'u to annex or overshadow as many of the orthodox states as possible, so that Ts'u's undoubtedly high literary output, in later years, is easily accounted for: in other words, Ts'u's northern population was now already orthodox Chinese. Moreover, it must not be forgotten that, even before the Chou conquest, one of the early Ts'u rulers was an author himself, and had been tutor to the father of the Chou founder: that means to say Ts'u was possibly always as literary as China.

Meanwhile Ts'u and semi-barbarian Wu were contesting possession of Ch'en, and the King of Ts'u tried to secure by presents the services of Confucius, who had prudently transferred himself to a safe place in the open country lying between Ch'en and Ts'ai The ministers of these two orthodox states, fearing the results to their own people should Confucius (as he seems in fact to have contemplated) decide to accept the Ts'u offer, with a police force surrounded the Confucian party; they were only able to escape from starvation by sending word to the King, who at once sent a detachment to free the sage. He would have conferred a fief upon Confucius, but his ministers advised him of the danger of such a proceeding, seeing that the Chou dynasty conquered the empire after beginning with a petty fief, and that the great kingdom of Ts'u itself had arrived at its present greatness after beginning with a still smaller fief. Accordingly the sage decided to return to Wei (489), where several of his disciples received official posts, and where Confucius himself seems to have acted as unofficial adviser, especially in the matter of a contested succession. All this competition for, or at least jealousy of, Confucius' services proves that his repute as an administrator (not necessarily as a philosopher) was already widely spread. The following year the King of Wu appeared before the Lu capital, and one of Confucius' former disciples holding office there (the one who went in advance in 492) just succeeded in moderating the barbarians' demands, which, however, only took the comparatively harmless "spiritual" form of orthodox sacrificial victims.

In 484 Confucius was still in Wei, for in that year he is stated to have declined to discuss there a question connected with making war. In the year 484 or 483 the disciple sent by Confucius to Lu, as stated, in 492 conducted an expedition against Ts'i: this was the shameful period when orthodox Lu, in compulsory league with barbarous Wu, was playing a double and treacherous game under stress, and the question of recalling Confucius to save his native country was on the tapis. Hearing of this, and despite the heavy bribes offered him to stay by the ruler of Wei, Confucius started with alacrity for Lu, where he arrived safely after fourteen years of wandering. He is often stated to have visited over forty states in all; but it must be remembered that each of the important countries he visited had in turn a number of satellites of its own; as, for instance, the extremely ancient "marquess state" of Ki, or K'i, subordinate to Lu, which, though possessing great spiritual authority, had no weight in lay policy. An interesting point to notice is that Confucius' travels almost exactly coincide with those of the Second Protector 150 years earlier (see Chapter XXXIX); both of them ignored the Emperor, and both of them visited Ts'i, Ts'ao, Sung, and Cheng on their way to the Ts'u frontiers; but Confucius was not able to get much farther west so as to reach the Ts'u capital; nor was he able to get to Tsin; not to say the still more distant Ts'in. In other words, the limited centre of orthodox China remained for many centuries the same, and the vast regions surrounding it were still semi- barbarian in the fifth century B.C. Now it was that Confucius, seeing that the imperial power had diminished almost to nothing; that the Odes and Book, the Rites, and the Music no longer possessed their former influence; employed himself in making systematic search for documents, in re-editing the Book (of History), and in endeavouring to ascertain the exact ritual or administration of the preceding dynasties. "Henceforth the Rites could be understood and transmitted,"—from which we may assume that, up to this time, they had been practically a monopoly of the princely caste. He did not go further back into the mythical period than the two emperors who preceded the Hia dynasty, nor did he bring the Book farther down than to the time of Duke Muh of Ts'in, which practically means the time of the first Protectors. He really did for rites and history what he had blamed Tsz-ch'an for doing with the law: he popularized it. He also attempted with persistent study to master the Changes, to which incomprehensible work he added features of his own— very little more understandable than the original texts. As to the Odes, 3000 in number, he used the pruning knife much more vigorously, and nine-tenths of them were rejected as unsuitable for the purposes of good didactic lessons or conservative precedents. If we substitute, as we are entitled to do, the vague word "religion" for the equally vague word "rites" (which in fact were the only ancient Chinese religion); if we substitute the empty Christian churches of to- day, and the too little scrupulous ambitions of rival European Powers, for the neglected tao of the Chou ideal, and for the savage rivalry of the great Chinese vassals; we obtain an almost precisely similar situation in modern Europe. If we can imagine a great Pope, or a great philosopher, taking advantage of a turn in the European conscience to bring back the simple ideals of Christianity, we can easily imagine this European Confucius being universally hailed in future times as the saviour of a parlous situation; which, in Europe now, as 2000 years ago in China, entails on the people so much misery and suffering. Confucius was, in short, in a way, a Chinese Pius X. declaiming against Modernism.

Confucius' only certain original work was the "Springs and Autumns," which is practically a continuation (with the necessary introductory years) of the ancient Book edited or, as some think, composed by him. He brought the former, this history of his, down from 722 to 481 B.C. and died in 479. His pupil Tso K'iu-ming, who was official historian to the Lu court, annotated and expounded Confucius' bald annals, bringing the narrative down from 481 to 468; and Tso's delightful work forms the chief, but by no means the sole, basis for what we have to say in the present book of sketches.

CHAPTER XLV. CONFUCIUS AND LAO-TSZ

Apart from the fact that reverence for rulers was the pivot of the Chou religious system, or, what was then the same thing, administrative system; official historiographers, who were mere servants of the executive, had to be careful how they offended the executive power in those capricious days; all the more had a private author and a retired official like Confucius carefully to mind the conventions. For instance, two historians had been put to death by a king-maker in Ts'i for recording the murder by him of a Ts'i reigning prince; and Ts'i was but next door to Lu. Hence we find the leading feature of his work is that he hints rather than criticizes, suggests rather than condemns, conceals rather than exposes, when it is a question of class honour or divine right; just as, with us, the Church prefers to hush up rather than to publish any unfortunate internal episode that would redound to its discredit. So shocked was he at the assassination of the ruler of Ts'i by an usurping family in 481, that, even at his venerable age, he unsuccessfully counselled instant war against Ts'i. His motive was perhaps doubtful, for the next year we find a pupil of his, then in office, going as a member of the mission to the same usurper in order to try and obtain a cession of territory improperly held. This pupil was one of the friends who assisted at the arrangement made in Wei in 492. Confucius' failings—for after all he was only a man, and never pretended to be a genius—in no way affect the truth of his writings, for they were detected almost from the very beginning, and have never been in the least concealed. Notable instances are the mission from Lu to Ts'u in 634; Confucius conceals the fact that, not courtesy to barbarian Ts'u, but a desire to obtain vengeance against orthodox Ts'i was the true motive.

Again, in 632, when the faineant Emperor was "sent for" by the Second Protector to preside at a durbar; Confucius prefers to say: "His Majesty went to inspect his fiefs north of the river," thus even avoiding so much as to name the exact place, not to say describe the circumstances. He punishes the Emperor for an act of impropriety in 693 by recording him as "the King," instead of "the Heavenly King." On the other hand, in 598, even the barbarian King of Ts'u was "a sage," because, having conquered the orthodox state of Ch'en, he magnanimously renounced his conquest. In 529 the infamous ruler of the orthodox state of Ts'ai is recorded as being "solemnly buried"; but the rule was that no "solemn funeral" should be accorded to (1) barbarians, (2) rulers who lose their crown, (3) murderers. Now, this ruler was a murderer; but it was a barbarian state (Ts'u) that killed him, which insult to civilization must be punished by making two blacks one white, i.e. by giving the murdered murderer an orthodox funeral. Again, in 522, a high officer was "killed by robbers"; it is explained that there were no robbers at all, in fact, but that the mere killing of an officer by a common person needs the assumption of robbery. It is like the legal fiction of lunacy in modern Chinese law to account for the heinous crime of parricide, and thus save the city from being razed to the ground. Once more, at the Peace Conference of 546, Ts'u undoubtedly "bluffed" Tsin out of her rightful precedence; but, Tsin being an orthodox state, Confucius makes Tsin the diplomatic victor. We have already seen that he once deliberately broke his plighted word, meanly attacked the men who spared him; and, out of servility, visited a woman of noble rank who was "no better than she ought to have been." There is another little female indiscretion recorded against him. When, in 482, the Lu ruler's concubine, a Wu princess (imperial clan name), died, Confucius obsequiously went into mourning for an "incestuous" woman; but, seeing immediately afterwards that the powerful family then at the helm did not condescend to do so, he somewhat ignominiously took off his mourning in a hurry. All these, and numerous similar petty instances of timorousness, may appear to us at a remote distance trifling and pusillanimous, as do also many of the model personal characteristics and goody-goody private actions of the sage; but if we make due allowance for the difficulty of translating strange notions into a strange tongue, and for the natural absence of sympathy in trying to enter into foreign feelings, we may concede that these petty details, quite incidentally related, need in no way destroy the main features of a great picture. Few heroes look the character except in their native clothes and surroundings; and, as Carlyle said, a naked House of Lords would look much less dignified than a naked negro conference.

As a philosopher, Confucius in his own time had scarcely the reputation of Tsz-ch'an of Cheng, who in many respects seems to have been his model and guide. Much more is said of Tsz-ch'an's philosophy, of his careful definition of the ritual system, of his legal acumen, of his paternal care for the people's welfare; but, like his contemporaries and friends of Ts'i, Tsin, Cheng, Sung, Wei; and even of Wu and Yueh; he was working for the immediate good of his own state in times of dire peril; whereas Confucius from first to last was aiming at the restoration of religion (i.e., of the imperial, ritualistic, feudal system); and for this reason it was that, after the violent unification of the empire by the First August Emperor in 221 B.C., followed by his fall and the rise of the Han dynasty in 202 B.C., this latter house finally decided to venerate, and all subsequent houses have continued to venerate, Confucius' memory; because his system was, after Lao- tsz's system had been given a fair trial, at last found the best suited for peace and permanency.

Not only is Lao-tsz not mentioned in the "Springs and Autumns" of Confucius, as extended by his contemporary and latter commentators, but none other of the great writers and philosophers anterior to and contemporary with Confucius are spoken of except strictly in their capacity of administrators. Thus the Ts'i philosopher Kwan-tsz of the First Protector's time, 650 B.C.; the Ts'i philosopher Yen-tsz of Confucius' time; and the others mentioned in preceding chapters, notably in Chapter XV. (of whom each orthodox state of political importance can boast at least one); based their reputation on what they had achieved for the state rather than what they had taught in the abstract; and their economical and historical books, which have all come down to us in a more or less complete and authentic state, are valued for the expression they give to the definite theories by which they arrived at practical results, rather than for the preaching of the counsels of perfection, We have seen that Yen-tsz expressed rather a contempt for the (to him) out-of-date formalistic ideals of Confucius, though Confucius himself had a high opinion of Yen-tsz. Lao-tsz is first mentioned by the writers of the various "schools" brought into existence by the collapse of Tsin in 452 B.C., and its subdivision into three separate kingdoms, recognized as such by the puppet Emperor in 403 B.C. The diplomatic activity was soon after that quite extraordinary, and each of the seven royal courts became a centre of revolutionary thought; that is, every literary adventurer had his own views of what interpretation of ancient literature was best suited to the times: it was Modernism with a vengeance. There is ample evidence of Lao-tsz's influence upon the age, though Lao-tsz himself had been dead for a century or more in the year 403. Lao-tsz is spoken of and written about in the fourth century B.C. as though it were perfectly well known who he was, and what his sentiments were; but as, up to Confucius' time, state intercourse had been confined to traders, warriors, and officials of the princely castes; and as books had been unwieldy objects stored only in capitals and great centres; there is good reason to assume that philosophy had been taught almost entirely by word of mouth, and that something must have occurred shortly after his death to cheapen and facilitate the dissemination of literature. Probably this something was the gradual introduction of the practice of writing on silk rolls and on silk "paper," which practice is known to have been in vogue long before the discovery of rubbish paper A.D. 100. Confucius himself evidently made use of the old-fashioned bamboo slips, strung together by cords like a bundle of tickets; for we are told that he worked so hard in endeavouring to understand the "Changes," that he "wore out three sets of leather bands"; and it will be remembered from Chapter XXXV. how the Bamboo Books buried in 299 B.C., to be discovered nearly 600 years later, consisted of slips strung together in this way.

Confucius' movements during the fourteen years of his exile are very clearly marked out, and there seems to be no doubt that his visit to the Emperor's court took place when he was a young man; firstly, because Lao-tsz ironically calls him a young man, and secondly because he went to visit Lao-tsz with the son of the statesman who on his death-bed foretold Confucius' future distinction; and there was no Lu mission to the imperial court after 520. In the second century B.C., not only are there a dozen statesmen specifically stated to have studied the works of Lao-tsz, but the Empress herself is said to have possessed his book; and a copy of it, distinctly said to be in ancient character, was then stored amongst other copies of the same book in the imperial library. The two questions which the Chinese historians and literary men of the fifth, fourth, third, and second centuries B.C. do not attempt to decide are: Why is the life of Lao-tsz not given to us earlier than 100 B.C.? Why is that life so scant, and why does the writer of it allude to "other stories" current about him? Why is it that the book which Lao-tsz wrote at the request of a friend is not alluded to by any writer previous to 100 B.C.?

As not one single one of these numerous Taoists or students of Lao-tsz expresses the faintest doubt about Lao-tsz's existence, or about the genuineness of his traditional teachings, it is evident that the meagreness of Lao-tsz's life, as told by the historian, is rather a guarantee of the truth of what he says than the reverse, so far as he knows the truth; otherwise he would have certainly embellished. The essence of Lao-tsz's doctrine is its democracy, its defence of popular rights, its allusion to kings and governments as necessary evils, its disapproval of luxury and hoarding wealth; its enthusiasm for the simple life, for absence of caste, for equality of opportunity, for socialism and informality; all of which was, though extracted from the same Odes, Book, Changes, and Rites, quite contrary in principle to the "back to the rites" doctrine of Confucius. Therefore, there could be no possible inducement for Confucius, the pruning editor of the Odes, Book, etc., or for his admirers, to mention Lao-tsz in either his original work, the "Springs and Autumns," or in the other works (composed by his disciples) giving the original words and sentiments of Confucius. Besides, during the whole of Lao- tsz's life, the imperial court (where he served as a clerk) was totally ignored by all the "powers" as a political force; the only persons mentioned in what survives of Chou history are the historiographers, the wizards, the ritual clerks, the ducal envoys, now sent by the Emperor to the vassals, now consulted by the vassals upon matters of etiquette. Lao-tsz, being an obscure clerk in an obscure appanage, and holding no political office, had no more title to be mentioned in history than any other servant or "harmless drudge." That his doctrines were well known is not wonderful, for Tsz-ch'an, his contemporary, and this great man's colleagues of the other states, also had doctrines of their own which were widely discussed and, as we have seen, even Tsz-ch'an was severely blamed for the unheard-of novelty of committing the laws to writing, both by Confucius of Lu and by Shuh Hiang of Tsin (imperial clan states). It is reasonable to suppose, therefore, that the traditional story is true; namely, that Lao-tsz's doctrines were never taught in a school at all, and that he had no followers or admirers except the vassal envoys who used to come on spiritual business to the metropolis. We have seen how these men used to entertain each other over their wine by quoting the Odes and other ancient saws; when consulting the imperial library to rectify their own dates, they would naturally meet the old recluse Lao-tsz, and hear from his own mouth what he thought of the coming collapse anticipated by all. He is said to have left orthodox China in disgust, and gone West—well, he must have passed through Ts'in if he went to the west. At the frontier pass (it is not known precisely whether on the imperial frontier or on the Ts'in frontier) an acquaintance or correspondent on duty there invited him to put his thoughts into writing, which he did. Books being extremely rare, copies would be slowly transmitted. This was about 500 B.C., between which time and 200 B.C., when a copy of his book is first reported to be actually held in the hand by a definite person, the great protecting powers, and later the seven kings, were all engaged in a bloodthirsty warfare, which ended in the almost total destruction throughout the empire of the Odes, Rites, and the Book in 213 B.C. Remember, however, that the literary empire practically meant parts of the modern provinces of Ho Nan and Shan Tung. The "Changes" were not destroyed; and as the First August Emperor himself, his illegitimate father, several of his statesmen, and his visitors the travelling diplomats, were all either Taoists or imbued with Taoist doctrines (their sole policy being to destroy the old ritual and feudal thrones), there is ground to conjecture that Lao-tsz's book escaped too, and was deliberately suffered to escape. We know absolutely nothing of that; assuming the truth of the tradition that there was a book, we do not know what became of the first copy, nor how many copies were made of it during the succeeding 300 years. No attempt whatever has ever been made by the serious Chinese historians themselves to manufacture a story. It is, of course, unsatisfactory not to know all the exact truth; but, for the matter of that, the existence, identity, and authorship of Confucius' pupil and commentator Tso K'iu-ming, the official historian of Lu, is equally obscure; not to mention the history of the earliest Taoist critics who actually mention Lao-tsz, and quote the words of (if they do not mention) his book. When we read Renan's masterly examination into the origins of our own Gospels, and when we reflect that even the origin of Shakespeare's plays, and the individuality of Shakespeare's person, are open to everlasting discussion, we may not unreasonably leave Chinese critics and Chinese historians to judge of the value of their own national evidence, and accept in general terms what they tell us of fact, however imperfect it may be in detail, without adding hypothetical facts or raising new critical difficulties of our own. No such foreign criticisms are or can be worth much unless the original Chinese histories and the original Chinese philosophers have been carefully examined by the foreign critic in the original Chinese text.

CHAPTER XLVI. ORACLES AND OMENS

Consulting the oracles seems to have been a universal practice, and there are numerous historical allusions, made by statesmen of the orthodox principalities, to supposed interpretations attached to this or that combination of mystic signs or diagrams from the "Changes," together with arguments as to their specific meaning or omen in given circumstances. Doubtless the Chinese of those dates, like our own searchers for religious "analogies" and mysteries, examined with perfect good faith combinations of the Diagrams which to us appear arrant nonsense; and there can be no doubt of Confucius' own individual zeal, though the fact that he thought fifty years' study at least would be necessary for full comprehension points to the tacit confession that he had totally failed to understand much of the mystery. The Changes are supposed to have been developed by the father of the Warrior King when (about 1160 B.C.) he was in prison under the tyrannous suspicions of the last Shang emperor; and we have seen that the ruler of Ts'u was his tutor, at a time when Ts'u was not yet vassal to Chou. Like the Odes, Book, and Rites, the Changes were Chou literature, though possibly the unwritten traditions of earlier dynasties may have contributed to that literature; which, indeed, seems very likely, as Ts'u was already able to teach Chou.

Another form of augury was the examination of the marks on the carapax of a tortoise; thus the Martial King in 146 consulted, and found unfavourable, such marks—this was before attacking the last Shang emperor; and it was only at the earnest instigation of his chief henchman (afterwards vassal king and founder of Ts'i) that he was prevailed upon to proceed. Possibly he borrowed Eastern ideas from this founder of Ts'i too. Later on, the Martial King's younger brother, the Duke of Chou, consulted the oracle along with the same Ts'i adviser: this was done before the three ancestral altars of their father, grandfather, and great-grandfather, in order to ascertain if the Emperor (i.e. the Martial King) would recover from a sickness. In 1109 the Martial King's son and successor sent one of his uncles or near relatives to examine the site of modern Ho-nan Fu, with a view to transferring the metropolis thither, and, the oracles being favourable, the Nine Tripods were removed to that place, and it was afterwards called the "Eastern Metropolis" (the original or western capital was not moved for over 300 years after that). It was at the same time foretold that there would be thirty more reigns, of 700 years in all: this was "Heaven's decree." On the other hand, when the Duke of Chou died during a tempest, the young Emperor was advised not to consult the oracles as to what the storm signified, because his uncle's virtues were so manifest that Heaven itself had, by the agency of a tempest, spontaneously announced the fact.

Astrology was another form of soothsaying. In 780 B.C. the imperial astrologer (one of those two men, by the way, whom erroneous tradition 1000 years later confused with Lao-tsz) foretold the rise of Ts'i, Tsin, Ts'u, and Ts'in, upon the ruins of the imperial power; in 773 the same astrologer repeated the prophecy to the imperial prince then recently enfeoffed by his relative the Emperor in the state of CHÊNG. In 705 the imperial astrologer, when passing through the orthodox state of CH'ÊN, foretold from the diagrams that a scion of the CH'ÊN house would obtain the throne of Ts'i (which actually took place when the maire du palais, to the horror of Confucius, assassinated the last legitimate duke in 481 B.C.); this particular prophecy is doubly interesting, because the diagrams from the Changes, thus cited in detail in Confucius' history, correspond exactly with the diagrams of the Book of Changes as we have it now, since Confucius manipulated it—proof that no change has taken place in this part of the text at least. The ruler of Ts'in in the year 762, nine years after receiving the western half of the Chou imperial domain, and being recognized as a first-class vassal, consulted the oracle as to whither he should move his own capital. In the year 677 the oracles once more decided the then reigning ruler to shift his capital to (the modern) Feng-siang Fu in West Shen Si; the oracles added: "And later you will water your steeds in the Yellow River"; which came to pass after the conquests and annexations of 643 B.C., as already related. In 374 B.C. the imperial astrologer (the second man whom tradition, 300 years later this time, erroneously confused with Lao-tsz) then on a visit to the now royal Ts'in court said: "After 500 years of separation Ts'in is reunited to our imperial house; in 77 years more a domineering monarch will arise." Seven years later the "raining down of metal" (probably some natural phenomenon not clearly understood at the time) was considered a good omen in connection with the new capital, now placed on the south bank of the River Wei. After Ts'in had conquered China, there are numerous other instances of oracles, omens, and so forth, all supposed to have had political significance.

In 645 the ruler of the neighbouring state of Tsin consults the oracles in order to ascertain who will be the most suitable war charioteer. A few years before that the court diviner foretold the future success of the petty Ngwei sub-principality of Tsin, which in 403 B.C. actually became a separate vassal kingdom. In 575 Tsin dared not, at the moment, accept the battle challenge of Tsu, because the particular day was a dies nefas, being the last day of the moon. Meanwhile the spies of the Ts'u army discerned that the Tsin leaders were consulting the oracles before the tablets of their ancestors in the field tent. In 535 the Ts'in administration consulted its own astrologer upon the point: "Will the state of Ch'en survive?" The answer was: "When it secures Ts'i, it will perish." As just explained, a scion of the Ch'en house did practically obtain Ts'i in 481 B.C., and the very next year Ch'en was annexed by Ts'u. In 510 the Tsin astrologer prophesied the destruction of Wu by Yiieh within forty years, and also the predominancy of the Lu private family so intimately connected with Confucius' troubles. There were not lacking sensible men, even in those days, who ridiculed the science of astrology: for instance, Shuh Hiang of Tsin—the man who so strongly disapproved Tsz-ch'an's written laws, and the man who discussed with the Ts'i envoy, the philosopher Yen-tsz, the worthlessness of their respective dukes—said on one occasion when the "course of the heavens towards north-west" was supposed to indicate a success for Tsin: "The course of the heavens, as that of our success, lies in the qualities of the prince, and not in the situation of the stars."

Tsz-ch'an of Cheng himself pooh-poohed oracular warnings, and said that he preferred to do his best, and leave omens to do their worst. On one occasion, outside the south gate of the Cheng capital, two snakes (one from the city, one from outside) were observed fighting; the one from the inside was defeated. Sure enough! the exiled duke six years after that returned to his own. So, in the state of Lu, the children sang: "When the thrushes come and make their nests, the ruler will go to a place on the Tsin frontier; when the thrushes settle here, the duke will be abroad"—in allusion to the future ejecting of the reigning prince by the powerful family above referred to.

And, again (480 B.C.), in the state of Sung, whose terrestrial position was supposed to be "invaded" by the then peculiar celestial position of the planet Mars: it was suggested, however, to the ruling prince that he might "pass on" the threatened disaster to his ministers, to his people, or to their harvests—a solution the duke declined to avail himself of. 'Yours are indeed the words of a sage,' said the astrologer.

We now come to the semi-civilized state of Ts'u, which seems to have had its oracles with the best of them, at all events after 560 B.C. At that date it was explained to the King that "the ancient emperors would at times consult the oracles for five years before deciding upon an expedition, or fixing the date of it; they were content to await patiently the decrees of Heaven." In 537 the Ts'u king, having a prince of Wu in his power, sent to ask him ironically if he had duly consulted the oracles. "Yes," said the prince, "every ruler has his tortoise, and it is easy to demonstrate by our oracles how injurious it will be for you if any harm comes to me." This presence of mind saved his life. In 528 a Ts'u usurper invited a man who had once assisted him to name any post he would like. The man chose that of diviner, which, it appears, was an office of the first rank. The father of this king had secretly arranged with a concubine, notwithstanding the Ts'u rule (or possibly in accordance with it) that one of the youngest sons should succeed, to "sacrifice from a distance to the gods in general, and ask of them which of five sons should sacrifice to the spirits of the land"; then he buried a jade symbol of rule in the ancestral temple, and ordered the five sons to enter after proper purification; the three sons who happened to touch the spot reigned one after the other. In 489 the King of Ts'u, then engaged in assisting the orthodox state of Ch'en against the attacks of Wu, interrogated the imperial astrologer (who must have been there on a visit): "What is the meaning of that halo, like a bird's wings, on each side of the sun?" The astrologer replied: "It presages calamity, but you can transfer it to your generals." The generals then offered to consult the gods themselves, and even to sacrifice their own persons if necessary; but the King declined (on the same ground as the Duke of Sung above mentioned) because "my generals are my own limbs." It was then proposed to transfer the calamity to the Yellow River. "No, the Yellow River has never played me false: ever since we received our fief, we have never at full moon sacrificed beyond the River Han and Yang-tsz." Confucius registered his approval of this answer. It will be remembered that just at this time Confucius was hanging about Ch'Ün and coquetting with Ts'u, so that possibly this approval had something to do with his own prospects.

In recording these instances of prophecies and omens (which might be multiplied tenfold), it is desired to show how one main set of ideas pervaded the whole. We should not be too ready to ridicule them, or to hint at "after the event." Our own Scriptures are full of similar prophecies, and what is good for us is good for the Chinese. If the celestial movements can be foretold, why not corresponding terrestrial movements, each corner of the earth being on the meridian of something? In the infancy of science, it is rather a question of good faith than of truth; and even the truth, if we insist on expecting it, was rudely guessed at by such great thinkers as Tsz-ch'an and Shuh Hiang.

CHAPTER XLVII.RULERS AND PEOPLE

A feature of the times was the remarkably personal character of the wars, and the apparent utter indifference to humble popular interests; Quidquid delirant reges, plectuntur Achivi; stress is laid upon this point by the democratic philosopher Lao-tsz, who, however, in his book (be it genuine or not), is wise enough never to name a person or place; probably that prudence saved it from the flames in 213 B.C.

In 684 B.C. the ruler of Ts'ai (imperial clan) treated very rudely his own wife's sister, married to a petty prince (imperial clan) close by; the sister was simply passing through as a traveller; the result was that this petty prince, her husband, induced Ts'u to make war upon Ts'ai, whose reigning prince was captured, and died a prisoner. In 657 the ruler of Ts'ai had a sister married in Ts'i. The First Protector, offended at some act of playful disobedience, sent her back, but without actually divorcing her. Her brother was so angry that he found her another husband. On this Ts'i declared war, and captured the brother, who, however, at the intercession of the other vassal princes, was restored to his kingdom. In 509 and 506 B.C. Ts'ai induces Tsin to make war on Ts'u, and also assists Wu in her hostilities against Ts'u, because a Ts'u minister had detained the ruler of Ts'ai for refusing to part with a handsome fur coat. It is like the stealing of the Golden Fleece by Jason, and similar Greek squabbles. In 675 B.C. the Emperor, for the third time, had to fly from his capital, the immediate cause of the trouble being an attempt on his part to seize a vassal's rice-field for including in his own park—a Chinese version of the Naboth's vineyard dispute. Nothing could better prove the pettiness of the ancient state-horizon; no busily active great power could find time for such trifles.

When the Second Protector came to the throne, the orthodox states of Wei, Ts'ao, and Cheng (all of the imperial clan), which had treated him scurvily as a wanderer, had all three of them to pay dearly for their meanness. In 632, when the Protector had secured the Tsin throne, the ruler of Ts'ao was promptly captured, and part of his territory was given to Sung (where the wanderer had been well treated). The same year Tsin wished to assist Sung, and accordingly asked right of way through the state of Wei, which was curtly refused; the Tsin army therefore crossed the Yellow River to the south of Wei: as a punishment for this refusal, and also for the previous rude treatment, Wei also had to give part of her territory to the favoured Sung. In 630 Tsin induced Ts'in to join in an attack upon Cheng, the object being, of course, to revenge similar personal rudenesses; however, Cheng diplomacy was successful in inducing Ts'in to abandon Tsin in the nick of time: this was one of the very few cases in which Ts'in interfered, or was about to interfere, in "orthodox" affairs. In 592 Tsin sent a hunchback envoy to Ts'i; it so happened that at the same time Lu sent one who was lame, and Wei a third who was blind of one eye. The Ts'i ruler thereupon appointed an officer mutilated in some other way to do the duties of host to this sorry trio. The Tsin envoy swore: "If I do not revenge this upon Ts'i, may the God of the Yellow River take note of it!" Reaching his own country, he tried to induce the ruler to make war on Ts'i; but the prince said: "Your personal pique should hardly suffice for ground to trouble the whole country": and he refused.

The principle of the divinity that doth hedge a king was early established, but there are certainly more numerous evidences of royal absolutism in Ts'u than in orthodox China, where responsibility of rulers before Heaven and the People (symbolical of Heaven also) was an accepted axiom. For instance, in 522 B.C., an officer, knowing that the King of Ts'u was sending for him in order to kill him, said to his brother: "As the king orders it, one of us two must go, but you can avenge me later on." When the next Ts'u king was a fugitive, and it was a question in a subject's mind of killing him because his father had taken a brother's life, it was objected: "No! if the king slays one of his officers, who can avenge it? His commands emanate from Heaven. It is unpardonable to cut off the ancestral sacrifice of a whole house in this way."

In still more ancient times, when the last Emperor of the Shang dynasty was being warned of the rising popular feeling in favour of the rising Chou power, he remarked: "Have I not Heaven's mandate? What can they do to me?" When the Martial King achieved his conquest, he smeared the god of the soil with the sacrificial victims' blood, and announced the crimes of the dead tyrant to Heaven. In the war of 589 between Tsin and Ts'i, the ruler of Ts'i, who had changed places with his charioteer in order to escape detection, was hotly pursued; but his chariot caught in a tree. Seeing this, the Tsin captain prostrated himself before the chariot, and said: "My princely master's orders are to assist the states of Lu and Wei" (i.e. not to attack your person). Meanwhile the disguised charioteer ordered the disguised king to fetch a drink of water, and the king thus escaped even the humiliation of a favour from his generous victor. When in 548 a worthless Ts'i ruler was assassinated, the philosopher Yen-tsz said: "When the ruler dies or is exiled for the gods of the land and its harvests, one dies or is exiled with him; but if he dies or is exiled for private reasons, then only his personal friends die with him." He therefore contented himself with wailing, and with laying his head on the royal body. The same Tsin captain who was so tender to the Ts'i duke in 589 had an opportunity fourteen years later of taking prisoner the ruler of CHÊNG in battle; but he said: "Evil cometh to him who toucheth a crowned head! I have already committed sacrilege once against the ruler of Ts'i; preserve me from committing this crime a second time!" And he turned promptly back. During the same fight, the King of Ts'u's body-guard was attacked by the Tsin generalissimo, who, when he discerned the king in the centre of the guards, got out of his chariot, doffed his helmet, and fled in horror, "such was his respect for the person of royalty." It was a ritual rule in China for the distinguished men not to remove the official head-covering in death; for instance, in 481, when one of Confucius' pupils was killed in war, his last patriotic act was to tie his hat-strings tighter. Though rulers were supposed to owe duties to the gods in general, yet the power of the gods was limited. Thus when Tsz-ch'an of CHÊNG was sent as envoy to Tsin in 541, the sick Tsin ruler asked him: "How can the two gods who, they say, are responsible for my malady, be conjured?" Tsz-ch'an replied: "These particular gods cannot injure you; we sacrifice to them in connection with natural phenomena, such as drought, flood, or other disaster; just as in matters of snow, hail, rain, or wind we sacrifice to the gods of the sun, moon, planets, and constellations. Your illness is the result of drink, over-feeding, women, passionate anger, excessive pleasure." Shuh Hiang approved this common-sense view of the situation.

ANCIENT CHINESE LAW

APPENDIX I

In the spring of the year 536 B.C., Tsz-ch'an, one of the leading statesmen in the Chinese Federal Union, decided to publish for popular information the Criminal Law which had hitherto been simply "declared" by the various rulers and their officers according to the circumstances of each case. At this time the different premiers and ministers used to visit each other freely, generally in the suite of the reigning prince who happened to be either receiving or paying a visit from or to some other vassal prince. The Emperor himself, now shorn of his power, was only primus inter pares amongst these princes. Shuh Hiang, one of the ministers at the neighbouring court of Tsin, addressed the following remarkable letter to the colleague above mentioned who had introduced the legal innovation. It is published in exteso in Confucius' own history of the times, as expanded by one of his pupils:—

"At first I used to regard you as a guide, but now all this is at an end. Our monarchs in past times were wont to decide matters by specific ordinance, and had no prepared statutes, fearing lest the people should grow contentious. Yet even so it was impossible to suppress wrong-doing; for which reason they employed justice as a preventive, administration to bring things into line, external formality to secure respect, good faith as an abiding principle, and kindness in actual treatment. They appointed certain ranks and emoluments with a view to encouraging their officers to follow the course thus sketched out for them, and they fixed certain stern punishments and fines in order to fill these officers with a dread of arbitrariness, fearing that otherwise they might fail in their duty. Thus admonition was given with every loyalty; fear was inspired by personal example; instruction was conveyed as occasion required; employment in service was accompanied by suavity; contact with inferiors was marked by a respectful demeanour; the executive arm was firmly applied; and decisions were carried out with virility. Yet, with all this, it was never too easy to secure wise and saintly (vassal) princes, clever and discriminating ministers, loyal and trusty officials, or kind and affectionate instructors. Under these circumstances, however, it was possible to set the people going, and China was at least free from revolution and misery.

"But when the people themselves become cognizant of a written law, they will cease to fear their superiors, and, moreover, they will acquire a contentious spirit. Having book to refer to, they will employ every device to elude the letter of the law. This will not do at all. It was only in times of anarchical rule that the founders of the Hia and Shang dynasties (2200 B.C. and 1760 B.C.) found it necessary to issue (to their officers) the collections of laws which still bear their two respective names; and it was also only in anarchical times (1000 B.C.) that one Emperor of our present dynasty found it necessary to publish (for his officers) the so-called Nine Laws. In other words, the advent of written law has on all three occasions connoted a decay in government. You, sir, are the chief minister of CHÊNG state (part of modern Ho Nan); you made a few years ago some new regulations about the parcelling of land; next you placed the system of your taxation on a fresh basis; and you now proceed to embody the three special collections just cited in a new popular code, which you have had cast in metal characters. If you are doing it with a view to pacify the people, surely you will not find this an easy matter? The 'Book of Odes' says: 'King Wên (the virtual founder, 2200 B.C., of the then reigning Chou dynasty) took virtue as his guide, and thus gradually pacified the four quarters of the world.' It also says: 'The methods of King Wu (son of the virtual founder) secured the confidence of all the other countries.' Where were the written laws in those times? When people begin to get the contentious spirit upon them, they will have done with the principles of propriety, and only stickle for the letter; they will haggle upon every tiny point accessible to knife's edge or awl's tip. We shall witness a flood of litigious accusations; bribery and corruption will be rampant. Do you think the state of Cheng will last out your life? I have heard it said: 'When a country is about to collapse, there are many conflicting administrative changes.' Will this apply to present conditions?"

The reply returned was:-

"With regard to what my honourable friend has been pleased to say, I am afraid my humble capacities are not sufficiently great to take the interests of posterity; my action has been taken in the interests of the state as I find it, and as I have to govern it. Though, therefore, I cannot accept tour commands, I shall be careful not to forget your kindness in proffering advice."

Though the exact words of the above-mentioned Code in Brass have not come down to us, they are (like the Twelve Tables of Rome, eighty years later in date, were in relation to Roman jurisprudence) the foundation of Chinese Criminal Law as it exists to-day, modified, of course, dynasty by dynasty. At this time Confucius was a mere youth; but later on, as minister of a third vassal state, that of Lu, he also expressed his disapproval of a written code, much though he respected the author, whom he knew personally. Shuh Hiang's letter is of interest as showing the pitch of philosophy, common-sense, and international courtesy to which the statesmen of China had attained 2400 years ago.

APPENDIX II

In 539 B.C. the Ts'i statesman and philosopher Yen-tsz was sent on a mission to Tsin in order to negotiate a political marriage. At this period Han K'i, also called Han Süan-tsz, was the premier of Tsin, and he despatched the minister Shuh Hiang with a complimentary message to the Ts'i envoy, accepting the offer of a suitable wife. At this time the diplomatic relations of the Chinese states were particularly interesting, because, apart from the fact that intellectual premiers ruled all the great states, most of them were personal friends, acquaintants, or correspondents of Confucius, who has left on record his judgment upon each. After the official marriage negotiations were over, Shuh Hiang ordered refreshments, and he and Yen-tsz sat down to a nice quiet little chat by themselves.

Shuh Hiang. How is Ts'i going on?

Yen-tsz. These are bad times. I don't know what I can say about Ts'i, except that it appears to be falling into the hands of the CH'ÊN family. The prince neglects his people, and consequently they turn to the CH'ÊN family for protection. In former times Ts'i had three grain measures, each a four multiple of the other—etc. four pints, sixteen pints, sixty-four pints—and finally there was a large measure containing ten times the last, or 640 pints (or litres); but the three measures of the CH'ÊN family have each been raised by one unit, so that three successive fives multiplied by ten give 800 pints, and their plan is to make loans of grain with their private 8oo-pint measure, and then to take back payments in the prince's measure. The wood from the mountains is sold in the market-place as cheaply as on the mountains; fish, salt, clams, and cockles are sold in the market-place as cheaply as on the shore. On the other hand, two-thirds of the produce of the people's labour go to the prince, whilst only one-third remains for the sustenance of the producers. The prince's stores rot away, whilst our old men die of starvation. False feet are cheaper than shoes in the market-place (owing to the number of people punished with amputation of a foot); the people are smarting with a sense of wrong, and are longing for the advent (of the CH'ÊN family), whom they love as a parent, and towards whom they tend, just as water runs downhill. Under these circumstances, even if they did not want to gain the people over, how can they avoid it? The last surviving member of that branch of the CH'ÊN family who traced his descent to previous dynasties has still left his spirit in the land of Ts'i, though the representatives of the family are nominally subjects of Ts'i.

Shuh Hiang. Yes. And even our ruling house of Tsin has fallen on degenerate times. Armies are no longer equipped, and our statesmen are not ready for war. There is no one to lead the chariots, and our battalions have no competent commanders. The common people are utterly exhausted, whilst the extravagance of the palace is unbounded. The starving folk line the roads, whilst money is squandered upon female favourites. The commands of the prince are received by the people as though they longed to escape the clutches of a bandit. The representatives of the eight leading families who have served the state so long and faithfully are reduced to the most insignificant offices. Government is administered in certain private interests, and the people have no one to whom to appeal. The ruler shows no sign of amendment, and endeavours to drown his cares in excessive indulgence. When did the ruling house ever before reach the low depths of to-day? The warning oracle inscribed on the tripod says: "However early you may get to zealous work, your descendants may be lazy." How much more, in the case of a man who will not reform, is disaster likely to be impending soon!

Yen-tsz. What do you propose to do?

Shuh Hiang. The ruling house of Tsin is about exhausted. I have heard it said that when a ruling house is about to fall, its family members drop off first, like the branches and leaves of a stricken tree; and the ruler himself, like the trunk, follows suit. Take my own stock, for instance, which formerly contained eleven family or clan names. The Sheepstongue (cf, English Sheepshanks) clan is my clan, and the only one now left; and I myself have no son fit to be my heir. The ruling house is arbitrary and capricious, so that, even if I am fortunate enough to die in my bed myself, I shall have no one to perform the sacra for me.

In 513 B.C. two generals of the Tsin state carried their arms into the Luh-hun reservation (in modern Ho Nan province), whither, in 638 B.C., the Tartar tribe of that name had been brought to settle by agreement between the two Chinese powers whose territories (Ts'in and Tsin) ran with the Tartars; "and then they drew upon Tsin state for four cwt. of iron, in order to cast a punishment tripod upon which to inscribe the law-book composed by Fan Süan- tsz (a minister)." Confucius said:—

"It looks as though Tsin were about to perish, as it has made a mistake in its calculations. The state of Tsin ought to govern its people by maintaining the ancient laws and ordinances received by their ancestor who was first enfeoffed there (in 1120 B.C.), when the officers of state would each observe the same in their degree. Thus the people would know how to respect their superiors, and the ruling classes would be in a position to maintain their patrimonies. The proper balance between superior classes and commoners is what we call 'ordinance.' The ruling prince W&n (who assumed the Protectorship of China in 632 B.C.) for this reason established an official body of dignitaries, and organized the annual spring revision of the laws of his ancestors as Representative Federal Prince. Now Tsin abandons this system, and makes a tripod, which tripod—will henceforth govern the people's acts. How can they now respect their superiors (having book to go by)? How can the superiors maintain their patrimonies? If superiors and commoners confuse degree, how can the state go on? Moreover, Süan-tsz's punishments date from the spring revision (of 621 B.C.), when confusion and change was going on in Tsin state; how can they take this as a fit precedent?"

APPENDIX III

About twenty-five centuries ago—in 546 B.C., to be precise—the Chinese Powers had a "Hague Conference" with a view to the reduction of armaments. This is how Confucius' pupil, Tso K'iu-ming, tells the story in the "Tso Chwan," or expanded version of Confucius' "Springs and Autumns" (for convenience the names of the ancient States are changed to those of the modern provinces corresponding with them):—

"A statesman of Ho Nan, being on friendly terms with his colleagues of Shan Si and Hu P&h, conceived the idea of making a name for himself by proposing a cessation of armaments. He went first to Shan Si, and interviewed the Premier there; the Premier consulted his colleagues in the Shan Si ministry, and one of them said: 'War is ruinous to the people, and a fearful waste of wealth; it is the curse of the smaller Powers. Although the idea will come to nothing, we must consent to a conference; otherwise Hu P&h will consent to it first, in order to gain favour with the Powers, and thus we shall lose the predominant position we now occupy.' So Shan Si consented.

"Then (the narrative continues) Hu Pêh was visited, and also consented. Then Shan Tung (the German sphere now). Shan Tung did not like the idea; but one of the Shan Tung Ministers said: 'Shan Si and Hu P&h have agreed, and we have no help for it. Besides, the world will say that there would be a cessation of armaments were it not for our refusal, and thus our own people will vote against us. What is the use of that?' So Shan Tung consented. Next Shen Si was notified. Shen Si also consented. Then the whole four great Powers notified the minor States, and a great durbar (of fourteen States) was held at a minor court in Ho Nan."

The curious part of it all is that the representative of the Emperor (whose political position was not unlike that of the Popes in Europe since 1870) did not appear at the Conference at all, though all the Great Powers maintained the fiction of granting precedence to the Emperor and his nuncios, and even went through the form of accepting investiture from him and taking tribute presents to the Imperial Court-when it suited them.

This celebrated Peace Conference closed the seventy-two years of almost incessant war that had been going on between Tsin and Ts'in (Shan Si and Shen Si), apart from the subsidiary war between Tsin and Ts'u (Hu Pêh).

Made in the USA
Lexington, KY
25 January 2017